ROULE BRITANNIA

William Fotheringham writes for the *Guardian* and *Observer* on cycling and rugby. A former racing cyclist and launch editor of *procycling* and *Cycle Sport* magazines, he has reported on over twenty Tours de France as well as Six Nations rugby and the Olympic Games. His biography of Tom Simpson, *Put Me Back on My Bike*, was acclaimed by *Vélo* magazine as 'the best cycling biography ever written'.

Also by William Fotheringham

Put Me Back on My Bike: In Search of Tom Simpson
Fallen Angel: The Passion of Fausto Coppi
Merckx: Half Man, Half Bike
Cylcopedia: It's All About the Bike
A Century of Cycling
Fotheringham's Sporting Trivia
Fotheringham's Sporting Trivia: The Greatest Sporting
Trivia Book Ever II

ROULE BRITANNIA

A History of Britons in the Tour de France

William Fotheringham

YELLOW JERSEY PRESS
LONDON

Published by Yellow Jersey Press 2012

2 4 6 8 10 9 7 5 3 1

Copyright © William Fotheringham, 2005, 2010, 2012

William Fotheringham has asserted his right
under the Copyright, Designs and Patents Act 1988
to be identified as the author of this work

First published in Great Britain in 2005 by
Yellow Jersey Press

This edition published in 2012
by Yellow Jersey Press
Random House, 20 Vauxhall Bridge Road,
London SW1V 2SA

www.vintage-books.co.uk

Addresses for companies within The Random House Group Limited
can be found at: www.randomhouse.co.uk/offices.htm

The Random House Group Limited Reg. No. 954009

A CIP catalogue record for this book
is available from the British Library

ISBN 9780224092104

The Random House Group Limited supports The Forest Stewardship Council
(FSC®), the leading international forest certification organisation. Our
books carrying the FSC label are printed on FSC® certified paper. FSC
is the only forest certification scheme endorsed by the leading
environmental organisations, including Greenpeace. Our paper procurement
policy can be found at www.randomhouse.co.uk/environment

Typeset by Deltatype Ltd, Birkenhead, Merseyside
Printed and bound in Great Britain by
CPI Group (UK) Ltd, Croydon, CR0 4YY

To my father, Alex, who would have loved to have seen a first British victory on the Tour.

Contents

Acknowledgements

This book could not have been written without the assistance of the riders who gave up their time for interviews, in some cases on several occasions, over the last few years. My most sincere thanks are therefore due to Bob Addy, Chris Boardman, Stan Brittain, Mark Cavendish, Vin Denson, Malcolm Elliott, Derek Harrison, Tony Hewson, Tony Hoar, Barry Hoban, Graham Jones, Ken Laidlaw, Colin Lewis, Bob Maitland, David Millar, Robert Millar, Bernard Pusey, Alan Ramsbottom, Harry Reynolds, Brian Robinson, Paul Sherwen, Shane Sutton, Geraint Thomas, Adrian Timmis, Paul Watson, Charly Wegelius, Bradley Wiggins and Sean Yates.

For providing background information and memories, many thanks are also due to Phil Anderson, Martin Ayres, Billy Bilsland, Sally Boardman, Jean Bobet, Dave Brailsford, Mike Breckon, Philippe Brunel, Arthur Campbell MBE, Guy Caput, Jeff Connor, David Duffield, Rod Ellingworth, Alasdair Fotheringham, Sandy Gilchrist, John Herety, Peter Keen, Jean-Marie Leblanc, Richard Moore, Matt Parker, Robert Rodrigo, Jean Stablinski, Neil Storey, Roger St Pierre, Scott Sunderland, Mike Taylor and Les Woodland.

The magazines *Cycling Weekly*, *Cycle Sport* and *procycling* were useful sources of reference throughout, as were *L'Equipe* and *www.cyclingnews.com*. Martin Ayres's retrospective on British cyclists at the Tour in *Cycling Weekly* in 2002 was of great assistance, as were Tony Hewson's 1959 article in *Cycling*, 'Ice-cold in Flanders', the late Dennis Donovan's interviews of 1992 with Brian Robinson and Barry Hoban in *Cycling Weekly*, and Jeremy Whittle's interview of March 2000 with David Millar in *Procycling*. The special editions of the magazine *Cycle Sport* devoted to Robert Millar and Sean Yates in January and February 1997 were also valuable.

Ray Pascoe's video account of British cyclists' experiences in the Tour, *The Britpack*, was a goldmine of information. Granada Television's 1986 film about Robert Millar, *The High Life*, provided various other insights. Both are available through Bromley Video. I should also like to thank Richard Allchin at Sport and Publicity for the loan of Barry Hoban's autobiography *Watching the Wheels go Round*. Mark Cavendish's autobiography *Boy Racer* (Ebury 2009) was of value, as was Tim Lewis's interview with the Manxman in *Observer Sport Monthly* in December 2008, and Bradley Wiggins's *In Pursuit of Glory* (Orion 2008).

Since the beginning of the Team Sky project, many individuals within that organisation and within British Cycling have been of considerable help. I would particularly like to thank Rod Ellingworth, Dave Brailsford, Shane Sutton, Fran Millar, Sean Yates – again – Tim Kerrison and Matt Parker for their assistance over several years now.

I remain indebted to Tristan Jones for his hard work and patience in producing the initial edition of this book, and to his successor at Yellow Jersey Matt Phillips for his assistance in producing updated and extended versions. Thanks are also due to successive sports editors at the *Guardian*, Mike Averis, Ben Clissitt and Ian Prior for putting the paper's resources behind sending me to the Tour from 1999 to 2012, and to my agent John Pawsey for his continued support.

As ever though, it is to Caroline, Patrick and Miranda that I owe the most, for putting up with many absences over the years and many hours when I have been chained to my desk.

List of Illustrations

ANC team, 1987 Tour de France (Photosport International)

Robert Millar, 1986 and 1990 Tours de France (Offside/ L'Equipe)

Sean Yates, 1990 and 1994 Tours de France (Offside/ L'Equipe)

Chris Boardman, 1994, 1996, 1998 Tours de France (Photosport International)

David Millar, 2002 and 2003 Tours de France (Photosport International)

Mark Cavendish, 2009 Tour de France (Offside/ L'Equipe)

Bradley Wiggins, 2012 Tour de France (Getty)

Le Tour en Angleterre 1994 (Photosport International)

'Roule Britannia'
     Headline, *L'Equipe*, 7 July 1962

Rouleur: [*Sports*] a cyclist who can
maintain a rapid, regular pace.
                    Le Petit Robert

Prologue

The sky was a clearest blue above the Champs-Elysées on Sunday 22 July 2012. We crushed onto the barriers by the finish line, waiting for the final moments when the long string of cyclists would fly towards us for the last time. We knew Mark Cavendish would lead them in, and so it proved as he raced up the slight slope, close to the right-hand side of the road, stage victory in his sights. A few seconds later, well back in the heart of the bunch, it was the turn of Bradley Wiggins, his arms in the air as he turned to his teammate Michael Rogers, with the pair embracing on their bikes as they passed us. The Tour de France was won. The first British victory in the race was complete. And on they went for a few yards, before Wiggins climbed off his bike and was suddenly lost in a sea of cameras, only his yellow crash hat in the throng showing that he was there at all.

I walked back down the Champs a few minutes later, towards the team buses parked on the Place de la Concorde. As I did, I turned to watch Christian Knees, Wiggins' German 'watchdog', who had spent kilometre after kilometre on the front of the peloton, and was now enjoying his moment of glory: as the crowd cheered on either side of the boulevard, he zigzagged from one side to the other to wave at them and milk the applause, his face crushed into a massive grin.

It is rare for journalists covering the Tour de France to schlep down to the Champs. By the final day of the Tour battle fatigue has set in, and the lengthy trip there and back from the press centre at Porte Maillot cuts into writing time on a day of tight deadlines. And there was far more than usual to be written on this particular Sunday: the life story of Wiggins, how he had transformed himself from Olympic track gold medallist into Tour de France winner, how he and Team Sky had come to rule the greatest, toughest cycle race in the world. That story would dominate the British press the following day.

But on this occasion the trip had to be made. As a cycling fan I had waited thirty-five years to see this, ever since the day my late father bought me the book *The Great Bike Race* by Geoffrey Nicholson. As a writer I had waited twenty-two years since covering my first Tour de France, back in the days when we followed the fortunes of Robert Millar and Stephen Roche. I had seen the Tourmen pass for the first time, on a back road deep in the lush Normandy countryside, and over the years the connection between me and the stars on two wheels had changed, subtly and strongly.

In 1984, when I watched Robert Millar and Stephen Roche pedal past, along with Paul Sherwen, the hero of my teenage years, the link was different. At the time, I was trying – in a far less significant way and ultimately to no great effect – to do what they had done: come to France, live the cycling life, race hard, and see how far my passion would take me. 'Living in a cold-water flat, trying to be a pro,' was how Millar put it. That in turn kept up a connection that went back thirty years, to the time when Brian Robinson, Tom Simpson and Barry Hoban had crossed the Channel to, in the words of Robinson 'live like the French did, and learn from them'.

I admired all of them, because I had an idea of what they had achieved. I could not begin to imagine the sporting side, but the leap in the dark that they had all made was the same: packing a bag and a bike, getting on the ferry to go somewhere you barely knew, throwing yourself on the mercy of people you had never met at a time of life when you had never lived away from home, all on the strength of a single letter and a phone call, and with the hope that the people waiting would not prove to be charlatans or crooks. For all of us who got the ferry, at whatever level, the leap of faith was the same. You bought your ticket; you hoped it would work out on the opposite side of the Channel. The stakes were different: my livelihood would not depend on it, although the experience was formative. But certain things were the same: the language and cultural barriers, the need to learn rapidly, in spite of those barriers; the isolation, the need to save one-franc pieces for the weekly phone call home, the need to last the days until the next race through fatigue, injury, illness and solitude. As Millar said, 'if the French didn't make it they could go back to their parents. If we went home, everyone would say, "You weren't good enough".'

With Wiggins, the connection was different. It was a matter of shared history, moments when our paths had crossed. With other bike racers in West London in the late 1990s, I had discussed the phenomenal junior from the Archer Road Club who would massacre us all if we were unlucky enough to come across him at a race somewhere (I never did, so cannot boast to having taken a kicking from a teenage 'Wiggo'). I had commiserated with a close friend – and remonstrated with the relevant coach – when young Wiggins was selected for the junior world championships in 1998 and my friend's son wasn't. I had ghost-written his columns for the *Observer*, listened on the phone when he ranted about this or that, shared coffees in the start village of the Tour, crucified myself to stay with him when we rode up the climb to Val d'Isère on the rest day of the 2007 race, and got seriously disillusioned with the whole of cycling when he had to leave the Tour with the Cofidis team later in the race after one of their number tested positive. I had seen him win his gold medals in Beijing and Athens, and I still get shivers up my spine when I remember the best Madisons he ever raced: in Athens with Rob Hayles, and in

Manchester at the 2008 world track championships with Mark Cavendish. I had wondered, a little sceptically, when he told me in 2009 he wanted to finish in the top ten of the Tour. As he would say, it had been emotional. The journey didn't end on the Champs-Elysées, but the end of that part of the journey was a moment that had to be lived.

The original reason for writing this book was to trace the path taken by British cyclists in the Tour from the 1950s over the half-century that ended with Chris Boardman and David Millar. The stories of Robinson – who was there to see Wiggins's ride up the Champs in yellow – Simpson, Hoban and all the others, stars and obscurities alike, did not deserve to be forgotten. The British legacy in the Tour, I wrote in 2004, was a rich one, embracing glory, tragedy, joy, scandal, courage and bankruptcy. It still is, but it now includes overall victory, that goal which eluded Robert Millar, which killed Simpson and frustrated Boardman.

There was another reason to go to the Champs. Earlier in the summer of 2012 my father died suddenly. I remembered, always, the cycling memories he had passed on to me: most of all, his tale of watching Tom Simpson race on the other side of the Seine at the Velodrome d'Hiver. Simpson had gone. So had the great velodrome. But the memory remained, and it had been handed down from him to me. So there was no option but to make the effort this time, so that I could place those new images in my mind: a man in yellow hugging a man in black as they crossed a finish line, a yellow Kask helmet in a sea of cameras, a blissful *domestique* weaving down an empty road. I can tell my children, and perhaps, one day, my grandchildren: I was there.

CHAPTER ONE

The First Great Prize

In small French villages, even on the cosmopolitan Côte d'Azur, new and peculiar things do not stay unnoticed for long. And there was much that was new and peculiar about the group of British cyclists who turned up in Les Issambres, halfway between St-Tropez and St-Raphaël, in early February 1955.

Their bikes and jerseys bore a name that any half-educated Frenchman knew was that of a mythical hero with the strength of ten men: Hercules. But strength is not always enough: as they rode in an elegant crocodile along the coast roads and up the hills of the *arrière-pays* in the thin winter sun, each man carrried a Michelin map tucked into the back pocket of his jersey. Clearly, they feared getting lost. None of them spoke French fluently, although some had learned a smattering at school, and the chances were they wouldn't be able to understand any local who tried to explain the way back to La Finca, their pink rented villa down by the shore.

They were pioneers, strangers in a foreign country. When they sat down to dinner, wine was placed in front of them. Finding it not to their liking, they mixed it with water and sugar. It turned from red to blue, like a school chemistry experiment. But they were pioneers in a sporting sense as well, preparing to do something that no British team had ever done before: ride the Tour de France, and finish the race.

The Riviera was where the French professional teams came to prepare for the first races, held locally as soon as the weather warmed up. In the villa next door were none other than the double Tour de France winner Louison

Bobet and his brother Jean, together with their team. They saw the English group as a curiosity, joked about them at the dinner table. When they heard that the new arrivals were preparing to ride 'their' Tour, an event which they all adored and feared, they found that even more peculiar. As far as they were concerned, Englishmen did not race bikes, let alone in *le Tour*. If Englishmen appeared in France at all, they were tourists, or an army landing to liberate them from the Germans.

A contemporary French view of the English and cycling is found in Pierre Daninos's *Les Carnets du Major Thompson*, an affectionate fictional account of a stiff-upper-lipped Englishman's discovery of France and things French. The hero comes across the Tour one July and is shocked that the traffic is stopped for hours, shocked at the attire of the cyclists, and shocked that world affairs (and particularly Commonwealth matters) are driven off the front pages by blanket coverage of the Tour.

Thompson concedes that there is a Tour of Britain, but it is a very different proposition. 'Our cyclists do not cause the traffic to be halted, but race right in it. They stop at red lights, *comme tout le monde*; they are amateurs who are sheltered from the dirty deals done by sponsors, who say "excuse me" as they pass an opponent, and get off their bikes for tea; last but not least these young people, to whom no one pays any attention, are properly dressed.'

What the amused, mystified French professional cyclists witnessed on the Côte d'Azur that February was the moment when the two cultures met and began to shed their received ideas. The scene would be repeated again and again, but in different parts of France, and rarely again involving a whole team. British cyclists would turn up in France to race their bikes, not speaking the language or knowing quite what to expect, but determined that their end goal was the country's great Tour. Over time, however, the ambitious *Britanniques* and the great national sport would subtly adapt to each other, like partners in a marriage. The outcome? Not true love or total understanding perhaps, but at least a shared acceptance of mutual need.

In the next half-century only two Tours de France would take place without at least one Briton on the start line. The Tour would twice visit British shores, and would arrange a trip to the British capital. Millions of British fans would travel to watch the race. Over fifty British cyclists would take part, although less than half would manage to reach the finish in Paris. Only seven would make a major impact. One, Tom Simpson, would die in the attempt.

In Les Issambres that January, the more thoughtful French cyclists, such as Jean Bobet, noticed that the strangers didn't look like bad bike riders. They had a strong and purposeful air. And like any other bike riders, they made the same jokes, teaching the maid and cook who looked after them that the English for '*bonjour*' was 'bollocks'.

Jean had studied English in Aberdeen, and he had accompanied Louison to London the previous winter for an award ceremony. There, they had been struck by the glamour, the black ties and dinner suits, and the mass of well-dressed club cyclists on their big night out. British cycling was insular, but it was clearly flourishing.

For the Bobet brothers' *équipiers*, however, the issue was less complex. It was hard to imagine a group of young *Anglais* taking their sport seriously. Some knew the team manager Syd Cozens's past career as a track racer; they knew nothing of his protegés. Wait for the first races: *on verra bien*. We shall see.

Recent history made scepticism the more prudent course. The first cycle road race, from Paris to Rouen in 1869, had been won by an Englishman, James Moore, but from the turn of the century to the Second World War, British cycling had been a backwater. It was teeming with life, but it existed on its own, with little connection to the wider two-wheeled world. While on the Continent the great races such as the Tour de France, Giro d'Italia and Tour of Flanders flourished and drew huge crowds, road racing had been banned in Britain since 1897. British cyclists' main activity was time trials, 'alone and unpaced' against the watch at the crack of dawn in remote places on code-named courses to avoid any police interest.

Racing on the banked velodromes drew big crowds, while time trialling was massively popular. The awards night the Bobet brothers had been invited to attend was the Road Time Trial's Council's Champions' Gala, so prestigious and well funded that it was held at venues such as the Albert Hall. But British cycling bore no relation to cycle racing as the Bobets knew it. It was a pastoral world of gentle cycle touring and races ridden by Brylcreemed heroes wearing anonymous black alpaca jackets, and the ethos was largely amateur: the big cycle companies – Raleigh, Hercules, BSA – had a mutual agreement that professionalism would be discouraged to avoid the high costs involved.

The isolation was not total. One Briton, Bill Mills, rode for a Paris-based professional team in the 1930s. Two more, Bill Burl and Charly Holland, had been invited to the Tour in 1937. Towards the end of the 1930s, British teams were invited to ride the world road race championships, and 'massed start' events were run on airfields and, famously, at the Brooklands car-racing circuit. Mills founded a magazine, *The Bicycle*, in 1936 and hired a young journalist by the name of Jock Wadley, and the pair of them set about informing the British about Continental cycle racing.

In the 1940s, as British cyclists became aware that there was another world across the Channel, the sport became bitterly divided. During the 10 years before the Herculeans landed in Les Issambres, British road-racing enthusiasts had begun to organise events Continental style, on the open

8

road, taking advantage of a lack of traffic during the war. However, the body which oversaw track racing and events such as Brooklands, the National Cycle Union, was fearful of anything that might upset the status quo. They banned the organisers and riders, who promptly formed a break-away group, the British League of Racing Cyclists.

The BLRC grew rapidly, and road racing based on the European model of place-to-place and stage events mush-roomed. Events such as the Tour of Britain and London –Holyhead were organised, to popular acclaim, and small professional teams began to appear. The sport was rapidly split three ways. The 'Leaguers' felt that Europe was the model to follow, the NCU traditionalists liked their quiet backwater, while the time trialists had an inverse snobbery of their own, centred on the Corinthian purity of the event, where the strongest rider always won, without the taint of professionalism.

The 'Leaguers' had their own uniform, imitating their European heroes, with tyres draped round the neck and motor-racing goggles. They read French magazines such as *But et Club* and *Miroir-Sprint*, passed around in the same slightly clandestine way that schoolboys might swap *Penthouse*. 'Up the League' they would shout as they whizzed past a group of slower moving Unionists. Many cyclists ended up joining two clubs and racing in both bodies' events. The legacy of the great schism is an enduring one: large British towns often have two or more cycling clubs, one of whose names has a 'continental' prefix (such as 'Vélo Club' or 'Groupe Sportif') or suffix (such as 'Coureurs') to denote its old BLRC allegiance. And time trialling has continued, pretty much unchanged in its basic principles and in its lack of connection to the broader cycling world, for almost a century.

Without the great post-war upheaval in British cycling, there would have been no British athletes capable of riding the Tour de France in 1955, and no professional teams capable of bringing them together to prepare for the event. The idea would simply never have occurred to anyone, let alone to the select group of men who gathered in a bar called Nino's in the Swiss town of Lugano on a warm evening in August 1953.

The whole of cycling – fans, racers, media, officials – had descended on the little lakeside town for the world championships. Before they watched the world professional road-race title, the great and the good of British cycling congregated in the bar, although the evening cannot have been particularly drunken, thanks to the presence of H.H. England, the austere editor of the official organ of all British life on two wheels, *Cycling*. With him were a smattering of British journalists, including Mills and his editor Peter Bryan, a cycle-shop owner, Rory O'Brien, and, critically, one 'Mac' McLachlan, a dapper little Scotsman who was publicity director of the Hercules bicycle company.

It is no longer clear precisely who said what or when. Most of those present are now dead; surviving memories are hazy. At some point during the evening, however, the idea of entering a British team in the Tour was mooted. It almost made sense. Hercules, Mac's company, backed a small but successful professional team; one of their four riders, the 'Pocket Rocket' Dave Bedwell, was competing in the professional race in Lugano and would finish twenty-third. That was part of a wider trend.

After being cut off from the mainstream for so long, in the post-war years British cyclists had done more than stay at home and imitate the Europeans. They were now competing internationally on a regular basis as amateurs, and were not disgracing themselves. The previous summer, for example, the Scotsman Ian Steel had won the toughest amateur race in the world, the Warsaw–Berlin–Prague 'Peace Race'. Why not aim higher?

British cycling was divided, but the injection of energy

that had come with the formation of the BLRC had inspired a feeling that anything was possible. After years of frustration, occasional 'massed start' events on motor test tracks and a few abortive trips to the world championships, British cyclists were suddenly travelling to places such as Mexico and the Communist bloc and competing more than honourably. Back home, an entire sport had sprung from nothing in the teeth of bitter opposition in a dozen years. A generation of young cyclists had appeared from nowhere and they looked as good as their European counterparts. Why not now aim for what England would refer to as 'the first great prize'?

There had been one, abortive, British foray to the Tour before. At the end of June 1937, England had been the only onlooker at Victoria station when Charles Holland and Bill Burl boarded the Golden Arrow for Paris and the great bike race. They were accompanied by 'very little luggage apart from two pairs of handlebars'; bikes, standard yellow, were provided by the Tour organisers.

They were handicapped partly by injury – Burl was getting over broken ribs, Holland a fractured collarbone – and partly by inexperience. The greatest bugbear, however, was that they had no experienced back-up or support staff and were constantly forced to ask for help from other teams. Holland had ridden the world road-race championship, but he and Burl started the Tour in almost total ignorance. 'The riders who live near the mountains practise, so I am told, coming round the bends at terrific speeds ... Cornering plays an important part. I hope to learn all about it!' wrote Holland before the start for England's magazine.

The Tour of the 1930s was as much a test of individual initiative as of physical strength. Burl and Holland were issued their race bikes only to find they were not in working order. The bikes were cloistered away before the start to avoid tampering; to enter the room to work on them the riders needed a pass from the race organisers, who, at the vital moment, were at a banquet. Cobbled roads, huge potholes nicknamed 'birds nests', unlit tunnels in the mountains and tramlines in town centres meant crashes were a constant danger. Most of the higher cols were unmetalled, and turned to mud as the snow melted. 'No matter what the weather, we always arrive at the end of a stage covered in mud, dirt or tar,' wrote Holland. Nicknamed 'Sir Holland' by the French, he lasted fourteen days as the lone representative of the three-man 'Empire Aces' team, two crashes in the first two days having put paid to Burl, while the Canadian Pierre Gachon disappeared soon after the race left Paris.

Holland's dispatches for *Cycling* have something of the tourist about them ('We left Digne, noted for its lavender'), and a little of the *Boy's Own* hero: 'In a large courtyard [in Toulon] we sat down to lunch . . . bread, vegetables, meat, fruit, mineral waters, beer, wine. This was some "bun fight".' Physically, Holland was able to stand the pace but in those days Tourmen had to repair their own bikes, and he was, in the end, let down by his equipment. In a two-wheeled variant of the horseshoe nail that lost the battle, a warped washer in his pump valve ended his race when he had a string of punctures in the Pyrenees.

Half a century later, Holland was still bitter at the way it ended. He was convinced the organisers had wanted him out. 'They didn't give me a fair do as far as helping me went. To have an organisation for one man was not their way. They had taken all the publicity they could out of me, and I had the impression they wanted me out because what would people think if I could finish the Tour without any help?'

Another factor must have been at the back of all those

British minds in Nino's bar. Post-war austerity was becoming a memory, and the universal optimism that would lead Harold Macmillan to proclaim Britain had 'never had it so good' extended to the British cycle industry. For men like McLachlan, famed for seizing on anything and turning it into publicity, and Bobby Thom, manager of the Viking Cycles team, competing in the world's greatest cycle race would have made sound economic sense.

With large-scale car ownership just around the corner, the mid-1950s would mark the last hurrah of the world-leading British cycle trade. Half a century on, with mass production of bikes extinct in the UK, it is hard to believe that in the first eight months of 1955, for example, over two million bikes were produced in Britain. The bulk of these were exported, mainly to captive markets in the Commonwealth. The leaders were Raleigh, with its vast complex in Nottingham, and Tube Investments, based in Aston, Birmingham, who owned Hercules.

McLachlan had already been behind Hercules's highly successful backing of the record-breaking time trialist Eileen Sheridan, marketed as 'the pocket Hercules'. The company was known mainly for producing cheap working men's clunkers; McLachlan was looking for a more glamorous, sporty image. At a time when the 'Leaguers' were avid for anything 'Continental', putting his bikes in the Tour de France would lend just the right veneer of glamour. And there would be a chance to break into the thriving European marketplace.

McLachlan was a flamboyant character, though sober in dress and with the quiet accent of a well-educated east coast Scot, and he was not inhibited when it came to publicity stunts. He knew little of cycling, but he understood what made men tick. One 'Mac' legend has him being driven – he famously took taxis or company cars wherever he went – alongside Bedwell as the latter attempted to win a stage in the Tour of Britain. He waved a wad of banknotes out of the car window: the 'Pocket Rocket' delivered.

Putting the first British team in the Tour also appealed to the race organiser, Jacques Goddet. He was an Anglophile, who had been educated at Oxford. There was even something British in his appearance, especially in the shorts and colonial pith helmet he wore on hot days in the Tour. As editor of the organising newspaper and sponsor *L'Equipe*, he was constantly looking for new ways to gain publicity for his event. He had already made attempts to broaden the international appeal of the race. From 1950 to 1952 a North African team had taken part, reflecting France's colonial interests. They earned their place in Tour legend when one team member, Abdel Kader Zaaf, fell asleep under a tree in the Midi and rode the wrong way up the road after he woke up.

The deal to ensure a British team would ride the 1955 Tour was sealed at the Earls Court cycle show in autumn 1954 by McLachlan, Jean Garnaud, the Tour's director of logistics, and Hugh Palin, head of the British Cycle Trade Manufacturers' Union. However, there remained one issue for Hercules. Because the Tour was contested by national selections rather than professional trade teams, the ten best British professional cyclists would be selected and there was no guarantee how many would be from Hercules. McLachlan's solution was to ensure that his riders were the best prepared, so that they would at least provide the bulk of the team. Hence the decision to send them to Les Issambres to train as the Continentals did, and to enter the team in the major European races which formed the build-up to the Tour.

When the ten-man British team finally assembled in Le Havre in late June, McLachlan's tactic had paid off. Six were from Hercules and had been racing the European professional circuit since the spring: Dave Bedwell, who had been with the team since its foundation in 1953, Tony Hoar, who had quit his job as an admiralty plumber at Portsmouth to join Hercules that year, Fred Krebs, Bob Maitland, Bernard Pusey and Brian Robinson.

The others were based in Britain: Stan Jones was a part-time racer, who worked in the office at Tube Investments, Ken Mitchell raced for Wearwell Cycles, and Ian Steel and Bev Wood rode for Viking Cycles. Jones had taken three weeks off work to train, but the others were racing full-time: Steel and Mitchell had both started that year's Tour of Spain in a Great Britain team managed by Bob Thom. Alongside Syd Cozens, the Hercules manager, the mechanics – Thom and the Frenchman Louis Debruycker – and the masseur Julien Schramm, they had a professional film crew with them; sadly, the footage has vanished into the ether.

McLachlan's wheeze was one of the most successful pieces of marketing cycling has ever seen. Half a century on, it remains fixed in the British cycling consciousness that Hercules was the first British team to ride the Tour. (Indeed, it is the only thing for which the Hercules name is still known.) That was, however, manifestly not the case: the 1955 squad was a British national team in a Tour ridden by national teams. The misapprehension is understandable. Robinson saw it this way: 'The Tour organisers provided the jerseys and as far as the French were concerned it was a national team, but personally I was riding for Hercules.'

In Le Havre, the *Britanniques* received their Tour kit from the race organisers, an echo of the days when everything down to bikes was provided in the interests of equity and in order to curb commercial sponsors. 'Two jerseys, a tracksuit, goggles, a waterproof jacket, two caps and a couple of compressed air bottles along with an aluminium case for the clothes. All was signed for and was to be charged if not returned.'

Opinions varied as to how they would fare. A three-page

article in *Cycling* in January 1955 was adamant that a team should not be sent until the following year, and that 1955 should be used to train up riders and gather information. 'We cannot send a team to the Tour unless we are willing to gamble heavily with men's reputations, our future in the race, and Britain's sporting prestige.' ... 'Any rider we could send in 1955 could know no more about the Tour than what he had read, heard, or imagined,' wrote Ken Bowden. 'It would fall far short of reality, for the Tour is unique in terrain, weather variation, racing technique and a hundred and one other things.'

There were more optimistic voices, such as the journalists of *L'Equipe*, who had at least seen the Hercules men in action. The novelist Antoine Blondin felt that Robinson would be on the attack in the opening week, that Maitland offered the best chance for the overall standings, and that Bedwell would be in the hunt for the green points jersey.

He was wrong on every count, even though the team had not raced badly in the build-up. Robinson had finished fourth in the Flèche Wallonne single-day classic and had taken eighth in Paris–Nice, then as now the toughest early-season race in Europe; Maitland was twelfth and took third on one stage. Pusey had finished third in a race in Marseille. Bedwell had finished fourth in the Tour of Calvados. Robinson had worn the leader's jersey in the now-defunct Tour of Six Provinces, a selection race for the Tour. Maitland had come in the top thirty in the Dauphiné Libéré, the hardest event in France after the Tour.

These were performances which, if not directly earning the Britons their place in the Tour, at least proved they had a right to be there. *Cycling* hedged its bets: 'What we can definitely bank on is the best display of British guts and tenacity in any foreign event so far. This is indeed a great moment in our sporting history ... Such participation today would have seemed a fantastic dream but a few years ago. It is an honour to be permitted to ride in such a race. That was the first great prize to be won.'

The headline in *L'Equipe*, 'RICHER IN COURAGE THAN IN EXPERIENCE', perfectly summed up the British team. This was evident in the second stage, the team time trial round Dieppe, when each squad raced together against the watch. The British team had done no training for the stage, were 'disjointed' according to one team member, and left Bedwell and Jones behind from the start, which can hardly have done wonders for their morale.

They were, says Maitland, not a happy team, more 'a lot of individuals put together, just a shambles'. Not all the squad would share his opinion, but it is clear that tensions arose from the fact that he and Cozens, a former star of the winter 'six-day' track races, had been brought in from BSA, Hercules's bitter rivals in domestic racing. There were factions within the team: Maitland and Hoar did not see eye to eye, neither did Robinson and Cozens, while Jones and Krebs just did not get on. At the stage finish in Namur, for example, Krebs ran out of energy, and Jones pushed him up to the finish in the citadel. Jones was fined by the judges, and said he had never paid a fine less willingly.

With considerable prescience, the writer Ken Bowden had pointed out that a British Tour team would suffer language difficulties, and would have trouble adapting to the diet and sleeping in rowdy stage towns. He predicted the punctures and crashes which would cut a swathe through the British team, and made the point that there was no manager in Britain capable of matching the best on the Continent. Cozens, for all that he spoke French, had no experience of road racing, but was a track-racing specialist.

In today's Tour, punctures are at worst an irritation, thanks to modern tyre technology and the fact that many French communities resurface the roads before the Tour passes through. In the 1955 Tour, however, the risk of punctures could not be taken lightly. Perversely, until 1956, team-support cars were not allowed to give their riders a spare wheel with a pumped-up tyre, so that they could simply dismount, change the wheel and ride on. (This was a throwback to the days when the only service cars were 'neutral', and at the very back of the race; then, riders would repair their own bikes as far as possible.) Instead, when a rider punctured, the team mechanic had to get out of the car with a tyre and wheel, and he was not permitted to begin putting the tyre on the rim until his feet had touched the ground. The rider would already have stripped off the old tyre, but fitting a new one on the rim and inflating it could take several minutes. However, to muddy the waters further, if a wheel was broken in any other way it could be replaced complete with tyre; a common mechanics' ploy was to damage a punctured wheel out of the referees' sight. In any case, the energy spent regaining the bunch or riding alone to the finish would take its toll. Maitland recalls chasing the bunch for two hours on one stage, after Jones had punctured on the start line.

The Britons were at a further disadvantage: the Dunlop tyre company had promised the team a £200 bonus for riding its tubular tyres, which were, unfortunately, not up to standard. 'The first question we asked was "Are the tyres mature?"' says Hoar. Like wine, tubular tyres improve with age. The rubber hardens and the cotton casing becomes stronger, making them more puncture-resistant, and to this end professional team mechanics and equipment-conscious cyclists keep them for up to two years, ideally in a dark cellar, or perhaps in the spare bed, before use.

'We were assured that they were [mature],' continues Hoar, 'but we had more punctures than any other team. We all got pissed off with it, so we cut them open – they had the date stamped on the inner tubes and they were only a few months old.'

'The tyres were shit,' recalls Robinson. He had brought

his own from Italy, while Maitland had got tyres of the standard he wanted through connections at Dunlop.

Pusey was worst hit by the curse of Dunlop. On stage two, from Dieppe to Roubaix, he waited for Krebs, who had punctured. As they rode up through the convoy of cars behind the bunch, he punctured himself. The British car was ahead in the convoy, so he put on the spare tyre that all riders carried, but within five miles he had punctured again. With no spare, he rode the final twelve miles on a flat tyre – barely able to control his bike on the bumpy cobbled roads of northern France – then found the gates of the velodrome where the stage finished shut because everyone had gone home.

Steel had a different problem. A hugely talented cyclist, still the only Briton ever to win the toughest amateur stage race in the world, the Peace Race, he fell victim to the conflict of interest that arose when a trade-team boss was in charge of a national squad. The Scot was riding strongly, but he was a member of the Viking team, Hercules's big domestic rival. When Cozens ordered him to drop back from the main group to support a teammate during a mountain stage, Steel protested that he was not willing to sacrifice his own chances. He was threatened with expulsion, and duly went home, his morale in tatters.

Fatally for the British, it was a hot summer: the temperature added to the suffering on the road, and made it hard to sleep amid the hubbub of the city centres after the race finished. 'You were wound up, it was difficult to sleep, and the biggest problem was thinking you hadn't closed your eyes, waking up feeling as though you hadn't slept,' says Robinson. Each stage was followed by the nightly *animation* – a glitzy spectacular, in which 'traditional' accordion music figured strongly, held in the centre of the day's stage town until the early hours of the following morning, so that fans would linger and spend their money.

Rampant commercialisation being integral to the Tour

then as now, the *animation du Tour* formed part of large sponsorship packages tied in to publicity in the sponsoring newspaper *L'Equipe*. Nescafé's *film de l'étape*' was a big-screen showing of a round-up of the day's action. Waterman et Simmons sponsored a '*Tour de chance de chanson*', a talent contest with daily rankings that aped those of the race. There were personal sponsors for individual stars such as Yvette Horner – the '*championne du monde de l'accordéon*' – whose waxwork preceded the race on a car in the publicity cavalcade. Fees were large: the singer Annie Cordy, for example, received 2.5 million francs for appearing throughout the 1955 Tour.

For a tired rider lying in a stifling hotel room with no air conditioning, wound up after the day's efforts and well aware that without sleep the next day would be even more demanding, Horner's *accordéon* and Cordy's caterwauling must have been the stuff of nightmare. Hoar is succinct: 'It was a riot, every night.' Today's Tourmen usually sleep outside town centres in anonymous executive accommodation, and the *spectacle du Tour* has been consigned to history since the early 1980s. Its passing is not widely lamented.

Day by day, the British team became 'small by degrees and beautifully less'. The puncture curse saw Pusey off on stage two. The next day, as Louison Bobet and the France team stamped their authority on the race, Bedwell and Wood abandoned, while Jones went on stage seven. The next two stages did for Steel and Maitland; the latter went over a wall on a descent, survived a broken bike, got through the first Alpine stage, which included the 8,000-foot Galibier pass, then crashed again the next day.

Mitchell and Krebs hung on until stage eleven, when the race climbed the redoubtable Mont Ventoux in Provence, a climb that would take on greater significance for British fans twelve years later. Mitchell had hit a wall in an unlit tunnel going down an Alpine pass – these were 'terrifying, like going at speed into a black hole and having nothing to steer with' – and both he and Krebs were suffering from boils. Mitchell had a large chunk cut out of his saddle in a vain attempt to ease the pain, and started the Ventoux stage with a tyre on the saddle to cushion the shocks from the road.

By stage twelve, the British team amounted to just Robinson, the Hercules team's strongest and cleverest member since they had begun racing in February, and Hoar, who was struggling. 'In starting this Tour, the Britons were willingly taking part in an experiment, and already we can give the result,' wrote Pierre Chany in *L'Equipe*. 'They are very courageous, but the British roadmen are not yet mature enough for a race as difficult and long as the Tour de France. Only Robinson is strong enough to contemplate finishing. For how much longer can Hoar manage to cling on by sheer heroism?'

Perhaps with a certain amount of poetic licence, Robinson says that most evenings he was 'in the hotel, massaged and bathed' by the time his teammate got there. Hoar was primarily a track racer, specialising in events such as the five or ten miles. While Robinson maintained a place in the top thirty, Hoar slipped towards the bottom of the standings. 'It was harder just finishing the Tour than winning a lot of the races I'd won. At the end of the day, you would be exhausted and the next day you'd still be tired when you started again.'

He finished in Paris in last place, as *lanterne rouge*. There is always a sentimental attachment to the last man in the Tour, and Hoar, who had been behind much of the ribald humour at the villa in Les Issambres, played up to it. Cozens found a miniature red lamp to attach to his saddle during the final time trial, and he posed for photographs with a larger red lamp alongside the race winner, Louison Bobet, and his 'rival' for last place, the Frenchman Henri Sitek.

The *L'Equipe* diarist Fernand Albaret took particular interest in Hoar, making much of his '*humour anglais*'. Albaret called his style 'conservative', 'economical in its efforts' and wondered if he might be a Scot. Seeing Hoar running across a cycle track in the rain, Albaret compared him to Chris Chataway, who would beat the world three-mile record in White City later that month. What had impressed him the most on the Tour, asked Albaret? 'The bikinis on the Côte d'Azur,' said Hoar, playing the role to perfection.

Hoar would not be the last Briton to make the news for his *bons mots* – Tom Simpson later raised his profile considerably by hamming it up for the cameras and the sketch writers – and his humour has to be put in context. This was a time when riders' principal income came from appearance money, and the ability to play to the crowds could earn more, bigger race contracts. There was another side to it too. Hoar got through thanks not to his jokes, but to his quick-wittedness. A first-year professional, he adapted rapidly. 'You would talk with the French guys, ride along with them, do what they did. If you were thirsty, and you often were, you would wait until all the *domestiques* stopped and went into a bar for water or lemonade and stop with them.'

He usually found himself with the same companion in the mountains, the Frenchman Bernard Gauthier. Neither were efficient climbers, and Gauthier would enlist help from the roadside for his British partner by asking the crowds to push him '*et l'Anglais aussi*'. On the Ventoux stage, it earned Hoar a fine of 1,000 francs (£10). The Hampshire cyclist came closest to disaster in an Alpine stage in which he rode alone for 120 miles, finishing four and a half minutes outside the day's time limit. He stayed in the race only because officials considered that he had been held up by traffic. 'I know what it is to die,' he said later. 'I died several times in the mountains.'

Having had his brief moments of glory, Hoar never raced for Hercules again. For a while he stayed in Belgium, going to races by train and bus because he had no car. He and Steel started the next year's Tour of Spain in a 'mixed' team, but soon realised they were not going to be paid. 'I thought, "to hell with it," and quit.' He did not touch a bike for almost twenty years, and ended up travelling the world, working on automation controls for oil refineries in Pakistan, Mexico, Central America and Chile. He eventually settled in Vancouver, and, at seventy-three, is still organising races for the British Columbia Masters Cycling Association, with a sideline building cycle frames, racing wheelchairs and sulkies for dog racing.

Although Hercules barely made an impact on the results sheets, they were welcomed with affection. The 'landing' of the British cyclists in Normandy came when the bloody *débarquement* just up the coast only eleven years earlier was fresh in all minds. Le Havre was 'still emerging from the nightmare of war', as *L'Equipe* put it, and was still only partly rebuilt. One team member, Pusey, was reported to have got off the boat with a Churchillian V-sign which made the front pages, although he has no recollection of it. Half a century later the subtext of the liberation is still there: when Jean Bobet recalls the arrival of the Herculeans, it is in the same terms he would use to describe soldiers swarming up a beach: *'débarquait une colonne . . .'* (a column disembarked . . .).

The notion that the great French institution was broadening its reach struck a chord as well. Antoine Blondin wrote that the British were viewed '. . . with the affectionate interest usually reserved for the turbanned delegation from Pakistan when they ride the world championships on postmen's bikes. Their unusual accent, more often heard in travel agencies, stood out among Mediterranean exclamations and Flemish curses.' He noted that in spite of 'looking like refugees' they fitted in to the extent that they 'forgot about teatime'.

The French newspapers treated the Britons with a mixture of affection and ribaldry. Blondin dug out every English stereotype he could find: 'Jones would have looked better as a clergyman; Hoar should have gone back to the pages of *David Copperfield*, from which he seemed to have escaped; Pusey would have done well to put his fox's profile in the service of the county hunt, Bedwell to pull pints of beer as red as his cockney hair, and Robinson himself to buy a top hat and waistcoat to visit his stockbroker in the City.' Cozens's 'round glasses and meditative attitude', he felt, 'belonged to Mr Pickwick'.

L'Equipe derided the lack of coverage in the British press. 'There were only two English riders left but the oh-so-proper *Times* devoted all of fifteen lines to the Tour de France. And the *Daily Telegraph* even deigned to publish the results. However, the *Observer* sent two correspondents for two days' – a day and a journalist for each cyclist – 'and published three-quarters of a page. Undeniably a huge effort.'

They had a point, although the British press was in a cleft stick: history was being made, but in an alien sport in which the plucky Brits were not faring well. There were plenty of British success stories competing for the back pages: the England cricketers Peter May and Denis Compton were batting on in the series against South Africa; on 17 July, as the Tour raced to Marseille, Stirling Moss beat Juan-Manuel Fangio in the British Grand Prix at Aintree; and on the other side of the Atlantic, Rocky Marciano was fighting Archie Moore.

The presence of the Britons opened up the Tour in another way. It was estimated that five hundred English cycling fans had come over with their bikes to watch the race. One report noted that they had slept 'in station waiting rooms, warehouses, hay barns and on the beach', and, milking the French cliché of the uncultured *Anglais* to the full, described two visiting club cyclists from the Bruce Castle Cycling Club in London. 'They certainly needed a shave and their shirts could have done with a trip to the laundry, but they still proclaimed, "I've never seen anything like this. The Tour is the best summer holiday I've ever had."' Half a century on, the British go over each July in their thousands, following the race on their bikes, in camper vans and in organised coach tours.

Precursors of those Tour packages had been run in the 1930s by *The Bicycle*, and another was put together in 1955 by Thomas Cook on behalf of *Cycling*, which plugged it relentlessly. The excursion cost eleven guineas, and as a reminder to us that this was an era when travelling abroad was not an everyday matter, the magazine noted, 'Passports (they cost £1 and are valid for five years) will be required'. One hundred and seventeen English cyclists went to Paris, 'including a sprinkling of vivacious club girls and wives'. Robinson's parents were among them. *Cycling*, ever the primmest of publications, noted: 'One small sightseeing party which included a keen but shy photographer insisted that he record for them the beautiful bikini-clad Parisiennes sunning themselves by the Seine – and what confusion followed!'

The 'Greatest ever 10,000-mile "Test-in-action" of British Bicycle Design', screams the four-page A3 publicity flyer printed on glossy paper. Superimposed on a photo of the snowy Alps, in a jersey bearing the Union Jack logo and the Hercules name, a cartoon cyclist has the stylised muscula-ture and set-jaw grin of action heroes in the *Lion* and the *Wizard* comics. The hyperbole is relentless. 'Never before achieved by a British Bicycle and Rider', 'Buy a Bicycle which has been "tested-in-action"', 'The Finest Bicycle built today'. The marketing hand of 'Mac' McLachlan is easy to spot. 'The severest test of man and machine in the world. The HERCULES cycles, which came through with flying colours' – even if their tyres did not – 'through this cruel ordeal, were built by design and not by accident . . . The result – a better bicycle for you.'

The flyer is dated November 1955, and followed the launch of the company's Tour de France Equipe bike at that autumn's Earls Court cycle show. The bike, priced at £27 15s 6d, 'embodied all the practical knowledge gained from the men who spent a season sampling Continental road-racing conditions', according to one tester.

The reality did not quite match up to the rhetoric. Maitland rode the Tour on his old BSA, painted in Hercules colours. He recalls: 'They couldn't build us a good bike. The frames were rubbish.' Pusey concurs: 'The bikes had been tested since the start of the season and were found wanting.' Cozens had new frames made by a French builder shortly before the Tour started; they were sprayed in Hercules colours and some of the team rode those. It is a trick that is commonplace among professionals who find that the sponsors may produce the monthly pay cheque, but they cannot make bikes just so.

For all that British cycling fans would in future years identify Hercules with the first British team in the Tour de France, and for all the marketing hype, the company and its cyclists derived little short-term benefit. Late in 1955 the riders were informed abruptly that the company would no longer be sponsoring them. From an accountant's point of view, it made sense.

'Mac' had always been liberal with his marketing budgets, and the team had been indulged lavishly. The management, says Maitland, 'believed that if you threw in enough money, you could win everything'. BSA had raced on a £9,000 per annum budget; Hercules had £100,000 to play with. Maitland recalls travelling first class to a race in Brittany; as they went to their hotel after the finish, he spotted their rivals catching the overnight train 'with wooden slat seats' back to Paris.

It was not completely clear where all the money had gone. There were suspicions among some of the cyclists that Cozens was feathering his own nest by double-charging for race expenses. He and his Italian assistant certainly dined lavishly enough on the company cheque. 'The attitude was that the goose would never stop laying the golden eggs,' says Maitland. 'A bandit,' is Robinson's view.

Hercules followed its team into oblivion. The company was swallowed up in the wave of mergers at the end of the decade, as the British cycle industry contracted owing to the spread of car ownership and the loss of its Common-wealth markets. Over the next fifty years, it would suffer the same lingering death as the British motorcycle and car sectors, with which it shared its origins and its names – BSA, Humber, Rover, Triumph.

Tube Investments, the conglomerate which included Hercules and its parent company the British Cycle Cor-poration, bought Raleigh in 1960 and created one giant company, based mainly on a vast site in the centre of Nottingham. TI then set about reducing the vast array of names it owned to just one, Raleigh. By 2005, however, Raleigh itself was merely a stamp on machines imported from Taiwan.

With no major professional teams on the road in 1956, the British Cycle Manufacturers' Union was unable to take up an invitation for that year's Tour. The Tour organiser Jacques Goddet began to explore the chances of inviting a mixed team from Eastern Europe. It would be five more years before another team bearing the Union Jack would line up at the start of a Tour, and in 1956 there would be a single Hercules survivor in the great race: Brian Robinson.

CHAPTER TWO
The Sage of Mirfield

Merely completing the Tour de France is a feat in itself. At the end of the 1955 race, when Brian Robinson rode over the finish line in the Parc des Princes in twenty-ninth place overall, he earned a place in British sporting history. Not that he had any real sense of the wider implications. 'I knew Charly Holland had started the Tour, I knew no one had finished before us, but when you're young and keen you just put your head down and go and don't read the history books.'

However, finishing well at the first attempt with no one to guide him spoke volumes about Robinson himself. In a mere six months, racing in a foreign land, he had effectively made the transition from greenhorn to seasoned professional. That is a tag surprisingly few cyclists ever earn, owing to the spectacularly high drop-out rate: the average professional career is said to be around two years.

Most cyclists have a fair amount of experience before they ride their first Tour. But Robinson rode the Tour with only half a season's full-time racing at the highest level behind him, and with no one to turn to for advice. Most Tour novices can learn from a senior professional or their team manager, but in that 1955 Tour there was no one on hand to warn how a day's racing would develop, advise on how to ride the mountains, or recommend how much to eat and drink. The British manager Syd Cozens's experience was limited to track racing, and the only source of meaningful information, Robinson recalls, was the *Daily Telegraph* journalist J.B. 'Jock' Wadley.

What Robinson achieved in a relatively short career – only six or so years – has to be seen in this context. Other

Britons riding later Tours would benefit from the experiences of their predecessors. Robinson was on his own, and that makes him all the more remarkable. He is one of just a handful of Britons to finish in the top twenty of the Tour. Only three Britons, Robert Millar, Bradley Wiggins and Tom Simpson, have bettered the fourteenth overall he achieved in his second Tour; only two, Michael Wright and Millar, have bettered his eighth place in the 1956 Tour of Spain.

Robinson was the first British Tour de France stage winner, in 1958, and the first Briton to win a place in a trade team among the European elite. His 1961 victory in the Dauphiné Libéré, the French stage race second only to the Tour for toughness, is on a par with Simpson's or Millar's best results. 'He was the pioneer, the ambassador, the man who made us aware of British cycling,' says Jacques Augendre, the Tour de France's official historian. For five years, he was the British flag carrier in a totally foreign sport, as likely back then as a Frenchman making a fine fist of county cricket.

Half a century later, Robinson does not look the type to boldly go where none has gone before. Rather than being a trailblazer, he seems the kind of man who might, perhaps, point the way carefully while quipping that you should be careful not to trip over your feet. He does not have the look of a pioneer, this balding, avuncular man, who punctuates his talk with self-deprecating asides in a gentle Yorkshire accent.

His contemporaries saw a different Robinson. 'He was utterly single-minded, to the point of keeping himself to himself at races, and he could ride himself into oblivion,' says Bob Maitland, a big rival in Britain and a teammate at Hercules. Maitland recalls racing against Robinson in their amateur days on a hill climb – a brief uphill time trial – when 'the race started in rain and finished in snow. He won, but when he crossed the line, he was out for a quarter of an hour.'

These days, Robinson gives few hints about the suffering involved in riding the Tour, but at the time, it clearly shocked him. 'I had no idea men could do this to each other,' he said after his first Tour. The hardest thing, he said, 'was the thought of not sleeping night after night. I didn't sleep from start to finish. It would be hot, my body temperature would be sky-high, and the sheets would be soaked through.'

He is a modest man. There are no trophies, no blown-up photographs of magazine covers or publicity shots in his impeccably cared-for house in the sleepy Yorkshire town of Mirfield. The bike is well hidden in the garage. He is diplomatic to the point of being guarded. There are no complaints, no regrets at things that might have been. For a man who succeeded in an intensely competitive little world where a chip on the shoulder or a large ego is par for the course, he seems unassuming, almost downbeat.

When Robinson achieved star status, for a few brief years at the end of the 1950s, European commentators continually remarked on his sangfroid. It was a quality they loved to project on to all Englishmen, but in Robinson's case there was a little more to it than mere nationalistic cliché. A cool head was only to be expected of a man who at the age of fifteen was laying out corpses for his father, the local joiner and undertaker.

Robinson had the kind of upbringing that breeds an independent personality. The family had moved to Mirfield in mid-war, 1943, from nearby Ravensthorpe. Both parents worked at the local factory producing parts for Halifax bombers, his father Henry on the night shift, his mother Milly on days. Daily contact between the two was a wave morning and evening as their paths crossed on the way to and from the factory, Henry on his bike, Milly on the bus.

Self-sufficiency was the order of the day: the family had a big allotment, thirty or forty rabbits, a couple of pigs. To keep the animals fed, the young Robinsons – Brian, his brother Desmond, their sister Jean – would pull dandelions in the hedge bottoms, while Brian's personal task was to queue in the market for vegetables once school was over.

Robinson is a man who knows his roots. As a continental professional cyclist he returned home each winter to work on the family business as it expanded into house-building. He was married early, to a local girl, and now lives in a house he constructed himself, in the town where he was brought up. He still rides his bike to the café in Langsett, up in the dales, with the same group of mates. They have grown older and slower together. There is an inner stability about him: he has comfortably straddled two contrasting worlds for half a century.

He handled retirement from cycling well, quitting the sport at the time of his choosing for the family building business, which was sold in the early 1990s. He attends Yorkshire cycling club dinners, takes lengthy cycle touring holidays, and appears at the annual meeting of old pros in the Alpine ski resort of Combloux.

It was no coincidence that Robinson succeeded where his teammates failed, in finishing that Tour and going on to greater things. When he started the 1955 Tour de France, aged twenty-four, Robinson already had the wherewithal to be a European professional. He had the ability to look after himself, to sift information and use what he considered worthwhile; he had the communication skills to make connections and use them, and the instinct to recognise the moment and seize it. 'I went to do the job, and whatever it took, I gave it.'

Robinson was no dreamer, but a man who spotted his chance when Hercules sent him and his nine teammates to Europe, and who worked to the utmost to seize the day. Those teammates from 1955 recall him being detached, interested only in what involved him and his racing, or, as he himself puts it, 'so focused on riding the race and doing well that nothing else seemed to bother me'.

While other riders in the Tour team punctured daily owing to the poor-quality Dunlop tyres, Robinson was riding his own superior models made by the Italian firm Clément. Getting hold of them meant a ride over the Franco-Italian border from the team's base on the Riviera to a bike shop in the town of Bordighera. He can still remember the name: Chez Barrale. Robinson had to pay for them himself, but it was all part of 'giving 100 per cent, as you would in a building contract where they wanted the job done as well as it could be'.

He took the same approach to the language problem, which has always bedevilled British cyclists racing in Europe. Cycle racing is demanding enough without being unable to understand a team manager, or teammates, or ask for what you want. Those who succeed tend to be the ones who quickly learn to communicate. Robinson, no natural linguist but well aware of what was needed, worked out his own solution: learning a sentence of French out of the conversation book every day.

His self-sufficient childhood played a part. So did two years spent in national service with the army. There were other factors. In his formative years, he had done all his training with his brother Desmond, three years his elder, and his mates, meeting outside Ellis-Briggs's bike shop in Bradford on Wednesday nights. 'As a junior, I trained at senior level,' he says. It was Desmond who had sparked Robinson's interest in the Tour in the first place. He raced as an amateur, and attended a training camp in France in 1950 at the invitation of the Simplex component company. Back with big brother came tales of Europe and the cycling magazines that gave the twenty-year-old Robinson glimpses of this far-off, exotic world.

Having ridden local time trials, like every young British cyclist, and watched his future teammate Bob Maitland ride the Olympic Games road race in Windsor in 1948, Robinson was captivated by images of the Tour peloton strung out on mountain climbs. 'It was not a fixation,' he maintains, but 'it was stamped on my mind, it was what I wanted to do'. Riding for a team selected jointly by the army and the NCU, Robinson's appetite was whetted further in the 1952 Route de France, a two-week amateur event that he describes as 'the baptism of fire, the eye-opener, two weeks hanging on'. Eventually, it would prove invaluable when he started the Tour: 'Many of the guys who had raced in the Route had gone on to turn pro, so in the Tour I knew who some of the better guys were, and knew a little of what to expect.'

That year, he was high enough up the British amateur ranks to be selected for the Olympic Games in Helsinki, and by 1954 he had gone from meeting his mates outside Ellis-Briggs to racing as a semi-pro in the shop's colours. This was an education in survival as well: he was a single rider 'fighting the big teams, ten guys who would try to nail you down'. Second place in that year's Tour of Britain attracted the attention of the two biggest British squads, Hercules and BSA. Robinson signed with Hercules, because he did not like the BSA manager, Cozens. To his dismay, Cozens followed him to Hercules shortly afterwards.

What Hercules ended up offering him was something unique: a pathway as a professional into the biggest race in the world. It was all the more important because, in the early 1950s, there was no obvious route for a British amateur cyclist to follow to a professional career in Europe. A small number of British cyclists went to Belgium to race, and British amateur teams were sent to major events abroad, but that was all.

Robinson, a newcomer in the Hercules team, saw that some of his colleagues had been softened by years of relative ease. 'They had it so easy. With the expenses, they could put

£1,000 a year away in the bank. That was the price of a good family car at the time. They had had several years on good money, so they weren't hungry. I came from nothing, and I was hungry. You have to seize the chance, do the maximum.' Almost forty years later, his former teammate Dave Bedwell made the same point. 'I wasn't really interested in riding the Tour, and I should have had the courage to say no. I had a golden opportunity, and I wasn't interested. Brian was, and he didn't let things upset him.'

Robinson still recognises the opportunity Hercules offered him and the others. 'It was the best thing they ever did for me,' he says now. 'We grew up with the Continentals. We had the same programme as the French, and we ate like the French. In fact, we probably overate because the food was plentiful, and we had a maid at the bungalow to do the cooking.' When not eating or chatting up the maid, the Herculeans raced, two or three times a week. Robinson soon turned into their mainstay. He was not overawed by the sudden transition from cocks of the English walk to bantams in a very large hen run. 'My view was that I was as good as they were.' His poor relationship with the manager left no room for complacency either. 'With Cozens not being on my side, I had to be the best, so that he couldn't throw me out.'

Robinson adapted well in other ways as well. Within a month, says Jean Bobet, who raced against Robinson and then wrote about him when following the Tour as a journalist, the Yorkshireman had learned cyclists' argot. 'He might not have been understood by a Frenchman in the street, but in the peloton any racer knew what he was saying. Brian was quiet, but he had *un esprit guerrier* – the mind of a warrior. He landed in February, and by April he had forced the European riders to respect him.'

Robinson was simply more single-minded than his nine Hercules teammates. 'I knew what I was going to do. I was glad I had the chance; I was not a guy to take anything for granted, like . . .' The sentence ends there: he does not want to speak ill of the others. 'They had been racing in England and were stuck in their ways. I was on the Continent, I was going to follow what the Continentals did. I had no preconceived ideas on diet, things like that. As far as I was concerned, I was going to eat what the locals did. I never had any difficulties. I never felt homesick. I never hankered after Yorkshire pudding.'

And yet, for all his adaptation to life in Europe, Robinson clearly had no desire to live there. What appears to have set him apart from the other Hercules racers was an ability to compartmentalise his life, which enabled him to concentrate on the job in hand with total attention to detail. He had a life in Yorkshire; when he was on the Continent he was there to earn money for that life. He wanted to finish the Tour, so he got on with it.

As his Great Britain teammates in the 1955 Tour disappeared one by one, Robinson rode on, eventually with only Tony Hoar for company. 'I recovered well, but as for the other guys, it plays on your mind, the whole thing, eating steak and spaghetti at six o'clock in the morning. It's a different life. It's noisy all the time. You're climbing a col and the fans are shouting in your lughole. It really got to me at first: you're going through a funnel of noise.'

Robinson did what successful Tour riders have always done: he cut himself off from all that was going on around him. 'I'm not one to rely on other people, so the way the others disappeared didn't affect me. Essentially, you spend every minute you can resting or relaxing. I was just as keen to get it over with as anyone else. I don't think I enjoyed it. There were always guys in a worse state, physically, so that was good for the mind. It was a relief to get to the finish every day. You'd always be relieved because you'd got in a reasonable group. I can't remember having a good day. You'd be a bit anxious, wondering if it was your turn [to go home].'

Professional cycling is utterly Darwinian: there is no room for the weak or for those lacking in survival skills. Robinson, however, was a fast learner. Just as he had learned French rapidly, he also learned quickly on the bike, for example on the vertiginous descent from Mont Ventoux, close to Avignon, which drops several thousand feet in only a few miles. The hairpins on its north side sweep from left to right in quick succession and can be tackled at up to 60mph by a confident cyclist.

Robinson was not confident, but he was dogged. On the climb, he overtook the Swiss Ferdi Kubler, who was suffering grimly in the heat, imploring the spectators to push him. 'He went past me like a rocket on the downhill, but I was determined that he wasn't going to leave me, as I'd gone past him going up. He was a born descender, so I glued myself to his back wheel.' The 'wooh!' that follows is more surfer than stolid Yorkshireman, but the point is made: that day, Robinson learned to go down hills quickly. Four years later, it would be a major factor in Robinson's second Tour stage win.

Unlike today, when the Tour de France is overwhelmingly larger than any other cycle race on the calendar in every way – spectators, media, stress, prize money, toughness – the 1955 Tour de France differed only subtly from the stage races Hercules had already ridden: Midi Libre, Paris–Nice, the one-off Tour of Europe. It was more tightly organised. The riders' food was laid out for them at the stage start. The cars were all Peugeots. The stages were slightly longer, started earlier, and would usually begin with forty or fifty miles at 'a nice speed, chatting', before an eyeballs-out run to the finish.

Yet the Tour was set apart in other ways which surprised Robinson even then and seem utterly incongruous now. As well as an expense allowance for the riders, the Tour organisers stipulated that the hotels should give the riders half a litre of wine with their breakfast and a litre with evening meals, whether or not they wanted it. The wine went to the masseurs, who were frequently drunk as a result; one, the late Julien Schramm, would yell 'lazy bastards' as he walked past the riders.

There was little knowledge of nutrition. Each day the race organisers doled out '*musettes*' – cotton bags with a strap that could be grabbed by the riders when they were handed up during the stage. '*Musette* one' contained a quarter-chicken 'or similar', ten prunes and ten sugar lumps. '*Musette* two', skipped the chicken, but doubled the prunes.

These were all throwbacks to the years between the wars, when the Tour organisers had a grip on every side of the race, and underlined the fact that Robinson's career spanned a period when the Tour teetered between two eras, ancient and modern. The 1950s saw the introduction of many of the features of the present-day race: the photo finish, the Tour's travelling bank, which for many years was the only bank in France to open on Bastille Day, the green points jersey, the first start outside France, the first transfers between one day's stage finish and the next day's start. Of greatest long-term significance, however, was the introduction of live television coverage, in 1958, when the cameras covered part of the race's passage up the Col d'Aubisque.

As European economies emerged from the post-war rebuilding, road surfaces, bikes and tyres were all improving rapidly, and mountains could be climbed more speedily as derailleur gears were perfected. In 1956, the Tour was run at a record average speed, close to 23mph. Immediately after the war, 20–21mph had been more typical. Considering that the stages were still up to 220 miles, and there were as many mountain stages as ever, this marked a rapid advance towards today's norm of 25mph.

Better road conditions and bikes meant fewer crashes and punctures, and that meant that the riders were only battling each other, not fighting through mud and potholes. As a result, the margin of victory for the unexpected 1956 winner, Roger Walkowiak, one minute, twenty-five seconds remains one of the narrowest on record. This was the start of a new trend for a more tightly contested race.

When racing was simply a matter of battling your way through mud and gravel, trying to stay upright and avoid punctures, it was largely every man for himself. The Tour organisers had liked it that way: the perverse ruling over punctures, which made life so difficult for the Britons in 1955, harked back to the time when outside assistance of any kind was banned but it was ended in 1956.

As the race became less of a lottery, the team element became steadily more important. If a leader could be reasonably certain of having teammates around him, and the race was, by and large, going to be formed of one main group, it was possible to put tactics into play: to organise a team to put a rival under pressure, to chase a dangerous escape, or to set a searing pace to prepare for an attack.

None of these tactics would have been possible without another 1956 innovation: Radio Tour, the short-wave radio system, still used today, which linked race direction, team-support cars and press vehicles, telling them what was going on in the race. It was brought in as the number of journalists on the Tour increased, and it no longer became possible for all their vehicles to travel close to the race. However, it became far more significant for team managers, who now knew what was going on as it happened and could supervise their squads accordingly.

The new era in cycling would also be marked by the first of the Frenchman Jacques Anquetil's five victories in 1957. Anquetil's approach was based on reducing the element of chance to a minimum, by focusing on particular stages – the time trials – and by putting a new emphasis on teamwork, diet and equipment. The Anquetil way was closer to that of

a modern-day cyclist than to the approach of the men who
had raced the Tour only a few years earlier.

But all that was still to come when at the end of the 1955
Tour Robinson and Hoar rode their lap of honour on the
Parc des Princes, then spent the evening at a plush
restaurant with Hercules's marketing manager 'Mac'
McLachlan. Robinson was a respectable twenty-ninth;
Hoar forty places lower and last. The next day, they did
what all the other Tour cyclists did in those days: they went
to Monthléry in the Paris suburbs, and raced.

The British team had not earned any prize money in the
Tour, but there were appearance fees on offer. That
summer, Robinson rode 'fifteen or twenty' criteriums,
exhibition races on small circuits, where the Tour stars sped
round for the public. He would 'get my head down and get
through', receive his £40 per ride, then catch the train to
the next town.

In November that year, Hercules ceased to exist, so the
following spring he and a teammate, Bernard Pusey, set off
for Les Issambres to train on their own, renting a smaller
villa. Robinson had a contract for a race at the end of
February, and they had 'about £105' between them. By
mid-March they were down to £5 and came home, before
Robinson returned solo for one last go, having sold his car,
a Vauxhall Velux, to finance the move. His father, solid
Yorkshireman that he was, thought this was 'a bit light-
hearted', and it was hardly a secure existence. 'I'm usually
calculating, organised in my mind, but I was footloose and
fancy-free back then. I didn't have any money anyway, so it
didn't matter. I'd done my apprenticeship, so I had a job to
go to if it went wrong.'

Robinson was riding *à la musette*. The slang term means
he was racing unpaid, for whatever he could win. 'You
turned up at the first race and got a ride, then you looked at
the paper where the races were listed, and called the

organiser. They were always glad to have foreigners, but there was no start money. If you got £10 travelling money you were doing well. You were riding for the prize money.'

By chance, he encountered one of the more celebrated team managers of the time, Raymond Louviot, a clever young man with a reputation as a talent-spotter. Louviot remembered him from the previous year's Tour, and invited him to race that spring's Tour of Spain, along with Hoar and another member of the 1955 British Tour team, Ian Steel. Louviot would be Robinson's boss for the rest of his professional career.

The Tour of Spain was light years from the relative luxury of the Tour de France. The team vehicles were ex-army jeeps. The riders would finish the day's stage, find their kit in the baggage wagon, and set off for their hotels carrying their bags on their handlebars. There were no masseurs. The Britons were riding for what purported to be the Swiss team. Flags of convenience were accepted practice at the time – Robinson would also wear the colours of Luxembourg, while Irishmen and Australians would later be co-opted on to British teams. By the end of the Tour of Spain there was no flag, however; Robinson ended with blank spaces on his shoulders where the Swiss cross should have been, after complaints that as a Briton he had no right to wear it.

Robinson repaid Louviot's faith by finishing eighth – the highest finish by any Briton in a major Tour until Simpson's sixth in the 1962 Tour de France – and subsequently taking eighth in the Tour of Switzerland. For a rider participating *à la musette*, long stage races such as these had one particular advantage: all expenses were paid.

Robinson's second Tour de France, 1956, was with a mishmash of a squad which illustrated perfectly the eccentricities of the system of national teams. It was named 'Luxembourg' because it was led by the principality's cycling star, the late 'Angel of the Mountains' Charly Gaul, but it included Robinson, an Italian and a Portuguese, together with an Italian driver and Belgian and Spanish masseurs. This was Robinson's breakthrough Tour: fourteenth overall, one place behind Gaul, who would go on to win the following year. He finished third on the first stage to the Belgian town of Liège, commenting wryly that he had earned more prize money in that day than in the whole of the 1955 race.

His best day came in an epic stage over the Alps from Gap to Turin, crossing the rocky wasteland of the Col d'Izoard: Robinson was sixth, racing with the best climbers for the whole 147 miles. The following day, back across the Alps over 156 miles and eight hours, he was seventh behind his leader, Gaul. Even half a century on, mountain performances like these are almost unheard of for a Briton. Only Robert Millar and Bradley Wiggins have climbed the great cols of the Tour with such consistency. That fourteenth place overall needs to be put in context too: only Millar, Wiggins and Simpson have bettered this, Millar finishing fourth and tenth overall in 1984 and 1989, Simpson taking sixth in 1962.

It was a spectacular improvement on Robinson's debut, placing the Briton just below the top of the two-wheeled hierarchy. He considers now that at the time there were three levels: the *grands coureurs*, who numbered perhaps a dozen and included the Tour winners and one-day classic winners; the *bons coureurs*, who were capable of holding down a team place and winning a stage or two of the Tour, and the *petits coureurs*, scrabbling at the bottom.

Robinson rightly saw himself in the *bons* category, but *Cycling* magazine waxed lyrical to the point of hyperbole, which was hardly surprising given his dramatic improvement. 'This lone Briton has done more for British prestige on the Continent than any sportsman since Reg Harris ... There has never been a British roadman abroad with such guts and so clear-cut an idea about where he is going.

Robinson should finish well up in the top ten [next year]. And the year after, in which he reaches [the age of] twenty-seven, the best year of a man's career? How far away is a British win or at least a [top three] placing?'

Spain, Switzerland, France: it had been a massive spell of racing – seventy days on the bike in the space of four months – and Robinson would never be as fit again. The difference between those first two French Tours, he explains, was 'knowing what to expect. In the first Tour I was going into the unknown, in the second I knew what I was at. I knew the riders and I knew how to look after myself mentally and physically.' Completing a first Tour strengthens a rider in every way, but the key, he says now, was that he had spent the early part of the previous winter working for his father, to bring in some cash. Most of the work was digging foundation trenches for houses, and his back and shoulders felt the benefit.

It was not the only winter Robinson would spend with a pick and shovel. The following year, having earned some cash, he built his own house in Mirfield. In fact, he ran out of time, and it remained unfinished while he was in France during the next racing season. A three-storey building, he recalls, it still had no stairs when he held the house-warming. 'I dread to think how many fell through from the landing at that party.'

After his year without a firm contract, Robinson at last found security in 1957, when he was paid monthly by a squad sponsored jointly by the aperitif St Raphaël and Géminiani bikes. Louviot was offered the team manager's job, and his protégé went with him. Soon he would be joined by the Irish pioneer Seamus Elliott, who had earned his spurs racing with the ACBB amateur club in Paris.

While that year's Tour de France was a disaster, with a crash and broken wrist on the fourth stage at Abbeville putting Robinson out, there was one further breakthrough.

Robinson's third place in the Milan–San Remo classic was the first time since the nineteenth century that a Briton had been remotely close to winning one of the great one-day classics.

Robinson's next great achievement, Britain's first stage win in the Tour, was achieved in anti-climactic style; after the referees intervened. This is not to say that the victory was not richly deserved, at the end of 106 miles through France's cycling heartland from Saint Brieuc to Brest on 2 July 1958. It was simply not very satisfactory.

As in 1957, Robinson was riding in the catch-all 'international' team, with four Danes, two Portuguese, two Austrians, two other Britons – Ron Coe and Stan Brittain – and an Irishman, Elliott. While Coe disappeared quickly and Brittain was merely trying to survive, Robinson and Elliott were hunting stage wins, both well aware that a stage victory would bring enhanced appearance money in the post-Tour races.

By the finish in the great Breton port, Robinson was well clear of the main group, riding along with the Frenchman Jean Dotto and the Italian Arrigo Padovan. He felt the strongest: the sprint up a gradual rise to the chequered flag would have been a formality had Padovan not adopted an understandable but illegal tactic. As Robinson came past, the Italian moved towards him, forcing him across the road, first to the right, then the left. A stewards' inquiry – by the cycling equivalent, the *collège des commissaires* – was inevitable, as was their conclusion. 'The cyclist Padovan, having manifestly obstructed in the last hundred metres of the sprint the cyclist Robinson, is relegated from first to second place and penalised ten seconds.'

Robinson and Elliott were having dinner in the Hôtel Vauban in Brest when they learned the news. 'I never thought I'd won,' recalls Robinson. 'There was no podium, no sash or flowers. But I was chuffed, because I knew I'd got my contract safe for next year and probably the year after.'

In a world where your market value depended on your last win, making history mattered less to Robinson than the implications for his bank balance.

Robinson had rapidly made the cultural adjustment from merely racing to racing for a living. He summed up perfectly the philosophy of the professional cyclist in a 1958 interview: 'Every man who rides the Tour is doing it for personal gain, nothing less, nothing more.' Even now, he regrets what could have been a historical win in the previous year's Milan–San Remo – missed by a couple of metres – largely because 'it would have doubled my money and put me on another plane'.

Considering the effort put in over a nine-month season, and the risks taken on the road, the rewards seem minimal by today's standards. Robinson was not at the top of the earning hierarchy, but he was established, with a reliable retainer. He reckoned to salt away roughly the price of a good family car – between £1,000 and £1,500 a season, say £20,000 in today's money. An established professional now might reckon to make ten times that.

While the manner in which the stage win was taken was not entirely satisfactory, there were plenty of spin-offs. By the end of 1958, Robinson was appearing in full-page ads for Dextrose ('Extra energy makes the difference, says Brian Robinson') and Elswick-Hopper bicycles, promoting the Tour Anglais Prima at £23 19s 6d. There were appearances in England, such as the Fausto Coppi meeting, when the Italian great was flown over to London's Herne Hill velodrome.

By the end of that year, there was more discussion back home about whether Robinson could win the Tour de France. The consensus was that a lack of team support would be his Achilles heel. In fact, his weakness was elsewhere: his stomach. In 1956, what cyclists refer to as 'gastroenteritis' had almost cost him his eighth place overall

in the Tour of Spain, and it put him out of the 1958 Tour
following the stage win.

It had nothing to do with the preponderance of prunes in
the Tour organisers' *musettes*. During the Tour de France,
the cyclists' immune systems are stretched to the limit,
making them more susceptible to infections of all kinds.
Until very recently, poor hygiene – in food preparation and
such habits as sharing bottles – exacerbated the problem.

In the Tour, physical weakening tends to make itself felt
first in a cyclist's digestive system, which is placed under
massive pressure owing to the vast amounts of carbohydrate
and liquid which have to be processed on a daily basis. Once
an infection has set in it is rare for a cyclist to be able to ride
on in the Tour, because he simply cannot get enough
energy into his muscles. The only cure is rest, and that is at
a premium.

The same trouble came close to putting Robinson out of
the 1959 Tour. Again he was racing with the international
team, again it was a melting pot of nations, although the
mix reflected the Yorkshireman's increasing stature: two
Austrians, two Danes, two Portuguese, a Pole, Elliott and
four Britons – Robinson, John Andrews, Tony Hewson and
Vic Sutton, also from Yorkshire.

It was the usual story: Robinson 'ate something dodgy
and spent the night on the toilet' after performing
impressively through the high hills of the Massif Central
between Albi and Aurillac. He rode through the next day,
when the race travelled across the Massif Central again to
Clermont-Ferrand, trailing behind the field in a desperate
battle for survival.

In hot weather, these are some of the toughest roads in
France, constantly rising and falling. Elliott remained with
Robinson, chivvying him, pacing him, pouring water on his
head as the Tour's doctor Pierre Dumas administered
glucose tablets. It was the kind of heroic spectacle the Tour
reporters loved. '*Robinson en perdition*' ran the next day's

headline in *L'Equipe*, which described Elliott's efforts as *'attentions de mère poule'* – the solicitousness of a mother hen. 'Nothing could be more moving than to see, on this French road, an Englishman and an Irishman battling together against fatigue and despair.'

Both men finished well outside the day's time cut and both expected to be eliminated. However, Robinson stayed in thanks to the astute manager of the international team, Sauveur Ducazeaux, who had masterminded Roger Walkowiak's totally unexpected overall win in 1956. The manager recalled an arcane rule which stated that a rider who started the day in the top ten could not be eliminated. Robinson had started the day ninth overall and stayed in, while Elliott went home. The mother hen was cooked; the chick avoided the pot.

Fortunately, the next day's stage was a brief time trial. It was a mere eight miles, admittedly up a very steep extinct volcano, the Puy-de-Dôme, but still infinitely more conducive to recovery than a long day in the saddle. Robinson duly rested up, survived the Alps and, in the final week, began thinking about another stage win.

Several days beforehand, rider and manager had set their sights on stage twenty from Annecy to Chalon-sur-Saône. It was a classic 'stage of transition', taking the riders from the Alps to Burgundy for the final time trial. It was hilly enough at the start to make it likely that riders would try to escape, long enough that the favourites would want to save their strength before the final *contre la montre*, which would settle the overall standings. The downhill trajectory – starting high in the mountains, finishing in the plains – would favour a lone rider with strength in his legs.

By now there were those who were calling Robinson *le sage* – and there was nothing of the ingénu about the way he escaped. Instead of his normal road-racing wheels, strongly built with heavier tyres, the wheels he would use for a time trial – lighter, more rigid, with special lightweight tyres –

had been put on his bike. He attacked on an early climb, the Forêt d'Echallon, in the Haut-Jura between Oyonnax and Bellegarde, the final ascent of the Tour counting for the King of the Mountains prize.

At the summit, Robinson surged past Jean Dotto, the third of the trio from the previous year's Brest stage. 'He was twenty to thirty yards behind, shouting to me to wait, but I knew he couldn't go down hills.' Robinson was on his own and he stayed that way: by the finish in Chalon ninety miles later, the peloton were over twenty minutes behind. It remains one of the biggest stage-winning margins in post-war Tours.

By the end of 1962, the year when Tom Simpson made his personal piece of Tour history by becoming the first Briton to wear the yellow jersey, Robinson had retired at the age of thirty-one. A restructuring of France's professional teams meant he would finally be separated from Louviot. St Raphaël had not found him a place in their team for the 1962 Tour. There were no regrets. The family building business was waiting. 'I was tired of living out of a suitcase. I had two kids who were growing up. I had to decide whether I was going to die on the bike or do something else.'

He had started racing late, turned professional late – too late, some said – and his flowering had been relatively brief. Befitting a builder, however, his legacy would be an enduring one: Robinson's solid presence near the top of his trade established a pathway for riders such as Simpson and Elliott, both of whom entered professional cycling as his teammates.

Before Robinson, there had been occasional interlopers in that small, closed world, notably the Australian Hubert Opperman and the Briton Charles Holland, but they were isolated individuals compared to the numbers who followed Robinson. The Tour de France organisers would hardly have invited Great Britain teams to the event in 1960 and 1961 if Robinson had not already proved that Britons could compete in the race on equal terms, could learn the language and do more than bring a touch of the exotic with them. The fact that Robinson and Elliott, to a lesser degree, had the ability to act as team leaders weighed heavily in the balance as well.

Equally importantly, Robinson had a high profile back home – in the cycling world if not the wider sporting world. He drew British fans to France. The experience of one, Duncan Hamman from Manchester, was probably typical in what it says about the average level of knowledge of the race. Having heard that Robinson missed hearing English voices cheering him on in the Tour, he and three of his clubmates decided in 1957 to make their voices heard on the Galibier pass, the highest point regularly crossed by the race. Hamman had no idea where the Galibier was, so he went to W.H. Smith, bought a map of France and enlisted the aid of the staff in locating the pass. He and his mates flew to Geneva only to find that Robinson had retired; they rode their bikes the hundred-odd miles to the pass and found that it had been closed by the police to let the race through, but they still managed to watch Anquetil at the foot of the climb as he rode to his first Tour win.

Robinson also drew talented cyclists from the UK to France in his wake, much as Simpson's successes would do half a dozen years later. He acknowledges: 'I hadn't been a great champion at home before I came over, so guys would look at my results in the Tour, think they were no worse and wonder if they could do the same.' By the end of the 1950s, there were little clusters of them in Brive, Reims and Brittany, living in caravans and campsites as they attempted to follow the Robinson trail. Some were directly inspired by meeting Robinson or reading about him, while the brightest star of them all, Tom Simpson, was Robinson's protégé, initially at least, and would sign his first professional contract under the watchful eye of the pioneer himself.

CHAPTER THREE

A Question of Nationality

When Brian Robinson won his second Tour de France stage in 1959, that day's racing was sponsored by a wine company, Cepno. His team won the stage's Martini International Challenge. His food (not just his coffee) was provided by Nescafé. During the race he drank from a bottle supplied by the Vittelloise water company, and after the race he glugged down Perrier.

He was timed into the finish by Lio watches, and when he had his day of suffering in the Massif Central he was tended by Dr Dumas from the Aspro medical car. If he were staying in the centre of the stage town, he might be kept awake by the singers and accordionists of La Parade du Tour, sponsored by Butagaz. The team car driven by his manager was supplied and modified by Peugeot.

There has never been much space for the amateur spirit on the Tour. The event was devised as a publicity stunt to sell newspapers and has been a largely happy marriage between commerce and sport for the century or so since it was founded. By the 1950s, sponsors' and suppliers' branding was almost ubiquitous on the Tour, backed up by advertising in the newspaper *L'Equipe*, which organised the race.

There was one contentious area where commercial and sporting interests could not be reconciled: who ran the teams. By the late 1950s, the Tour was one of a few races where professional cyclists were grouped into national and regional selections. The rest of the season, the cyclists rode in professional squads with sponsors which could be anything from a cycle manufacturer to a coffee-maker.

The Tour organisers had imposed the national team

system in 1930. Until then, the riders were organised into *'groupes sportifs'*, sponsored by cycle companies, and *'touriste-routiers'* who competed with no back-up. That lasted until the organiser Henri Desgrange became convinced that the cycle-makers who sponsored the riders were fixing the race and it needed to be 'purified'.

The principle was simple, the practice arcane. The teams for the Tour were selected by national federations after complex horse-trading in which the organisers of the race had a considerable amount of influence. To start with, it was Jacques Goddet and his assistants who would decide how many teams there were and how many riders each would include. The 'international' or 'Luxembourg-mixed' team for which Brian Robinson rode four Tours was set up to ensure that there was a place for stars from countries that were not strong enough to field a full team. The riders applied for places, and their allocation was negotiated between the national federations involved and the organisers, who nominated the manager.

The arrival of Robinson and the Britons in the Tour came at a time of intense debate about whether the national teams should be abandoned and the race opened to the trade squads. During the 1950s, the professional teams had become increasingly vocal as the cycle companies which had been their backers gradually gave way to *extra-sportif* sponsors from outside the cycle trade. Nivea was the first company to put its name to such a team, effectively turning its cyclists into travelling sandwich-board men, and other companies followed, making up for a lack of funds from the cycle companies. *Extra-sportifs* did not look for a lengthy commitment to a team, as a bike company might: their purpose was to get maximum publicity, then depart. The professional sponsors' case against national teams in the Tour was simple: they paid the riders all year round, so why should they be excluded from the biggest shop window of the year?

Initially, race organisers across Europe were against the *extra-sportifs* because they feared competition for sponsorship income, so they banned them from the races. The sponsors, however, controlled the riders, and could dictate where they rode. Faced with the threat of having no riders in their races, by 1959 most of the organisers had given way, apart from the most powerful of them all: Jacques Goddet, the director of the Tour de France.

National teams were popular with the public, who found them easy to identify with. The intense speculation about who would be in the national teams raised the race's profile, while the plethora of French regional teams brought in to keep the numbers up – five in 1955, for example – ensured that every part of France felt involved. So deeply involved, in fact, was the cycling public that the France team manager, Marcel Bidot, would receive threatening letters from fans who felt he had selected the wrong men.

The average Frenchman found the system easy to understand, but the managers of bigger national teams had to tiptoe through a diplomatic minefield each year as they attempted to make sworn rivals race in the same team. A 'summit' meeting had been necessary to bring the two Italian stars, Fausto Coppi and Gino Bartali, together under the national banner in 1949, and matters came to a head in the 1958 Tour with a dispute over whether Louison Bobet, Jacques Anquetil or Roger Rivière should lead the France team.

Even though the Tour organisers had imposed national teams to reduce the sponsors' influence on the racing, under-the-table deals were actually made more likely. There was vast potential for secret collusion between teammates who rode for the same commercial team for the rest of the year but were put in different national or regional teams for the Tour. The conflict of interest was all too obvious: for example, an Italian *domestique* who rode for a French trade team with a French leader eleven months of the year would be foolish not to help out his trade team leader in the Tour, even if he were riding for Italy and his leader for France.

The same conundrum applied to professional team managers. If they ran national teams in the Tour, there was every chance that they would favour their own riders, so the teams had to be directed by outsiders who did not work for a trade team. In 1955, the presence of Syd Cozens, manager of Hercules, at the helm of the Great Britain squad caused howls of protest among the French cycle trade, who felt the British were bending the rules. To guarantee their neutrality the team managers – Marcel Bidot of France, Alfredo Binda of Italy – tended to be ex-cyclists of stature who had built a career outside the sport. The manager who guided Robinson to his 1959 stage win, Sauveur Ducazeaux, had a day job running a Parisian restaurant called the Bordeaux–Paris. The day the Tour finished, he was back in the kitchen.

The strongest argument against national teams, however, was that the nations were not there. Professional cycling's heartland was limited to half a dozen European countries; only the French, Belgians and Italians were strong enough to produce teams with true strength in depth, and thus they would have two or three teams each. Smaller cycling nations such as Luxembourg, Spain, Holland, Switzerland and Portugal either fielded far weaker squads or were combined in the 'international' teams. Sometimes, the outcome was totally incoherent: in the 1960 Tour, for example, France, Italy, Belgium and Spain had fourteen-man teams, while nine other squads, including four 'regional' French teams, had only eight riders, putting them at a serious disadvantage.

Once Brian Robinson had proved that British cyclists were capable of competing in Europe, the national team system provided an obvious pathway for those with ambition who wanted to progress beyond domestic racing. That entailed travelling to France and racing well enough to earn a place in the international team on the Tour or, later, to be selected for Great Britain. The transition from British to European racing was a tough one, but those who made the move were helped by being able to register as 'independents', a category halfway between amateur and professional. 'Indies' were often attached to amateur clubs and had the right to ride all but the biggest professional races and the better amateur events, and they could revert to amateur status after two years if they wished.

The new opportunity drew men such as Stan Brittain, the best British amateur stage racer of the time. The Liverpudlian had finished third in the Peace Race and won the Tour of Sweden, and he moved to the south of France in 1958, along with the former Hercules rider Bernard Pusey. As Robinson had in 1956, Brittain was riding *à la musette*. He had the name Helyett-Leroux on his jersey but was receiving no money, and in the winter he returned to his job as a joiner and pattern-maker.

That year, Brittain became the third *Britannique* to finish the Tour, and his experiences say much about the eccentricities that stemmed from the national team system. He turned up at the 1958 Tour start in Brussels – only the second *départ* outside France – knowing only three of his eleven teammates in the 'international' squad: Robinson, Ireland's Shay Elliott and the other Briton, Ron Coe, who was a prolific winner in England. Their *équipiers* were truly 'international': two Austrians, two Portuguese and four Danes. Each had been selected by his national federation; in the Britons' case, the National Cycling Union. The best rider in the team was the Austrian Adolf Christian, who had finished third the previous year.

Robinson would have preferred to race the Tour for his trade team, St Raphaël. He spoke for many other Tour cyclists when he said that as a professional whose job was to earn himself a living, he was put at a disadvantage by being thrown together in the most lucrative race of the year with riders who were not as strong as his trade teammates. And he did not like switching from his trade team to ride the Tour for the 'international' or 'Luxembourg' squad: 'You get a "feeling" (call it team spirit, or whatever you like) in stage races when riding with your trade team which makes the task much more pleasant than when you are riding with a mixed crowd who may speak different languages.'

Brittain saw at first hand what happened when riders were thrown together in this way. 'Robbo wasn't very keen on the Portuguese, and the Danes were very self-contained. I turned up and Robbo said he would go and see Christian and ask if he wanted to ride with us, split the prize money. He saw him, and Christian didn't want to know.' Brittain, Robinson, Elliott and Coe formed their own team within a team. They ate at their own corner of the dinner table, and Elliott and Robinson would talk tactics in their shared hotel room. Brittain and Coe were delegated to work for the two stars, waiting if they punctured, helping them move through the bunch. The little band was not together long: on the day that Robinson won stage six to Brest, Coe retired, while Robinson himself was struck down by stomach trouble five stages before the finish. In spite of breaking a rib in a crash, Brittain battled through to finish sixty-ninth.

Making the mental leap from the cosy world of British domestic racing has always been a precondition for Britons who want to succeed in European professionalism. Merely crossing the Channel and racing is not enough; since Robinson, those Britons who have succeeded have accepted that what they achieved at home counts for nothing. Brittain clearly recognised this when he said: 'Locked in a little country, sticking by tradition, we think we can ride bikes. We think we're good if we do well in the Tour of Britain and we think the Tour of Britain might one day become like the Tour de France. It makes me laugh. We will never get to know what this sort of thing entails until we break open the gates of our tight little world and come over here and live with it.'

Brittain would, however, never finish another Tour. He missed the 1959 race after breaking a wrist and was put out by food poisoning in 1960. Even so, he continued in France until 1961 – 'It was a living, we were never short of money; if I wanted to go home, I would just go to the airport.' After which he returned to Britain to race out his career with the Viking team.

Another who 'came over and lived with it' was Victor Sutton, a slender youth with wispy blond hair from the lowlands of South Yorkshire. He set off for France in 1958 with two other Britons, John Andrews and Tony Hewson, in a three-ton Austin ambulance. It was 'built for desert warfare', bought cheaply in a breaker's yard near Chesterfield and kitted out with four folding beds. Sutton was a boat-builder by profession, and did the joinery; Andrews made the mattresses.

'We had no idea where to go, how the system worked, or how to get our hands on prize money other than *primes* [cash prizes at the event],' recalls Hewson. Life in an ambulance was not ideal: the roof rack would bring down electric cables in the campsites and the 'code of conduct' for living in their cramped quarters included the rule 'not more than two people to make beds, dress, undress or stand up at any one time'. The trio settled in Reims, where the *Bicycle Club Rémois* paid their expenses and transported them to events. They became minor local celebrities, attracting crowds of curious onlookers as they stripped the engine of the ambulance with the help of the instruction book.

At the end of the season, Andrews finished thirteenth in the world road-race championship, and became the second Briton after Robinson to earn a professional place with a

French team, racing with Louison Bobet's Mercier squad. Having worked the winter in Britain, all three earned places in the 'international' team for the 1959 Tour, along with Robinson and Elliott. Andrews abandoned on stage three across Belgium; four days later, it was Hewson's turn. The nine-stone Sutton showed unexpected climbing ability, which helped him move from 109th place at the end of the first week to thirty-seventh when the race reached Paris. He was the first Briton to show that hallmark of the pure climber, the ability to change pace rapidly by spinning a small gear at speed on the Tour's high mountain passes. He also had a Nelsonian ability to understand only what he wanted to; when asked by his team manager, Sauveur Ducazeaux, to assist a Danish teammate on the fastest stage of the race, he replied, '*Non compris*'. Hewson, who did understand, and therefore had to wait, was unable to regain contact and withdrew.

In the Pyrenees, Sutton climbed alongside Bobet, Anquetil and the eventual winner, Ercole Baldini, and in the Alps he was not far behind the two best climbers of the day, Charly Gaul and the 'Eagle of Toledo', Federico Bahamontes. On the time-trial stage to the Puy-de-Dôme, an extinct volcano in the Massif Central, he topped the leader board for an hour, and managed sixteenth place. He was the climbing revelation of the race, yet his inexperience meant he was terrified when it came to going down the mountains: on the biggest Alpine stage he lost six minutes on the sinuous series of hairpins descending from the Petit St Bernard Pass, to the fury of his manager. When the team car overtook him, and the mechanic tried to hand him a spare tyre, he was unable even to take one hand off the handlebars.

The following year, Sutton was one of the leaders of only the second Great Britain team to start the Tour. He was tipped to match Gaul and Bahamontes in the mountains, but he started the Tour over-raced, having finished fifth in the Tour of Switzerland a few days before the start. He collapsed on the final Alpine stage, following what appeared to be a minor heart attack. He was told he should not race again, but by the time the doctor's letter reached him in Reims he was already competing, and he saw out the season. It was, perhaps, a premonition of the heart trouble that would eventually end his life in the summer of 1999, not long after he had finished the Étape du Tour as a celebration of what he had achieved forty years earlier.

The invitation to an eight-man Great Britain team for the 1960 race came partly because cycling in the UK was now united, formally at least. The previous year the BLRC and NCU had buried the hatchet and joined forces to form the British Cycling Federation. The Tour organisers could now be certain that the team would be selected from all the best British cyclists, in theory without prejudice. Moreover, the progress made by British cyclists – and the Irishman Shay Elliott – since 1955 underlined that interlopers could compete and integrate. Sutton, Hewson, Andrews and Brittain had all played their part, but Robinson had led the way with his stage wins and his all-round presence, and had been good enough for long enough to be considered as team leader.

Ironically the Yorkshireman was not bothered what flag he was flying as he raced to twenty-sixth place. 'I was just doing my job by then. There was no sentiment. The target was the same whether or not you rode for Great Britain: to do something and get your contracts. I had to jolly the others along and hope they made it. They all used to moan about the food. I'll always remember Vic Sutton saying he could murder some of his mother's Yorkshire pudding, and to me that means he was thinking the wrong thoughts.'

Compared to the ten pioneers of 1955, the Great Britain team of 1960 was battle-hardened. Robinson was the leader; Brittain and Sutton had both finished the race before;

Andrews had ridden the previous year, while Tom Simpson had shown colossal promise in less than a year as a professional, and would arrive in Paris an exhausted twenty-ninth. Harry Reynolds and John Kennedy were also based in France, as was Norman Sheil, a talented track racer.

Brittain and Reynolds were part of another cluster of British racers, based in a caravan parked in a farmer's field near Brive. They had a '10 per cent man' who would enter the Britons as a group in two or three races a week, averaging £15 a race. With *primes*, it made for a good living, at a time when the average wage in Britain was about £10 a week, and Reynolds sent money back to his wife in Birmingham. The Brive bunch shared their winnings and also reached an informal understanding with Sutton and his mates that they would not ride against each other.

For Reynolds and Brittain, the Tour was quite a luxury after their hand-to-mouth existence in Brive. They were, in theory, being paid £10 a day, and had masseurs and mechanics to look after them. But gastroenteritis saw off Brittain, while a broken collarbone ended Reynolds's race. To add insult to injury, the Britons had signed an agreement with the manager, Ducazeaux, that he would deal with the money, but Reynolds for one never saw a cheque. There were little cultural differences as well: Ducazeaux banned them from drinking tea, British style, with milk. Instead, they were told to take herbal brews, so they adopted a strategy of persuading the maids to smuggle them 'proper' tea in a pot. Major Thompson would have approved.

The insecurity and lack of support when racing *à la musette* meant it was not a long-term way of life for émigré British cyclists. They either moved forward by obtaining a professional contract, as Andrews did, or returned to England after a season or two. Reflecting the rapid turnover of riders, in 1961 Brittain had three fresh companions in Brive: Sean Ryan from Liverpool, Ken Laidlaw from the

Scottish border town of Hawick and a tall young man from Cheshire, Vin Denson. The Brive quartet were duly selected in the largest Great Britain team to start the Tour: its twelve members also included Simpson, Robinson – riding his last Tour – Elliott, whose Irish nationality was conveniently ignored, the sprinter Albert Hitchen, who was to carve out a career in Holland and Belgium, and four British-based riders: Ron Coe, Ian Moore, Pete Ryalls and George O'Brien.

Riders in GB teams always succumbed rapidly in the opening stages of the Tour, but the British were not alone in this. All the weaker national and regional teams suffered similarly, and Robinson, for one, believed that the ability range in the Tour was actually wider than in other major events. By stage five, in 1961, two-thirds of the British team had disappeared; those left were Elliott, Robinson, Denson and Laidlaw, who had virtually no experience of racing at this level – he had moved to France just six weeks earlier on a temporary professional licence solely to ride the Tour, having used the Peace Race as preparation.

He had already come within an ace of being eliminated. From the start, the team had expended a good deal of energy trying to assist Simpson, who had started the race with a knee injury that had been troubling him since the spring, and on stage four, across the heart of Belgium to the town of Charleroi, Laidlaw was delegated to nurse him through. Simpson was unable to hold the pace early in the stage; Laidlaw duly waited, but realised that Simpson was going nowhere and that if the pair of them continued together they would both finish outside the day's time limit. 'I swore at him, and said if he didn't buck up I'd be out of the Tour. He swore back, was really pissed off with me, and tore my legs off for twenty kilometres. We went up the Mur de Grammont' – a one-in-four cobbled climb that is a key part of the Tour of Flanders route – 'and spotted three Italians. He said, "Stay with them, and you're in the Tour," and got off his bike. I never saw him again, and rode on with the Italians.' Over forty years later, Laidlaw can remember that they were exactly twenty-two seconds outside the time limit. 'They didn't dare eliminate a quarter of the Italian team, so we were kept in.'

A few days later the Scot was again close to abandoning after he caught gastroenteritis. He dropped back into the convoy of vehicles behind the peloton, and was caught up by a car containing the British journalist 'Jock' Wadley, who had been a father figure and adviser to British cyclists on the European circuit since the Hercules days. Laidlaw said to Wadley that he was quitting, and was told, 'You'll regret it all your life if you do.' It is an exchange that seems inconceivable over four decades on, and is a reminder that the Tour was then a small, almost family affair, not the impersonal monster it is now.

Wadley was right: in Paris Laidlaw finished sixty-fifth, having come close to winning the sixteenth stage through the Pyrenees. The seven-hour haul from Toulouse ended with a twenty-kilometre climb to the ski station of Superbagnères: Laidlaw took the lead at the mountain's foot, only to be caught with three kilometres to go and left with the meagre consolation of the £95 prize for 'most combative' rider of the day. It was a promising first Tour, but the following year Laidlaw quit professional cycling, largely because the event had adopted trade teams. He could not find a slot in a professional team, so he returned to England and raced for the Viking team, 'a huge step backwards'. A year later he learned he could earn five times his carpenter's wage in New York, so he crossed the Atlantic 'an angry young man' and never returned.

Chances like those offered to Victor Sutton, Ken Laidlaw and Stan Brittain were about to become far more rare. The 1961 Tour had taken place amid increasing pressure from the *extra-sportif* sponsors, with one team, Liberia–

Grammont, threatening to forbid their star rider Henri Anglade to start for the France team. Ten weeks after the race ended, Jacques Goddet and Félix Lévitan summoned a select group of twenty-two journalists to the *L'Equipe* office in Paris. It seems curious now, but the Tour was not going to take the major step of reverting to trade teams without the approval of those who wrote about the race. This was partly public relations, partly a reflection of the fact that Goddet and Lévitan were, as editors of *L'Equipe* and *Le Parisien* respectively, journalists themselves.

Not all their colleagues agreed with the change Goddet and Lévitan proposed. Maurice Vidal, director of the magazine *Miroir-Sprint*, wrote: 'Since when has the intrusion of money been any guarantee of honest behaviour? Cycling needs to be a sport rather than a business.' Goddet and Lévitan also had misgivings: they feared that rich sponsors would be tempted by the idea of hiring as many major names as they could and putting them in the same team. This is precisely what happened, and still does. The Tour organisers recognised that the reversion to the trade-team formula would make it harder to open their race to new nations, and in particular the rapidly emerging East European countries, and so Goddet and Lévitan founded the Tour de l'Avenir. The Tour of the Future ran alongside the great race as a showcase for amateur cyclists from around the world.

An initial plan to run the Tour with national teams every four years was stillborn and apart from a brief reversion in 1967 and 1968 the era of national teams on the Tour was over. From now on, the only major race where professionals would have to swap trade for national loyalties was the world championship.

This drastically reduced the openings available to Britons in the Tour. Being a good British cyclist who raced at a reasonable level in France would no longer be enough to earn a ride in the great race. To get in the Tour, a cyclist would now have to earn a trade-team place, then earn a place in that trade team's squad for the Tour. To load the dice further, in the era before the global economy and with import duties still high, few European sponsors had products that needed publicity in the UK, so there was no incentive to hire Britons unless they could make a major impact in Europe.

The British also fell foul of an agreement between the Tour organisers and the trade teams that limited a Tour team to three or four riders from outside the country where the team was registered. This was intended to ensure that the teams had a 'national' flavour, but it meant a British cyclist would always be the last to be chosen. That was made clear in 1962, when St-Raphaël deemed that Brian Robinson was surplus to requirements in spite of his pedigree.

A year later, through his magazine *Sporting Cyclist*, Jock Wadley was already calling for the Tour to return to the national system. 'The public prefer a national struggle and it is the public whose interest keeps the Tour going,' he wrote. Wadley felt that the *extra-sportif* sponsors were buying up the strong riders to guarantee results all year round, which meant that with only nine or ten in a Tour team, big names were being left out of the race.

The Britons, he felt, had been put at a disadvantage with the end of national teams. '[They] enabled Brian Robinson to come to the front, to be signed on by a Continental firm; it was in a national or international team that he won his two stages,' wrote Wadley. 'It was the national team system which gave Vic Sutton the chance to ride the Tour and to shake us all by topping an Alpine col with Bahamontes and Gaul and all the field strung out behind. Perhaps the abandoning of trade teams would reveal some new talent.'

One man who had good reason to share Wadley's view was Alan Ramsbottom, a laconic, bespectacled sewing-machine mechanic from east Lancashire, nicknamed the 'Clayton le Moors demon'. He had met Brian Robinson at a North Lancashire Road Club dinner in Blackburn ('He rolled up looking cool in a Ford Consul or whatever'), was duly inspired, and arrived in Troyes in early 1960, with £80 in his pocket, 'enough for two months'. The main amateur club in the town, UV Aube, had advertised in *Cycling* for British riders; Ramsbottom's clubmate and mentor, the journalist Harry Aspden, put him in touch. Having missed out on the Olympic shortlist, Ramsbottom had no reason to stay in England, so he drove over with two other Britons, got his bike out of the car fifty miles from Troyes and rode in, to the delight of the French.

The club was run by Marcel Bidot, a legendary figure in French cycling, whose professional career spanned the 1920s and World War II, and who had become established as the manager of the French team in the Tour. Bidot rang up the mayor of Troyes, who promptly found the Britons a flat. After two years, he helped Ramsbottom and Vin Denson, who arrived in Troyes in 1961, to professional contracts with the squad backed by Lejeune cycles and the beer company Pelforth. Ramsbottom rode from Troyes to Dunkirk for the team launch, some 250 miles. ('How long did it take?' I ask. 'Well, we got there before dark,' is the answer). That was not enough to win over the team manager, Maurice de Muer. After Ramsbottom finished in front of his team leader Jan Janssen in the Liège–Bastogne –Liège one-day classic, de Muer castigated the Dutchman for failing to beat *l'Anglais*.

Ramsbottom finished his first Tour, in 1962, in a respectable forty-fifth place. He had come close to catastrophe after an ill-timed stop to answer nature's call cost him half an hour, had been shocked by descents in the Alps where the road was merely loose stones, and had lost so much weight that he 'looked like something out of Belsen'. Yet several thousand *Troyens* turned out to welcome him home to a civic reception with brass bands. A popular local figure he may have been, but often his and Denson's monthly pay cheques did not arrive. 'I would have to go to the butcher's and ask for credit: it was humbling, embarrassing.' Sometimes Bidot would intervene, sometimes the pair would travel to Dunkirk to visit the manager to protest, at which he would upbraid them: 'All you English think about is money.'

Ramsbottom felt that de Muer did not want him to succeed. During the 1963 Tour, on the Col de la Forclaz in the Alps, the race leaders had slimmed down to about a dozen, with Ramsbottom riding alongside Jacques Anquetil, Raymond Poulidor and the best climbers. The Pelforth manager drove his car up alongside the group, and told the Englishman to stop, because the Pelforth team leader Henri Anglade was 'just behind' and needed support.

Ramsbottom knew that de Muer knew that he understood French, so feigning incomprehension *à la* Vic Sutton was not an option. So he pulled to the side of the road and sat on one of the concrete blocks that line mountain roads. And sat. And sat. It took six minutes for Anglade to catch him up, and when he did, the Frenchman was astounded. 'What are you doing here?' he asked. Once a Tour cyclist has 'exploded' on a climb, he is unlikely to regain contact.

The minutes that Ramsbottom lost on that key day turned what could have been a top-ten placing in the Tour into sixteenth overall. Only two Britons – Simpson and Brian Robinson – had finished higher in the Tour at the time. Today, that result in only his second Tour would have transformed his status, but at the time cycling was still rigidly hierarchical: riders who were outside the small group of accepted team leaders were expected to know their place.

Ramsbottom's relationship with his boss broke down completely the following year. The Briton was riding strongly in the Dauphiné Libéré stage race before the Tour began, when his wife called. A letter had arrived from the team saying that he was to ride the Tour of Luxembourg, but Ramsbottom knew he was also contracted to ride a race in the Isle of Man. 'I asked de Muer about it, and he told me to ignore the letter and go to the Isle of Man. When I got back it was all over the papers that de Muer was saying I'd gone there against his instructions and he was kicking me out.'

Ramsbottom upped sticks for Ghent, where Simpson found him a place at Peugeot for 1965, but again commercial interests worked against him. The final slot in Peugeot's Tour team was down to a straight fight between Ramsbottom and the German Karl-Heinz Kunde, who made the team because there was a strong market for Peugeot bikes in Germany, whereas taxes and import duties meant that bikes from Europe were priced out of the British market. A Belgian teammate, Georges Van Coningsloo, who had never ridden well in the Tour and hated it, requested that the Briton be given his place. Belgium was a Peugeot market as well, though, and the ploy failed.

In 1966 Ramsbottom returned home, and went back to sewing machines. For many years, as he criss-crossed the north of England in his car from one broken machine in a textile factory to another somewhere else, he brooded. 'I would see in my mind what I might have done if I'd ridden the Tour in 1964. You wonder what would have happened if I'd been in another team.' 'How long did it take to get over it?' I ask. He weighs his words: 'Well, it lessened over the years.'

There is no such bitterness for Vin Denson, one of the few Britons who made the crossover from the national team era and who had a lengthy career, spanning seven years and six Tours. Denson had learned about the Tour at secondary school from his French teacher, who indoctrinated his pupils with pictures of the peloton riding through snow-drifts in the Alps. Like Ramsbottom, Denson met Brian Robinson at a club dinner and decided to follow him to France, drawn by the fact that the British Cycling Federation was offering temporary professional licences for those interested in making up the 1961 Tour team. He lasted until stage sixteen, when he succumbed to a stomach bug, probably caught when he filled his water bottle from a roadside spring.

After his spell in Troyes with Ramsbottom, the pair turned professional for the Pelforth team in 1962. While Ramsbottom clearly had greater ability, though it was never fulfilled, Denson was the first Briton to make a career as a *domestique*, a team rider who is happy to subordinate his interests to those of his leaders. The best *domestiques* are highly valued, for their ability to be on hand with a spare wheel or to lead a chase for mile after mile. He was capable of winning on his own account – indeed, he was the first Briton to take a stage of the Giro d'Italia in 1966 at Campobasso, near Naples – but Denson was happy with a support role. 'I loved the idea of being well-respected and trusted, and not having too much responsibility.'

In his first Tour, 1961, he devotedly followed his hero Robinson, 'hoping that he would puncture'. Subsequently, being a team man meant letting team leaders such as the five-times Tour winner Jacques Anquetil and the great climber Julio Jimenez ride alongside with their hand on his thigh so that they didn't have to pedal so hard up the climbs; once, Henri Anglade dragged so hard Denson tore a buttock muscle. Denson raced his second Tour in 1964, for the Belgian squad Solo-Superia, alongside Rik Van Looy, the legendary Belgian 'Emperor', who won some four hundred races in an eighteen-year career. In the Tour that year, Solo had no interest in the overall standings, so the team members took it in turns to try to win a stage, eventually garnering six between them. Denson's allotted stage was the leg to Thonon-les-Bains, which he lost by just a wheel.

The following year, he acquired the nickname 'Vic' – under which he appears in the record books – and found his true niche with Anquetil in the Ford-France team, nick-named *l'équipe de rugbymen* because the riders were all heavily built. Denson spent four years alongside Anquetil, finishing the 1965 Tour for Ford.

On the road, the Frenchman's epic duel with his bitter rival Raymond Poulidor in 1964 set the standard by which most French fans of a certain age still judge the Tour. Off the bike, 'Master Jacques' represented professional cycling at its most glamorous. His taste for champagne, oysters and whisky was legendary, and he and his platinum-blonde wife, Janine, were regulars in the gossip columns.

Cycling's other extreme – drudgery and official indiffer-ence – is epitomised by Denson's account of a day spent looking after his teammate Michael Wright, a Belgian of British extraction who raced for Great Britain in the 1967 Tour. The stage in question went over two of the longest passes in the Alps, the Croix de Fer and Galibier. Wright had crashed the day before and broken two ribs; for nine hours, from start to finish, Denson nursed him through, shouting to the fans to push him, pulling him by the jersey himself and constantly checking the time limit with the journalists on their motorbikes.

They made the cut by two minutes, but that was merely part one of the saga. At the finish in Briançon, Wright got into the race ambulance, and Denson sat down in the passenger seat of the British team car alongside a mechanic, Ken Bird. 'We got off the pavement, and all the publicity caravan were coming past. A local policeman stopped us and let two or three vehicles pass, and I said, "For Christ's sake, Ken, I've got to get to the hotel, I'm going to die." Ken got out of the car and told the gendarme to move, but he was a bit timid because it was his first year on the Tour.

The gendarme just sat on the bonnet of the car and said, "When I say move, you move." I said, "I've been nine hours on my bike, and all I want to do is get to my hotel." He replied, "Get back in the car, you English." I said, "What right have you got to sit on the Union Jack?" and spun him off the bonnet, then he started blowing his whistle. I had some rice cake in my back pocket so I threw it at him, and took off my race number and threw it at him.' The next morning, Denson was summoned into the presence of Jacques Goddet, the Tour organiser, who 'looked like General de Gaulle, all epaulettes and so on. He said, in perfect English' – and, perhaps, with Major Thompson on his mind – '"Denson, I'm very disappointed in you. I always saw you as the perfect English gentleman."' The gendarme brought charges against Denson, who was eventually fined £150.

The minor diplomatic incident involving a rice cake was put into perspective by the trauma that Denson would go through a few days later, with the death of his close friend, the Great Britain team leader Tom Simpson. They had first met in 1954 or '55, and had trained together in Yorkshire, where Denson was doing national service. They had briefly been teammates in the Tour in 1961. When Denson's deal with Pelforth fell through two years later, Simpson had found him lodgings in Ghent, where Vin and his wife Vi opened a bar – simply named 'Vic Denson' – with team jerseys hanging from the ceiling in a swathe of fishing net. They travelled to criteriums together, and Simpson had tried to find Denson a place in his Peugeot team, while Denson had helped Simpson to win the world title in 1965.

That they were riding together again in 1967 under the Union Jack was purely due to a quirk of history. The Tour's return to national teams was short-lived, unsuccessful and controversial. It stemmed partly from Goddet's belief that the Tour should occasionally revert to the old system, even though the interval was six years rather than the suggested four. Primarily, however, Goddet's assistant Félix Lévitan believed that the commercial sponsors had been behind a riders' strike at Bordeaux in 1966 against the imposition of dope tests. 'Trade teams [are] close to producing all the same problems, all the same defects, all the dishonest compromises that led Henri Desgrange to take his brave decision [to adopt the national team formula] in 1930,' said Lévitan. The 1967 Tour, he wrote, would be *moralisé*. It would, ironically, end up producing the sport's most poignant morality tale.

CHAPTER FOUR

Lost Illusions

On 29 June 1959, after the finish of the Tour de France stage in the Breton city of Rennes, Brian Robinson was called down from his hotel room. Downstairs, his manager Raymond Louviot was with another Englishman, a slender, bright-eyed stripling of twenty-one, whose nose looked too big for his face and who spoke poor French with a vaguely Midlands accent. It was Tom Simpson, a miner's son from Nottinghamshire, who was in the process of signing his first professional contract with Robinson's Rapha–Gitane team.

Robinson was required to translate as terms were agreed, and was disconcerted to find that this complete novice was being paid 800 francs (£80) a month, which was more than he was earning in his fifth season on the circuit. Louviot was not being extravagant, however. If he was willing to pay so much to hire Simpson after the youngster had spent a mere three months racing as an independent in the coastal town of St-Brieuc, then that spoke volumes for the rider's talent and potential. It underlined that what Robinson witnessed in the hotel in Rennes was the start of a breathtaking career.

Simpson would soon become the most celebrated British cycling star of all time, rapidly outstripping the pioneer Robinson, his mentor in his early years. With two months' racing as a professional behind him, he finished fourth in the world championship. In his first full season as a professional, 1960, he came within one stage placing of winning the yellow jersey in his first Tour de France. Each season after that, Simpson went where no Briton had been before.

In the 1962 Tour, he wore the *maillot jaune* for a day, and finished sixth overall. That remained the best British performance until Robert Millar managed fourth twenty-two years later, while no Briton would wear the yellow jersey for another thirty-two years. He took four of cycling's greatest one-day races – the Tour of Flanders (1961), Bordeaux–Paris (1963), Milan–San Remo (1964) and the Tour of Lombardy (1965), this last a few weeks after the world road-race title that remains the crowning point of his career. No Briton would win any of those events until Mark Cavendish took Milan–San Remo, thirty-five years later.

Of all the Britons who have forged successful careers in cycling, only Cavendish can match Simpson for ambition, courage and charisma. While Simpson's results speak for themselves, no Briton managed to build anything to rival his public profile across Europe until Cavendish made his incredible leap to stardom in 2008 and 2009. Simpson was the first Briton to achieve star status, and the only one in that category for over forty years. He was also the first Briton to make serious money out of road cycling, going far beyond Robinson's laudable ambition of earning a family car's worth each season.

Simpson was the first British road cyclist to make mainstream British sports fans and press truly aware of European road racing and the Tour de France. After winning the world road title in 1965 he was voted Sports Personality of the Year three times over, by the BBC, the sports writers and the *Daily Express*. But it was in Europe that he made the biggest impression on hearts and minds. A quarter of a century after Simpson had spent his brief spell in Brittany in 1959, most Frenchmen of a certain age still associated any English cyclist racing in their country with Simpson. As the twenty-first century began, new British stars such as David Millar were still being hailed as '*le nouveau Simpson*'. In Millar's case, the tag would prove ironically apposite.

Today, however, Simpson's legacy is compromised: all that he strove for and achieved is overshadowed by his tragically premature, self-inflicted death on stage thirteen of the 1967 Tour de France due to the overuse of amphetamines. Ironically, riding himself to oblivion helped to ensure his immortality: such an event in one of the world's toughest endurance events could not fail to capture imaginations. In 2002, Simpson's death was rated by the magazine *Observer Sport Monthly* among the hundred most striking events in the whole of sport.

Simpson's lofty ambitions in the great race were obvious within two days of his debut in 1960. He was only twenty-two years old, an age at which most cyclists are considered too immature for the Tour, and Louviot did not want him to ride as he felt it would be harmful in the long term. There was a place available alongside Robinson in the Great Britain team, however, so Simpson was able to go against his manager's advice. By the end of the first day, a double stage in Brussels, he was in fifth place overall, and on day two, down the North Sea coast to Dunkirk, he forced his way into the winning escape. At the finish, there was a time bonus of thirty seconds to be deducted from the time of the second-placed rider on the stage. That would have been enough to put Simpson in the yellow jersey, in his first Tour, but he was outsprinted by the wily Frenchman Jean Graczyk.

Simpson had begun the race by crashing on a cinder athletics track in Brussels, and he fell off again on the descent from the Col d'Aubisque when the race entered the Pyrenees. Even so, later in the same stage he had the nerve, and initially the strength, to attempt to stay with the Italian climber Gastone Nencini when the latter made what was to be the race-winning attack, close to the top of the Col de Peyresourde. But Simpson ran out of strength just 1,500 metres from the summit, 'drained of energy, as weak as a kitten', as he put it, and the field caught him up again. In the Alps, there was another crash, in which a rider ran over Simpson's right calf, so that he spent the rest of the race able to pedal with only one leg. By the finish in Paris, where he finished twenty-sixth, he had lost two stone.

His 1961 Tour was a disaster owing to a knee injury, but by 1962 Simpson was fitter, older and wiser. That Tour was ridden in trade teams for the first time since 1929, and Simpson was the joint leader of the Gitane-Leroux squad, sponsored by a bike manufacturer and a supermarket chain and managed by Louviot.

As on his debut Tour, he rode aggressively from the off, and by the first stage in the Pyrenees he was third overall. That paved the way for him to take his place in history by becoming the first Briton to wear the yellow jersey. On the following day, the race crossed the Cols du Tourmalet, Aspin and Peyresourde en route to St-Gaudens. Simpson had done the hard work in the preceding days; the two riders ahead of him in the overall standings, Willy Schroeders of Belgium and André Darrigade of France, were not climbers, and when they were unable to keep up he simply had to maintain his place in the front group to take the overall lead.

The rest of Simpson's Tour showed promise, but betrayed the recklessness that would be his undoing. He actually wore the *maillot jaune* for less than an hour, the time it took to lose his overall lead the following afternoon in a short mountain time trial to the ski resort of Superbagnères, but he raced well to remain third overall by the final Alpine stage. Here, he attacked the field on the descent from the final climb, the Col de Porte, lost control on a patch of gravel and flew off the road on a hairpin bend, landing, with his bike, in a tree on the hillside below. He climbed out of the tree, a television cameraman rescued his bike, and he continued with a broken finger. The next day, with the finger in a cast, he could barely hold the handlebars, but his sixth place overall in Paris was still a fine achievement for a rider of only twenty-four.

The rest of Simpson's Tours never quite lived up to this showing, however. In 1964 he finished fourteenth, suffering from the effects of a tapeworm, in 1965 he rode himself to a standstill, his entire body gradually becoming more heavily infected by a poisoned wound in his hand. He eventually had to be taken off the race and to hospital. The end of Simpson's penultimate Tour de France, in 1966, as world champion, epitomises his do-or-die approach. A flat-out assault on the yellow jersey in the Alps ended in disaster with a high-speed crash on the 60mph descent from the Col du Galibier, leaving him with a horrendously deep cut in his elbow. At the finish in the fortress town of Briançon, he nearly fainted from loss of blood.

He started the following day's stage across the mountains into Italy in spite of the fact that he could barely hold the bars, let alone use the brakes, because to abandon wearing the world champion's jersey would have been dishonourable. Eventually he was forced to climb off his bike in tears. 'Each pedal stroke gave birth to a new line in his face ... Hollows opened beneath each eye,' wrote Guy Lacorce in *L'Equipe*, adding this eerie premonition: 'We felt we were watching a man shorten his life.'

The European media had liked the exotic touch that Brian Robinson, and before him the Australian Hubert Opperman, had brought to cycling. Simpson, however, was not content with merely being given the same tag as his predecessors, and was exotic in image and deed. His alter ego, 'Major Simpson', conceived by the riders' agent Daniel Dousset, appeared in 1960 at a photo shoot in which Simpson was dressed up in a sharply tailored suit and bowler, which enhanced his lanky figure and expressive face. He carried a brolly and briefcase, and had a *Times* tucked under his arm: Pierre Daninos's Major Thompson made flesh. (The Thompson tag had already been used for Robinson, but it had not stuck. He was not the acting type.)

Simpson was a showman, and he had to be. This was an era when the bulk of a top cyclist's earnings came in appearance money at track races or circuit events, and performance meant more than mere athleticism. He delivered quotable quips for the gossipy 'in brief' sections of sports newspapers. He donned hats of every ilk for the photographers: panamas, sombreros, berets, policemen's helmets. He gurned over vast ice creams on hot days. He would act up for the crowd, pretending to pull a rival's saddle or cycling in the wrong direction, but was more than a mere ham: his speech to a crowd including the Prime Minister on accepting the sports writers' award in 1965 was delivered in impeccable, self-deprecating style. Harold Wilson, Simpson noted, was 'also in the saddle, but I hope his bottom doesn't hurt as much as mine'.

Where Robinson was solid, cool-headed, Simpson was impulsive, constantly asked questions and was given to sudden enthusiasms. Soon after Simpson turned professional, Robinson sent him to the Peugeot dealers round the corner to buy a car, something cheap, but the new boy came back with an Aston Martin, 'half the price it would be in England'. His taste for fast cars was legendary, as were his shopping trips for fine clothes. He dreamed of living in a restored vintage train, of building a house with a tree growing through a vast entrance hall.

His rise to celebrity and fortune epitomised the wider social mobility that became evident in the 1960s. Simpson's father was a miner; the family were not well off. He caught the cycling bug from his brother Harry. By his early teens his bedroom walls were plastered with photographs of cycling stars of the early 1950s, and from then on his life was focused on joining their ranks. He bartered, begged and borrowed equipment, and he had a thirst for knowledge which led him to seek advice by letter from one of the best

British track stars of the 1950s, Cyril Cartwright, as well as from the runner Gordon Pirie and a great French cyclist of the 1920s, Francis Pélissier. He left the village of Harworth in spring 1959 to avoid national service, with £100, two bags and two bikes to his name. He returned driving a Jaguar.

The French writer Antoine Blondin was one of many who welcomed the upmarket touch which 'Major' Simpson seemed to bring to a largely working-class sport. The metaphors he chose played on a clichéd view of Englishness: 'He [Simpson] had tied an Eton cravat around the bars of a machine where many still see a postman's basket.' The Nottinghamshire mining village where Simpson grew up was, of course, light years from the privileged world of Eton, and Blondin was in fact projecting a Thompson-style education ('Rugby, Trinity, All Souls') on to the cyclist.

There was far more to Simpson than a natty suit and a finely turned umbrella. His racing style also won hearts. Fans and press have always preferred sportsmen who win occasionally but manage to lose heroically at least as often. Simpson had been a daredevil with scant respect for tactics or his own safety since he first began racing a bike in his teens; as a professional he crashed more than most, and made a habit of attacking early, often being caught before the finish and trailing in behind the leaders. His courage, inevitably, was seen as the British 'stiff upper lip', and '*le fairplay*'. His best wins came on the rare occasions when he restrained himself.

The French saw Simpson's single day in the yellow jersey in 1962 as a deeply symbolic moment. It was, thought Jacques Goddet, the moment when the Britons had truly become integrated into European cycling. *L'Equipe* called it 'a day unique in the well-filled annals of the Tour . . . a just reward for those who have worked for 15 years to throw a cycling bridge over the Channel'. After the finish, Jean Bobet went to Simpson's hotel to set up the picture that led the front page of *L'Equipe* the next day (see plate section). 'We got him sitting on an old staircase in the hotel, one of the better ones in the town, wearing his bowler hat, and with his umbrella. He was like a small boy who had just been given the most beautiful Christmas present. I remember his smile for us. It was totally genuine. It made a huge impression: this young cyclist, who had come from nowhere and was so happy to be there.'

The symbolism, of course, went beyond cycling: the French had only recently learned to love their old adversaries turned liberators. Simpson was inevitably nicknamed Tommy, even though he disliked the name. 'The Englishman, our dear and traditional enemy,' Blondin wrote ('This Dear, Hereditary Enemy' is the title of one of Daninos's chapters) the evening Simpson took the yellow jersey at St-Gaudens. Blondin added that it was only appropriate that an *Anglais* should triumph in France's south-west, the heartland of rugby, an English sport that the French had adopted.

The Major Thompson get-up fitted only up to a point. '*Tom Simpson-de-Doncaster*' was how *L'Equipe* described Simpson on that day, noting with delight that he had ordered a cup of tea as soon as the stage was over (but not observing that this was cited by Daninos's Thompson as being a habit of British amateur cyclists). The press loved Simpson to play the quintessential Englishman, but it was merely an act: Thompson is a bemused observer of the bizarre ways of the 'Frenchies', while 'Major Simpson' was utterly integrated. He learned French with grim determination and the help of his wife, Helen, and within a few years he was fluent in French and Flemish, with passable Spanish and Italian. His knowledge went far beyond mere *argot*: few Englishmen of any background or education master the art of the French *double entendre* as Simpson did.

The man who rode himself to death on one of the Tour's toughest climbs, Mont Ventoux, was not merely a cyclist with a stirring style on the bike and a natty suit off it. His death was all the more dramatic because here was a major figure in his sport across a continent, one of the top dozen stars of his time. 'An ambassador' says the marble memorial close to the top of the Ventoux, but that was only the half of it. Simpson was also comedian, European, dreamer, father, figurehead, entrepreneur, iconoclast; as Goddet put it, 'a champion in his own style'.

Eight years after helping Simpson take his first steps in professional cycling, Robinson was also present as he was laid to rest. He stood in the pouring rain with thousands of British fans in the churchyard in the shadow of the great pit heap at Harworth as Simpson was lowered into his grave. Simpson's jests were recalled then, and later, but with wistful half-smiles. 'The church was packed, and in a way I thought, "You silly bugger, Tom, you had it all there and you threw it away for a pill." '

The pills in question were probably brought to Simpson's hotel room by two Italians as the 1967 Tour reached the Alps. The drug was Tonedron, the Rolls-Royce of amphetamines, nicknamed Tonton by the cyclists. The box of speed cost him £800, a colossal sum at a time when a young professional cyclist might earn £16 a week; it held his 'year's supply of Mickey Finns', Simpson said lightly. He had a reputation for using the drug regularly and probably heavily; that is confirmed by riders who knew him well such as Vin Denson and Alan Ramsbottom.

Simpson's ambitions had always been greater than his physical ability. Soon after leaving school he collapsed at his job as a draughtsman after a particularly hard weekend's training and racing. He was known for overreaching himself as an amateur racer, and he turned professional in an era when cyclists did not think in the long term. In 1967, he was desperate to succeed in an event in which he had showed true potential only once in six starts.

Simpson was not truly a man of the Tour, but a specialist in one-day events who rode well in one Tour. He was 'capable of winning any event up to eight days but was without the robust health essential to see him through three weeks without a bad day', believed Jock Wadley, who knew him better than most. A race three weeks long simply did not suit Simpson's swashbuckling racing style or his unfortunate tendency to fall off at the wrong moment, both of which might have had more than a little to do with his use of amphetamines. His best opportunities came in the one-day classics, where he could race himself into exhaustion, as was his wont, without having to get up and do it again the next day, and the next.

In 1967, Simpson was convinced that he could put his poor Tours of 1965 and 1966 behind him. He had been enjoying one of his better seasons, with six major wins already to his name before he lined up for the start in Angers, including the best stage-race victory of his career, in the eight-day Paris–Nice.

The Tour had reverted to the national teams format, and he was the undisputed leader of the Great Britain team, a similar mix of riders to those in the squads of the early 1960s, but rather stronger, as three of its members had finished the Tour. Riding the Tour with his trade teams, Gitane–Leroux and then Peugeot, Simpson had been forced to race hard from the start to show he was worthy of the team's backing. With Great Britain there was no such pressure: the entire team was there to cater to his every need.

There were other pressures, however. At the age of twenty-nine he could not expect his career to last more than another three or four years, and he needed to earn money fast. He estimated that he had lost £40,000 the year before, when a broken leg had prevented him from milking his year as world champion for its true worth. He needed to bank a further £50,000 before he stopped, he said. He had bought an estate in Corsica, had property interests in Ghent and Yorkshire, and had put down a deposit on a new Mercedes 'for something to aim at'. As a final turn of the screw, the night before he died Daniel Dousset told him that if he did not perform his appearance fees would be cut.

At the start of stage thirteen from Marseille to Carpentras over the Mont Ventoux, Simpson was lying seventh overall, and needed to make the big push up the standings that would take him close to his target: a place in the top three overall or a spell in the yellow jersey. That morning the heat was intense as Simpson fooled around in a dinghy in the Vieux Port for the photographers. As he lined up at the start, he conducted a final radio interview. He apologised for the muffled tone in his voice, and opened his mouth, showing the journalist several white pills sitting on his tongue. 'That was just to get me up this morning,' he laughed.

The Ventoux is a bleached, white pyramid rearing up to 5,000 feet, that can be seen from many miles away, standing alone above the vineyards and olive groves of the Vaucluse. By the time Simpson reached the foot of the mountain he had emptied two of the three small, white pillboxes in his jersey pockets; he had also drunk part of a bottle of brandy passed up by a teammate, and had taken more alcohol from a roadside café.

On the lower slopes of the mountain, the road rises unrelentingly at between one in ten and one in eight. There are none of the hairpin bends that offer a moment's respite on other climbs, and there is no change in the gradient. The scrubby woods offer little shelter from the sun. At first Simpson rode strongly, but he hit trouble soon after the road reached the shoulder of the great peak and turned left at a cluster of ski huts known as Chalet Renard. Here the woods are left behind, and the road begins to cross a mass of limestone scree that lasts for four miles to the summit. Every now and then the tarmac curves into great hollows in the mountainside; in the hot sun these act as natural ovens, reflecting and intensifying the heat.

There were three men in the Great Britain team car that followed Simpson and the leaders up the mountain: the manager Alec Taylor, the driver Ken Ryall and the mechanic Harry Hall. As he crossed the scree, Simpson began to ride erratically, zigzagging across the road. For a moment, the men in the car thought he would drop off the edge, but eventually he went to the right, into the stones by the roadside, and fell awkwardly against the bank.

Hall was first to him. 'Come on, Tom, that's it, that's your Tour finished,' he said. But Simpson, coherent in manner and determined in tone, wanted to continue. 'I want to go on, Alec,' he told the manager. 'If he wants to go, on he goes,' said Taylor. 'We thought he might just get over the top, but after a couple of hundred metres the zigzagging started again,' recalls Hall, who jumped out of the car, ready to catch Simpson once more. By then the British leader had fallen, in the middle of the road. As his heart subsided, his fingers had gripped his handlebars in a desperate last spasm. They had to be unwound before he could be disentangled from the bike.

Simpson's last words are, famously, held to have been 'Put me back on my bike', but this is probably part of the myth. As Hall helped Simpson back on to his bike and pushed him away, he heard Simpson asking him to tighten up the straps that held his feet fast in the pedals – 'Me straps, Harry, me straps' – and he recalls that the British team leader faintly muttered, 'On, on, on.' 'Put me back on my bike' appears in a report of Simpson's death in *Cycling*, but the journalist who wrote it, the late Sidney Saltmarsh, used to say he had made it up. It seems most likely that he asked Hall or one of the others whether Simpson said anything and paraphrased the reply: 'He told us to put him back on his bike.'

All Hall, Taylor and Ryall could do was pick Simpson off the tarmac, lay him on the stones and attempt mouth-to-mouth resuscitation until the Tour's doctor, Pierre Dumas, arrived. He it was who found the three pillboxes, two empty, one half full, while he was rolling up Simpson's jersey to give him heart massage. He removed them, gave them to the Tour's head of police and refused permission for the body to be interred. His assessment to the press that evening was simple: 'It is not natural for an athlete in his prime to die in this way.'

Providing or using certain drugs, including amphetamine, had recently been made illegal under the French penal code, hence the need to involve the police. For the first time on the Tour, there were searches by the gendarmes, who rifled the British team hotel thirty-six hours after the tragedy, questioned Taylor and the team's masseurs through the night, and detained Hall the next day. They found a box, said to have belonged to Simpson, containing amphetamines.

It was not until 3 September 1968 that the inquest recorded an open verdict, although its initial findings released on 3 August 1967, confirmed that Simpson had died from a combination of amphetamines, alcohol, hot sun and intense effort. That concluded the formalities: the repercussions would be felt for years to come.

Simpson's death focused minds after a dozen years of ambiguity and calls for action that had begun in 1955, when the Frenchman Jean Malléjac collapsed in a similar way to the Englishman on the slopes of the Ventoux, amid strong suspicions that he had used amphetamines. Dumas took several minutes to revive him, and Malléjac had to be physically restrained in the ambulance after he regained consciousness. He never raced again. Tony Hoar, riding that Tour for Great Britain, recalled riding up the mountain, seeing the ambulance and 'the guy just lying there, with his eyeballs all dilated. It was a dead giveaway'.

The British team car stopped and gave Dr Dumas some water, which he poured over the rider's inert body. 'His eyes never flickered,' recalled the British mechanic, Bob Thom.

The Malléjac episode had come as doping in professional cycling was going through a phase of transition. The era of old wives' remedies such as bee stings and toads' venom, ether and cola was ending; they were being replaced by industrial quantities of amphetamines and painkillers. It was the start of the period when some professional cyclists began using the 'Anquetil cocktail' of opiate painkillers, amphetamines and sleeping pills. The first deadened the pain, the second counteracted the opiates, while the sleeping pills enabled the cyclist to rest in spite of the amphetamines.

By the early 1960s, the sport was a free-for-all. 'There were no controls, so the guy who had the best stuff did the business,' recalls Brian Robinson. 'In Belgium in the classics you would see them with a syringe in their hands during the races.' In another incident that foreshadowed Simpson's death, the promising French cyclist Roger Rivière rode into a ravine on a mountain descent during the 1960 Tour while under the influence of amphetamines, and broke his back. There were other occasions when riders keeled over on mountains in extreme heat and had to be revived by Dr Dumas.

Jean Bobet had given up racing at the end of the 1950s as drugs became more widely used. 'It was falsifying the results. I got absolutely fed up with it, with seeing guys who I knew were not as good as me coming past with a big smile on their faces.' Amphetamine, wrote Bobet, 'puts an individual into a trance, abolishes all sense of fatigue, will-power or pain. It suppresses the body's natural warning signals and a cyclist who accepts this can never know if he is going too far.'

The precise part played by amphetamine in Simpson's

death remains a bone of contention. No one can dispute that he used the drug: the autopsy findings confirm it. The dose was not strong enough in itself to kill him, but it was taken in order to override the fail-safe mechanisms within the body's metabolism. These should ensure that a human being cannot work himself to death as Simpson did. In addition, amphetamine raises the body's core temperature, which would have contributed to the heat exhaustion that caused his heart to stop. The picture is muddied by those who assert that Simpson was capable of riding himself to death with or without amphetamines, such was his determination. That is irrelevant: on this day, he took amphetamines to make himself ride faster up the mountain. Indeed, he probably took them in quantity because of his intense desire to succeed.

The Tour, of course, demands that its participants be superhuman; that is where its great fascination lies. As Goddet said: 'Excess is necessary.' Since its inception in 1903, the organisers had constantly made the race tougher and tougher, and the 1967 race was one of the longest post-war Tours, including one stage over 225 miles which took eleven hours. Drug-taking had played a part in the Tour since the earliest days, and by the 1960s it was also inevitable outside the Tour, where riders earned the bulk of their income in appearance events. The more of these a cyclist could do, the more he could earn. Thus it would be that a Tourman would finish the race and then begin travelling from one criterium or track meet to another. Early drug tests were actually regarded as unfair partly because the riders said they needed amphetamines to keep awake while driving between events.

L'affaire Simpson, 'the cruellest and most moving demonstration of the ravages of doping', as Goddet called it, was merely the first in a series of major drug scandals that would hit the Tour roughly every ten years. In its consequences it was as significant as the greatest scandal the Tour has seen, the Festina 'Tour de Farce' of 1998 (see Chapter 11). In 1967, even after amphetamines had been declared illegal in France and Belgium, tests were rare, and the authorities often had no stomach for a fight with highly paid stars such as Jacques Anquetil, who vehemently opposed testing. After Simpson's death they had no choice but to react; controls were rapidly brought in, although there would be no wholesale change of heart among professional cyclists.

The inquest verdict scotched the myth that taking speed was the cycling equivalent of a businessman's post-lunch coffee, a necessary and positively health-giving aid to get through the demands of the day, and that amphetamine could be used 'sensibly' with the advice of sports doctors. The doctors who 'advised' Simpson had not been on hand on the Ventoux to prevent abuse by an overambitious man who went beyond his physical limits as a matter of course.

The morning after Simpson's death, at the stage start in the little yellow-stone town centre of Carpentras, the atmosphere was funereal. The Tour de France is like a small mobile community, and a prominent, much-loved citizen had been suddenly taken away. 'It was silent handshakes, that kind of thing,' said Hall. 'No one had time for more. They kept coming up and saying, "Simpson . . . Oh!" or "*Quel catastrophe.*"'

The minute's silence 'lasted for ever', Hall said, with many of the cyclists in tears. In the front rank, as the field stood with heads bowed, were Simpson's four remaining teammates: his fellow Yorkshireman Barry Hoban, his great friend Vin Denson, and two British-based professionals, Colin Lewis and Arthur Metcalfe. En route to the town of Sète, across the baking roads of Provence, several of the cyclists – Denson, Lewis, his friend the Frenchman Jean Stablinski, for example – imagined they saw Simpson riding with them, but it would always turn out to be another rider in a Great Britain jersey. When Lewis went for a *prime*, two other riders held back to let him cross the line first.

Simpson earned an almost unique tribute from his fellows, who turned that day's race into a cortège paying homage to the fallen man, with victory going to his teammate, Hoban. Such an event would not be seen again on the Tour until 1995 and the death of the Italian Fabio Casartelli.

Not all those present were overwhelmed by sentiment, however. Although he had a Great Britain jersey on in the Tour, for the rest of the year Vin Denson was a member of the Bic trade team, and thirty-six hours after Simpson died he was approached by his *directeur sportif*, Raphaël Gémi-niani. 'Gem' told him that with no team leader in the British squad, he would now be expected to work for the Dutchman Jan Janssen. Denson abandoned, leaving Met-calfe, Lewis and Hoban to ride to Paris.

It must have taken considerable courage to do so, given the emotional upheaval they had been through, and given that two of them did not want to go on. 'I was in a right state,' Metcalfe told me before his death in 2002. 'I just stood on my own all night. I was crying. It was the emotional strain on top of the physical strain. There was a lot of talk about whether we should pull out. Alec [Taylor] felt we should stay in, so we just rode on. The rest of the race was a blur.'

The team voted over whether to go on or not, and were split, with Taylor – who had been told by the organisers that they would like the team to continue – putting the casting vote in favour of continuing. 'I was against carrying on,' said Lewis. 'I was totally wrecked. I spent the night crying. I was so low physically and mentally that I just couldn't handle it. It was a terrible, terrible night.'

They rode on, to great public sympathy. Lewis remem-bers being greeted with warm applause as he raced in the final time-trial stage to the Parc des Princes, but what followed struck him more. At the finish, he turned out of the track and was stopped by an old lady, in her eighties perhaps, wearing black. '*Vous êtes Anglais?*' she asked. Yes, he replied. 'This is in memory of Tom Simpson,' she said. 'I want you to have one each.' In her hand were three Victorian gold sovereigns wrapped in tissue paper.

Major Simpson was quietly laid to rest after 13 July: there wasn't much of '*le gentleman*' or '*le fairplay*' about riding yourself to death on speed. But Simpson destroyed far more than the Major when he made the fatal decision to take a few more pills than usual on that summer day. It might seem fanciful to suggest that it cast a pall over the British relationship with the Tour for years to come, but in the decade after his death only one Englishman turned professional and rode the Tour for a French team.

As new professionals, Lewis and Metcalfe were both deeply scarred by the event. 'I knew the scandal was coming,' said Metcalfe. 'I wasn't surprised. I saw something in the room [on the 1967 Tour] when I was waiting for a rub . . . a syringe and a couple of bottles of stuff. Living in England you wouldn't hear much about it, you'd hear about lads taking stuff and not take it seriously. What made it such a big jolt was that there was no concern about it.'

Lewis had also seen at first hand what was going on before Simpson's death. He roomed with Simpson, saw him take the foil-wrapped amphetamine tablets out of his jersey pockets after the stages, and looked on when the British leader bought his year's supply of 'Mickey Finns' at the room door. 'I was twenty-three; I was not totally naïve, but it was alien to me. When someone is taken from you by drugs, you can't accept it. I was a totally different person when I came back, because of the whole emotional experience.'

Lewis, Metcalfe, Hoban and Denson were already under immense physical and mental strain – all Tour cyclists are – and Lewis and Metcalfe's joint achievement in finishing that Tour cannot be overstated. They were the first Britons to do so who were not based full-time in Europe; they had raced in Belgium for a few weeks before the Tour started, but had not spent the season riding the long, tough races with which the rest of the field had prepared. When you add the shock of the death, and the drug connection, it is hardly surprising that Lewis wanted to quit the sport after the Tour. 'I was definitely thinking about it when I came back. My life was totally disillusioned and I didn't want to be part of it any more. I'd seen the doping thing in Brittany and with Tom, but I never knew the implications, what taking stuff did.'

Instead of hanging up his wheels, he rode the national championship the week after the Tour, largely through team duty, and won it. He is still racing though in his sixties, and only recently retired from running his bike shop in Paignton, Devon. In the long term, he says, Simpson's death did not alter his philosophy. 'I remained convinced that if I trained the way I did I could overcome riders who took drugs. I would race against guys who were drugged, and would think, "Even if you're better than me today, you are a short-timer, I'll have a long career if I ride the natural way," and I'm still going strong now.'

Hall 'did not want much to do with professional cycling' after Simpson's death, and took years to rekindle his enthusiasm for the sport. Jean Bobet, who was the last journalist to speak to Simpson before the start on the fatal morning, felt the same way. Denson quit his base in Ghent the following year and returned to England, after finishing one last Tour in 1968, for Simpson's sake. As for Metcalfe, talking about Simpson's death thirty-five years later still brought tears to his eyes.

Collectively, Simpson's death was traumatic for the entire sport in Britain, because of the man's status and because what he had achieved in his eight-year career went beyond a set of results. Through the strength of his personality, Simpson had brought British and European cycling closer together. A few months after 'Major' Tom's brief spell in the yellow jersey in 1962, Jacques Goddet, the Tour organiser and director of *L'Equipe*, was in London, at British time trialling's gala awards night at the Albert Hall. His visit, in the company of Simpson and the Bobet brothers, underlined that Britain had now ceased to be peripheral and was becoming integrated into the wider cycling world. The presence of the other British cycling pioneers, Charly Holland and Brian Robinson, made the occasion still more symbolic.

There were other such occasions: races such as the Manx International, London–Holyhead and the Corona Grand Prix at Crystal Palace, when Simpson would bring over a handful of European stars to do battle with the home-based British professionals in front of huge crowds. He was acutely aware that these events mattered massively to the British media and fans; on at least one occasion, having had flights cancelled, he hired a plane to get himself and the others to the race, although it ate up his entire appearance fee.

As well as bringing European cycling to Britain, Simpson had brought British cycling to Europe. He had lived in Brittany and Paris before moving to Ghent, where he had been made a freeman of the city and where he was officially mourned as intensely as in his home country. His supporters' club was based there, run by his rotund factotum Albert Beurick, who organised the Tom Simpson Grand Prix, helped Simpson run training camps in the city for aspiring English amateurs and took him to hospitals with bags of sweets to visit sick children. The flats Simpson built in the city are still standing, and his bust still stands at the Ghent cycling track.

Simpson also encouraged others to follow him. He and Beurick opened a hostel for English cyclists, who came in droves to wait on the great man, hoping, perhaps, to emulate him. He was the centre of a little community of perhaps ten or so British and Australian cyclists and their families. Denson, Hoban and Alan Ramsbottom all moved to Ghent from European bases to race with him; Metcalfe had done a spell there, and they were joined by other talented cyclists, such as Keith Butler and Bob Addy. With the loss of Simpson's bridgehead in Ghent, however, the movement of British cyclists to Europe slowed down to a mere trickle, increasing again only at the end of the 1970s.

Simpson was a man of massive patriotism, with plans to restructure his sport after he retired and to establish even stronger links between Britain and Europe; he certainly had the charisma, if perhaps not the staying power, to carry it all off. Since the start of his career he had campaigned to make more British cyclists race in Europe, and when he died plans were afoot to set up a team of Britons racing the professional circuit, through a combination of sponsorship and public subscription.

'We can beat the Continentals at their own game. I'm sure of it, and we are proving it here and now, Barry [Hoban] and Michael [Wright] and Vin [Denson] and Alan [Ramsbottom] and me,' he wrote in 1964. In one of his many articles in *Cycling* he eloquently made the case for a team of British cyclists on the Continent sponsored by a British company.

On 13 July 1967, British cycling was suddenly decapitated, a feeling summed up by the then editor of *Cycling*, Alan Gayfer. 'Tom Simpson, our own Tom is dead – what on earth shall we do without him? I am still trying to conceive of a world of cycling without the lively face and straightforward comments of 'Mr Tom', there to encourage, to guide and to lead. We had thought of the years to come, with Tom spearheading a professional assault with ever stronger British teams developing.'

In a letter to the magazine, N. Henderson of the Fulneek School CC wrote: 'Only a short time ago British cycling could envisage a future with confidence. Now the path has become obscure again, and there is a chance it could be lost.' Gayfer compared Simpson's assault on Europe with the strategy employed by Lawrence of Arabia, who 'became more Arabian than the Arabs, the better to dominate them, yet remembered all the time his English upbringing. [Simpson] had opened a whole new world of cycling to the insular British.'

CHAPTER FIVE

The Hangover

Following Tom Simpson's demise, all British cyclists who raced in Europe would ride in the shadow of the noble dead: inspired by Simpson or deterred by his fate, compared to him by the European media and in some fortunate cases tipped as his possible successor. The parallel was being drawn, only days after Simpson died, with a young British amateur named Derek Harrison, who was riding strongly in the Tour de l'Avenir. Yet being 'the next Simpson' seems to have brought Harrison little joy: he tells me he sometimes wishes he had never chosen cycling as a career. Where men such as Brian Robinson look back with affectionate nostalgia, Harrison is eaten from inside by might-have-beens that have festered untold for thirty years.

He is not at ease as we sit in a bar in the medieval French town of Uzès. Sometimes he seems close to tears, sometimes he clenches his fists as if shadow-boxing or punches one into the other to make his point. He has taken the trouble to drive many miles to give me his story, but however much he might want to tell it, there are moments when the telling looks like torture. There are events he does not want to relive, people now dead he does not wish to criticise too deeply.

'*Que de mauvais souvenirs,*' he mutters as he tells of ill treatment by team managers, a positive drug test, injuries. Just bad memories. But it's not that simple. The passion Harrison had for his métier, the joy he took in racing well, finishing his Tour alongside Eddy Merckx, still shines through. Harrison does not know it, but he is well remembered. Older fans still recall his smooth style on the bike, his impassive demeanour and a distinctive pair of sunglasses (which were in fact adopted through necessity, as he had worn spectacles from the age of nine). The most distinguished European journalists purr when they remember his riding in the first week of the 1969 Tour de France, or the stage he won in the Midi Libre ahead of the 1973 Tour winner Luis Ocaña.

'He was a fine climber and time trialist and not a bad sprinter,' recalls the journalist Guy Caput, whose father Louis managed Harrison at the Fagor–Mercier team in 1970. 'He was a real motorbike. After that stage win, my father believed he had the potential to win the Tour.' To sum up Harrison's class, Caput recalls a tale the Fagor riders told him about the man they called '*l'Eengleesh*': they were riding flat out at the front of the bunch one day, chasing down a dangerous break. Suddenly Harrison appeared from the back of the group explaining that he had just stopped to adjust a contact lens. 'They were suffering, going as hard as they could, but he had managed to stop for a few seconds, then catch them up again. That's how good he was.'

He is also the only British Tourman to have so totally immersed himself in France that he seems to have gone native. He still has a trace of his native Birmingham in his accent, but feels he was 'born to be French'. The hint of Brum is all that remains: as he sips his Perrier *menthe*, he is like any other recently retired Frenchman, if more slender ('I'm obsessed with my weight') and with a more distinguished, academic look about him, thanks to those spectacles.

We start the interview in English, but when he searches for a word to make a point it invariably comes first in French, and eventually we mix and match the two. Harrison had excelled in French at school and was at ease from the day he arrived in the eastern French town of Troyes in 1965, after throwing in his civil engineering studies at Manchester University. He married a French girl, and almost forty years after crossing the Channel he has taken to attending English classes to stop himself forgetting his native language. It would be harder to travel further from Daninos's Major Thompson.

Troyes, an elegant, half-timbered town on the edge of champagne country, already had connections with British cycling through Alan Ramsbottom, who had ridden for the local cycling club, UV Aube, and finished sixteenth in the Tour in 1964. Harrison spent three years living behind a butcher's shop, in what Jock Wadley termed a 'little shanty with a hitching rail', where he would hang racing jerseys to dry on the rails used to tie up the horses. They were 'the best years of my life'. All he wanted was to turn professional, 'make the grade'. In 1967 he won the Route de France, a good amateur testing ground for the Tour, and signed his contract with the Frimatic team. He was unpleasantly surprised by what came next.

Harrison's Tour debut in the Great Britain team of 1968, the year after Simpson's death, was not a happy one. He crashed, injured his knee, and had picked up an infection by the time he reached hospital the following day. He was in hospital for a month, and his legs would never quite regain their former strength. In 1969 he was riding on enthusiasm, rather than experience.

For the Tour itself, that was a watershed year. It was the start of the Eddy Merckx era, an eight-year spell in which the greatest cyclist of them all would dominate the event. Merckx would have five crushing victories, equalling Jacques Anquetil's record, and two heroic defeats, while his absence in 1973 and 1976 would merely result in speculation over what might have happened had 'the Cannibal' turned up. Harrison was fully aware that this was the birth of legend. It was a feeling shared by all those involved in that Tour. 'We knew we had a real phenomenon there in front of us, everyone knew it, a huge champion. It was clear at once.' Merckx and his team were sponsored by an Italian coffee company, Faema. Harrison and the rest used to joke that they could do with some of that coffee.

'Although we tried, there was nothing anyone could do most of the time,' says Harrison. 'He was like a machine. His legs were like pistons; the way he was sitting on the bike was just beautiful. But he was obsessed. He always had a spanner in his jersey to adjust his saddle height as he rode along. He would lift his saddle up in the middle of a race.'

Harrison rode what he now considers to have been the race of his life merely to stay with Merckx through the Vosges mountains. 'It was the stage I was really proud of: Merckx rode so hard over the climbs, everyone was hanging on for grim death. We got into the valley, and I looked around and thought, "What the hell am I doing here?"' All the 'heads' of the race apart from the 1966 Tour winner Lucien Aimar were in the fifteen-man lead group: the 1965 Tour winner, Felice Gimondi, the 1967 winner, Roger Pingeon, the 1965 world champion, Rudi Altig. Harrison clenches his fists as he recalls the effort it took to stay in the string of riders: 'I thought I would die, we were going that fast.'

There is no medical evidence that riding the Tour is prejudicial to health, but the riders cite their own figures: a 'bad' Tour is estimated to take three years off a life, a good one perhaps a single year. For most, it is not part of the equation. The best British Tourman, Robert Millar, told me: 'I accepted that the energy I was expending would probably mean I wouldn't live as long a life later.' In Harrison's case, he wonders if the heart trouble that has dogged him recently dates back to that afternoon of pushing himself beyond his limits alongside the great Merckx.

Faced with Merckx's tactic of attacking on every mountain as if the finish was at the top, Harrison developed his own strategy. He could not cope with the change of pace that came when Merckx decided to attack, so he would hang back, let himself recover, then attempt to rejoin the leaders.

The turning point of his Tour, and perhaps of his career, came on the Alpine pass of the Col de la Madeleine, thirteen miles of twisting hairpins through the high meadows between two vast peaks, the Lauzière and the Cheval Noir. 'At the bottom of the climb I said, "Don't worry, Derek, you'll come round," ' but I didn't, or not until the top.' By this time, however, it was too late, even though the Madeleine came early in the seven-hour stage running southwards from Chamonix to Briançon.

Harrison had found himself in the *gruppetto*, the band of non-climbers who would stick together for mutual support to complete the mountain stages within the day's set time limit. It took a rider of determination to break the unwritten rules of this little group, who knew that their only hope was to cling together. 'You need good morale to ride through the *gruppetto* and get to the front. I wanted to try to recover some time, *sauver les meubles*' – the French image is that of dragging the furniture out of a burning house – 'but everyone was pissed off, they got the hump. They don't want you to go away, they throw bananas at you, so you give up, you let it happen, you say, "If you want it like that, you can have it." If your mind is strong, you tell them where to go, but you're young, you're impression-able.' Lacking the contrary streak that sets the champion apart from the also-ran, Harrison gave up the fight.

By the great Pyrenean stage, as Merckx flew over the Tourmalet and the Aubisque passes en route to Mourenx, Harrison was merely attempting to get through the race. 'I try to forget that day, but I can't. I was going fast, on a big wide curve coming down the Aubisque, when I burst a tyre. I slid thirty yards on my backside, and was sitting by the road for twenty minutes waiting for the car to give me a new wheel. The first car was behind the lead group; I was waiting for the second car, but they had stopped for a drink.

I decided that day that I would just go to the stage finish, and I didn't care if I stayed in the Tour or not.'

He rode into Paris in a more than respectable thirty-second place, and is glad he did so. 'That day, I had said if I was eliminated I wouldn't care less, but when you get to Paris you appreciate what it is to finish the Tour. I would just say I was glad to finish. It is one of my best *souvenirs*. My wife was there to say *bonjour* to Eddy Merckx.' It was the day Neil Armstrong walked on the moon, and having earned his admittedly minor place in the Tour's record books, Harrison watched history being made from a restaurant on the Champs-Elysées.

When Harrison joined the professional ranks, he noticed a difference between the men who had nurtured him as an amateur and the trade-team managers, who could choose from any number of aspiring stars. 'As an amateur, they treat you like a rare bird; as a pro, when they realise you are not going to make it, you're in the dustbin.'

The man who brought Harrison to professionalism, the late Jean de Gribaldy, was a 'Jekyll and Hyde character'. Harrison does not like to talk about his former manager, in order not to speak ill of the dead, but says merely, 'He could be very, very *gentil*, or very, very *méchant*.' Nick-named '*le Vicomte*', because of a connection to the aristocratic Debreuil de Broglie family, de Gribaldy ran a large furniture company in Besançon and was a pillar of professional cycling for thirty years. He managed his own teams and discovered a legion of stars, sometimes from within his native France, more often from exotic locations, for example the Portuguese Joachim Agostino and most famously the Irishman Sean Kelly.

'De Gri' was 'always looking for a new star', says Harrison. He would invite the young Englishman to his home, a large house outside Besançon, and let him stay as long as wanted. He would lend him his car if he wanted to travel over the border to Switzerland. Yet he was a hard man 'with himself, his family and his riders', legendary, for example, for preventing his protégés eating any delicacy that might make them put on on weight. Failure was not tolerated. The story goes that after Harrison dropped out of the top ten in the 1969 Tour, he was punished by being made to ride over a mountain pass to his hotel, at a moment when, perhaps, encouragement and support might have served him better. Harrison remains bitter about his old mentor, but professional cycling has never been a nurturing sport.

In 1971, he returned to England to race for the Raleigh team, which was now splitting its activities between Britain and Europe. Disillusion was setting in, and a positive drug test in 1972 did not help matters. Like many other racers, Harrison took a cold cure which contained a small amount of the stimulant amphetamine. One season, it did not show positive, but when the drug controls were improved the next year he fell into the net.

It is not something he likes to talk about. Clearly, he still feels ashamed. 'It was like the bottom dropped out of my world. I can remember it as if it were yesterday. You feel terrible, the way your family look at you, what you read in the papers.' The only way round it was to get a medical certificate stating that the drug had been taken for therapeutic purposes: De Gribaldy made the attempt, but the doctor would not cooperate.

By then, Harrison recognised his career had become *'une galère'*. There is no English equivalent for this French term, which describes a constant struggle against events. 'After thirty you're playing with fire because you know you're going to have to stop and do something else. The further you go past thirty, the harder it is.' He had the chance to work in his father-in-law's tyre business in Troyes, and he took it.

Harrison remained in the town in eastern France, and the

town would retain its English cycling connections, largely through the UV Aube. Malcolm Elliott, who rode the 1987 and 1988 Tours, raced for the club as an amateur. A more permanent resident was Wayne Bennington, of Nottingham, who spent four years as a professional at the end of the 1980s with the Z and Système-U teams and now runs a taxi business in the town. Most distinguished of all, however, was Robert Millar, who lived near the town from 1988 to 1995. The Scot would buy his car tyres from Harrison, and when he raced in England he would bring Harrison wormkiller, which the old pro used to deter the moles that prevented him from achieving the perfect English lawn.

That, however, was the limit of Harrison's connection with his old life. He still rides his bike, but cannot push his heart on doctor's orders, so, to his frustration, cannot ride mountain-bike and road-touring events. Somehow, recently, he pedalled up Mont Ventoux without putting his heart over 120 beats per minute.

We meet on the rest day of the 2004 Tour de France. The Tour loves its *anciens coureurs*, and I know the organisers would make Harrison welcome after thirty-five years' absence. I offer to get him a guest invitation, so that the next morning he can go to the start and enter the race village, renew some old acquaintanceships, take in the atmosphere. He declines. Clearly, some ties are too painful to be renewed.

For the Britons, the 1970s would be a lean decade in the Tour. There was no Tom Simpson-style figurehead to draw cyclists across the Channel in his wake and to give British cyclists credibility in the eyes of hard-nosed team managers. There were no British national teams racing the Tour to give home riders exposure. The only major attempt to establish a European bridgehead came in 1971, when TI-Raleigh decided to race partly in Europe, partly in Britain. That venture eventually turned into a full-time, British-funded professional team racing the European circuit: TI-Raleigh in its various incarnations would be a force to be reckoned with by the late 1970s and early 1980s. However, the team was managed by a Dutchman, Peter Post, who did not feel that British cyclists were good enough and did little to nurture them. One Briton, Bill Nickson, did start the Tour de France for the team, in 1976, but he was eliminated in the Alps. The cash for Raleigh was British, the team essentially Dutch.

Only two Britons forged successful, long-term careers in Europe in the post-Simpson decade. Barry Hoban, who had been settled in Belgium since 1965, was the only survivor of the cluster of riders that had built up around Simpson in Ghent. He ended up riding more Tours and winning more stages than any of his countrymen: his story appears in the next chapter. The Bristolian Phil Edwards, meanwhile, established himself in Italy as right-hand man to the *campione* Francesco Moser. But Edwards and Hoban were essentially individuals who were not part of any wider trend.

Occasionally, Hoban was joined in the Tour by another cyclist with Great Britain after his name: Michael Wright. However, the Belgian cycling record book *Gotha* describes Wright as 'a typical native of Liège', although he was born in Bishop's Stortford. For all his very British name and British passport, he was, famously, the rider in the Great Britain jersey who could not speak English. Wright's father died in the war; his mother married a Belgian soldier and moved to the city of Liège with the three-year-old Michael. He still lives just outside the city on a high ridge overlooking the valley of the Meuse River and the giant steelworks founded by another English émigré, John Cockerill.

Tall and blond, Wright started out as a football player, and the sport remains his first love. When his stepfather died, leaving the large Belgo-British family short of finances, he realised there was no money in amateur soccer and took up cycle racing purely to earn some cash. Wright was too big-boned to ride well in the mountains of the Tour, although he managed fifth place overall in the 1969 Tour of Spain. He was, however, a fast enough finisher from a small group. 'He was not a super Tour rider, but he had super days, and he knew just how to take advantage of them,' says one contemporary. It was an outlook typical of professionals from the Low Countries.

Over the winter of 1967–8, during the Tour's brief return to national teams, he took evening classes to enable him to talk to his teammates, but his attitude to his British nationality was hardly sentimental. 'I saw myself as both Belgian and English. I never took Belgian nationality, and part of the reason was that I could go to the Tour and world championships ten times with the England team.' He was, in essence, an early cycling version of Greg Rusedski, and would be followed in the Tour in the 1990s by another Briton racing under a flag of convenience, the Italian Max Sciandri. 'Michael was Belgian, and we were English,' says Colin Lewis.

There were three stage wins in Wright's eight Tours, starting in 1965 at Auxerre, at the end of a two-rider escape with the Frenchman Michel Grain. In 1967, his stage win at Strasbourg was an early highlight for the Great Britain team. That was followed by a crash after he ran into a dog, which left him with broken ribs; he retired after his epic ride through the Alps with Vin Denson. His third Tour stage came on the asphalt running track at Aubagne, just north of Marseille, in the 1973 Tour.

In the late 1980s, I competed in a circuit race in a municipal park in Eltham, south London. The race itself was eminently forgettable, a brief, intense sprint around narrow park lanes. I did not win, which was par for the course. But one fact made the event memorable: on the start list, and well ahead of me in the sweating string between the horse chestnut trees amid the tower blocks, was a man who, I vaguely believed, had finished the Tour de France.

In fact, John Clarey had a minor place in British cycling history, as the third and last Briton from the home professional circuit to complete the Tour, in 1968, the year after Tom Simpson's death. That Tour marked the end of an era, as the dilemma over national and trade teams that the Tour organisers had faced since 1930 was finally resolved, owing to pressure from the commercial sponsors. The race started in Vittel, a sedate spa in the Massif Central. Clarey went into the hotel room occupied by another British-based professional, Bob Addy, lay down on the bed, and said, 'This is it, this is the big one, it's like playing in the FA Cup.'

Clarey's was the perfect metaphor. The national-team era had offered a brief window of opportunity for British-based pros, who resembled non-league soccer teams getting their annual chance of glory against the giants. For a few Tours between 1955 and 1968, the system gave the best of those racing the British domestic professional circuit, some of whom worked part-time, a chance to contest the world's greatest bike race, even though they had nowhere near the preparation of their European counterparts.

By the late 1960s, a quarter of a century after the formation of the BLRC and the introduction of road racing to Britain, professional cycle racing had developed a British subculture of its own. This had its roots in the rapid growth of road racing under the BLRC: there were races for professionals and independents, including Paris–London and a professional Tour of Britain. These were short-lived, but the successes of Brian Robinson, Shay Elliott and Tom Simpson gave the home circuit a major boost. The 'European' stars would be flown home occasionally to provide a touch of glamour at less than exotic venues such as New Brighton Promenade and Crystal Palace, and would top the bill in major road races such as London–Holyhead and in events on the Isle of Man.

The British calendar of professional races was not made up of the great place-to-place events seen on the Continent. Instead, the bulk of a British pro's racing consisted of short circuit events, which were easy to organise and a good draw for crowds, with occasional marathon one-day races such as the London–Holyhead, the Manx Grand Prix and the Vaux Grand Prix in County Durham. The biggest British stage race, the Milk Race, was key, although it remained strictly amateur. Because it included up to forty-five home cyclists in its international field, it provided a focus for emerging British amateurs and ensured there was a constant flow of talent. With nowhere to go once they had ridden the Milk Race, they would often turn pro.

The contrast could surprise top amateurs. Colin Lewis recalled turning professional in 1967, and going from riding major international amateur races such as the Tour de l'Avenir to whizzing round a one-mile circuit in an unsalubrious area of Birmingham. The races were largely at weekends, so it was possible to hold a British professional licence and have a job, as long as the employer was understanding. Bob Addy, for example, worked for the Inner London Education Authority, and took full advantage of school holidays. Even though the British bike industry was in steady decline from its post-war peak, the budgets involved in sponsorship were small enough to attract major bike manufacturers such as Carlton and Holdsworth, along with a plethora of smaller cycle- and component-makers and bike shops, and stranger additions such as Chris Barber's legendary jazz band, banana importers and a major toilet manufacturer.

The existence of the British professional circuit was another reason why few Britons raced abroad in the 1970s. The arguments for a career in the UK were reasonable enough: you could stay at home, have a life, earn a more than decent crust and race with people you knew. Aspiring amateurs would see the best Britons of the time, world-class riders such as Les West, Hugh Porter and Bob Addy, racing the home professional circuit, and they would feel that they needed to look no further.

There was also a fear among those who had grown up idolising Simpson that racing the Tour meant taking drugs, a fear which had put some off turning professional abroad even before Simpson died. It certainly deterred West, the most talented British cyclist of the post-Simpson generation. The days when BLRC men were in thrall to everything the Continent had to offer had ended with the reality check of 13 July 1967.

The shadow of Simpson inevitably hung over the British team in the 1968 Tour. Clarey and Vin Denson – riding his last Tour – would lie in their twin hotel beds in the evenings and talk about him. 'Denson would say that Tom dealt too much with drugs, that he was willing to take anything.'

With hindsight, there is a tone of misplaced optimism about the 1968 Tour de France. This was to be the '*Tour de santé*', the 'race of health', where the cyclists would turn over a new leaf and turn their backs on the pill and the syringe. As Jacques Goddet put it, they would ensure that Simpson's death had not been in vain. The choice of Vittel as starting point was symbolic as well as commercial: riding 'on water' is cyclists' slang for not using drugs. The evening before the race started, riders, managers and organisers met in the restaurant of the Grand Hotel and agreed that drug testing would be carried out by the French Cycling Federation.

It was a turning point. For the first time in Tour history, daily drug testing was introduced and the penalties for testing positive were properly enforced – two riders were taken off the Tour. The change in official attitude did not, however, end doping. Later, the sanctions were reduced to a level which now seem laughable – suspended bans, small fines – while the small number of tests compared to the number of race days and participants meant that drugs remained a gamble worth taking.

The British, Clarey recalls, were tested 'quite a few times'. There was concern among some of the team about a vitamin-based drink that they were given: Metcalfe was concerned that it might contain something that would show up in the tests. A positive result for one of the British contingent, would, of course, have been disastrous the year after Simpson's death, and they were closely watched. When Michael Wright had to have glucose through an intravenous drip, for example, Dr Dumas turned up to watch, 'to monitor him to make sure there was nothing dodgy going on'.

The philosophy of the Tour had changed subtly as well, if temporarily. The race would never again be so long, even though Goddet never lost his belief that doping had nothing to do with the distance ridden. The 1968 race would still include monstrous 'split' stages – two long races in one day, starting as early as 7 a.m. – but there were fewer mountains. The result was a boring race, and by 1969 the Tour had gone back to being as tough as ever.

Little was said about Simpson to Addy, Denson and Clarey by their fellow competitors, but they managed their own tributes to him. Barry Hoban scored a fine win in stage nineteen through the Alps to Sallanches, and two days later Michael Wright broke away in the final miles of the stage to Auxerre to finish second to the Belgian Eric Leman. Denson finished eighth in a chasing group, Hoban seventeenth, which meant that Great Britain won the day's team prize, worked out by totting up the times of the first three riders from each squad. The team, inevitably, saw it as a homage to Simpson, 'the icing on the cake', as Denson put it. The only Tour stage on which a British team had managed this before had been the day after Simpson's death.

Clarey was easy to spot that day in Eltham park: he was the only man there with a moustache. For reasons to do with sweat, snot and comfort, face fungus has never been popular among racing cyclists. But Clarey's moustache was more than a handlebar: it went down to his jowls. It would have looked less out of place accompanying a black leather jacket on a Harley-Davidson.

A more slender version of the moustache made quite an impression in the 1968 Tour, facial hair being almost as much of a crime against professional cycling aesthetics as unshaven legs. Clarey was in his first year as a professional. He had given up his job as a draughtsman to be a full-time cyclist at the age of twenty-eight, by which age most Continental professional careers are over.

Compared to previous British teams, the 1968 squad was relatively experienced. Barry Hoban, Michael Wright, Vin Denson, Arthur Metcalfe and Colin Lewis had all finished the race before at least once. Derek Harrison raced for the French team Frimatic, while Bob Addy, Hugh Porter, Derek Green and Clarey made up the British-based contingent. Manager Alec Taylor and mechanic Ken Bird had returned in spite of the Simpson trauma.

Clarey had been offered a bonus of £200 by his backer, the Clive Stuart chain of bike shops in south London, if he qualified for the Tour de France. The Tour could be a nice earner for a home-based British pro, even though in 1967 and 1968 the Great Britain teams had a unique way of sharing the prize money, to account for the disparity between the home riders and those based in Europe. Instead of pooling it and sharing it all out, as was customary, each rider kept 50 per cent of what he won, and the other 50 per cent went into the common pot. In 1967, for example, stage wins for Michael Wright and Barry

Hoban meant that Lewis came home with almost £350 in his pocket, a hefty addition to his weekly retainer of £4 from the Mackeson beer company.

There was, of course, something rather British about turning up at the world's longest and hardest bike race to compete with the greats of the day – who raced more in a week than many British-based pros did in a month – having prepared with a few extra-long training rides and a racing programme largely consisting of one-hour criteriums. Most could not deal with the extra workload, and returned to Blighty very rapidly. A few, such as Addy in 1968, were physically and mentally up to the task, but were merely unlucky to crash or puncture at the wrong moment.

The difference in standards was clear to both Clarey and Addy on day one. 'The first stage was into Roubaix, really fast, over the cobbles. At one point I lifted my head, and I was nearly last in the bunch,' recalls Addy. 'I turned round, J.C. was on my wheel, and we were the last two. "We have to move up," I said. "You move up," said J.C. So we moved up the line, and I lifted my head, and by then we were last in the queue again. We got to the track in Roubaix with the group, sat down and looked at each other: "What about that then? How the fuck did we hang in there?"'

Clarey believes that British cyclists projected a certain mystique on to European cycle racing because of their isolation from it, and this meant that many of his colleagues started with an inferiority complex. In an event that hinges on asking the mind to overcome the body's instinct for self-preservation, that immediately put many Britons at a disadvantage. 'Where a lot of people went wrong was that they thought the Continentals were superior. I thought I was pretty good, although obviously the Tour riders were the best.' Like Metcalfe and Lewis the previous year, and like Addy, he was not overawed. 'It was a hard race, but there was no big deal to it. You finished the stage, hopefully you hadn't punctured or fallen off, hopefully Michael

Wright or Barry Hoban had won something so you'd get a bit of money in the end, you'd eat your dinner and go to sleep.'

Burly in build, and with a fair turn of speed, Clarey rode into the top twenty in bunch sprints on seven stages. He was disconcerted to find that a number of stages finished on cinder athletic tracks, where the wheels would skitter about and a crash meant severe grazes. The main handicap in the Tour, he found, was his complete lack of experience. 'The thing I needed to learn about was getting in breaks. Every time I went for it, it was the wrong time, because I didn't know anyone.' He ended up staying in the middle of the bunch for most of the race, to the amusement of some of the French riders, who would make snide comments about Englishmen coming to their race on holiday.

Level-headed and confident in his ability he may have been, but Clarey did not totally qualify as a hard-nosed professional. He, Addy and Denson enjoyed sucking condensed milk from tubes – 'an excellent form of liquid glucose' – but he looked with envy at the Italian national squad, who were given chilled cans of Coke in their *musettes*, and he coveted the Italian national champion's jersey worn by the stylish Franco Bitossi, 'just like I'd seen in *Cycling*'. He offered Bitossi a few quid for it, but his teammate Derek Green had staked his claim several days earlier.

Clarey completed his Tour in sixty-third place, as *lanterne rouge*, one of only two Britons (along with Tony Hoar from the 1955 team) to enjoy that honour. Denson was one place ahead of him, and five places in front was an obscure French professional called Jean-Marie Leblanc, who still remembers spending time with Clarey at the back of the bunch and still recalls the moustache. The 'red lantern' did not bring any of the offers to race criteriums that usually came the way of the last finisher, for sentimental reasons, 'although Mrs Clarey did get a seat in the press box at the Parc des Princes' to watch her husband finish. That summer, although he did not know it at the time, was the high-water mark of John Clarey's career as a professional cyclist. He won the British national title the week after the Tour ended. A year later, an offer of a PE teacher's job came up, so he reverted to racing as an amateur – to a world of changing in village halls and sprinting for £5 notes on windswept hills, watched by three men and a dog – without a twinge of regret.

Jacques Goddet had wondered whether the end of national teams and their replacement by trade squads would kill the Tour. He was right to worry: in the short term, the result of the decision was stagnation. The race would barely change in the next ten years. In terms of increasing its international appeal, it actually went backwards. When the sponsors decided whether or not to send their teams and their stars to race the Tour, they did so purely for commercial reasons. The parochialism of Italian cycling in particular meant that its stars tended to stay away from the Tour; the domination of Eddy Merckx during the early 1970s merely encouraged many of the hopefuls to stay at home, and the number of starters in the Tour would fall steadily until 1978 and the start of the Bernard Hinault era.

After the major advances of the 1950s and 1960s, the British had returned to their insular ways, primarily because there was just enough racing in the UK for aspiring amateurs to turn professional and make a decent living without the sacrifices that racing in Europe demanded. During this long lean spell, the Union Jack carrier was Barry Hoban, who had been presented with his chance in the Tour the day after Simpson died and had grabbed it with alacrity. The 1970s would see Hoban establish himself as more than the great man's shadow.

CHAPTER SIX

The Quick Grey Fox

Wembley Arena was a place of bright lights and dark shadows that September night in 1979, filled with a vast wooden track – wall-of-death bankings, slatted pine boards and a rickety-looking bridge to access the centre. The twenty-two cyclists in the Skol Six-Day race whizzed round the 160 metres like so many hamsters in a vast wheel, to the strains of trad jazz pumped out by Alan Elsdon and his band.

Clad in a red jersey, grey-haired, with fine sideboards and a self-contained air, Barry Hoban was riding what looked to be his last race. At some point in the evening I descended the rickety bridge, hung over the barrier by the cabin where he changed and rubbed off the sweat between events, and presented my race programme, together with a pen borrowed from my father. The signature is standard sportsman's stuff, halfway to a scribble.

Hoban's was the one autograph I was interested in collecting that night. It represented a tangible connection with the man whose picture I'd seen in magazines such as *Miroir du Cyclisme* and, in a broader sense, with the Tour itself. It should have meant more: in those days, Hoban was a last pedalling link to the era of Jacques Anquetil, Raymond Poulidor and Tom Simpson. Sixteen summers. In a sport where the average career is said to last about two to three years, that is long indeed.

Hoban's 'farewell appearance in the UK' was not quite that: he was tempted by another year. But that did not affect the British records he had achieved in the Tour de France before I saw him at the Skol Six. He had finished eleven

Tours out of twelve, and had won eight Tour stages. Sean Yates and Robert Millar would ride almost as many Tours, but Hoban's tally of stage wins stood as a British record until the arrival of the phenomenal Mark Cavendish.

Moreover, few Tour cyclists have won a stage in quite the same emotionally charged circumstances that marked the first of Hoban's eight wins, as the French journalist Maurice Vidal's report in *Miroir-Sprint* magazine shows: 'Ah, hateful victory. At the end of Avenue Victor Hugo in Sète a lone figure appeared, a cyclist who kept his eyes concealed behind thick dark glasses. He crossed the finish line and removed the glasses like all cyclists do when they get off their bikes. Then we realised he was crying. Barry Hoban had won a stage of the Tour de France.'

The peloton had decided to turn stage fourteen of the 1967 race into a tribute to Tom Simpson, who had died the day before, and it had been decreed that one of Simpson's fellow Englishmen should win. Hoban's victory meant that he was the man who expressed the feelings of the whole peloton. Similar collective homage would be paid in 1995 to the Tour's other post-war fatality, the Italian Fabio Casartelli, but it differed in that all his teammates were sent ahead and no result was recorded for the stage.

The victory for Hoban, Simpson's friend and neighbour in Ghent, touched the right emotional chord at the time, but a bitter controversy endures about who should or should not have won on the day. In his autobiography, *Watching the Wheels Go Round*, Hoban wrote: 'I suggested that one of the British-based riders should be allowed to win, but the general feeling was it should be Vin Denson or myself. The stage was a promenade. We just rode along . . . Suddenly I looked round and there was nobody there. I was all alone. I hadn't jumped away . . . the others must have slowed down together. They had made their decision.'

On the day, he gave Robert Silva of *L'Equipe* a slightly different version from the one that appears in *Watching the*

Wheels: 'Everyone had decided that a Briton should win. All four of us were riding at the front. At one moment, I must have ridden more quickly than the others. I turned round and noticed a gap. After that, I didn't turn round again and rode as quickly as I could to the finish. That's all.'

Before the start, the Frenchman Jean Stablinski, who was the senior rider of the bunch, had gone up to Vin Denson, his teammate at the Bic squad, and said to Denson, Simpson's closest friend in the peloton, that the stage win was for him. '*En principe*, it was for Denson,' Stablinski told me. 'We said Denson, because he was older than Hoban. We thought Denson was supposed to win.'

'Stablinski came to me before the start and said, "We had a meeting last night, we didn't know what to do about the stage," ' says Denson. ' "We want to ride it as a homage to Tom, and we want you to go ahead with twenty to thirty kilometres to go." I said, "I can't stand on a rostrum today, and Tom would have wanted it to be a proper stage." Stab said, "No disrespect, but this is our international decision and can you see it through." I said I would be only too honoured, because I had loved Tom so much. Metcalfe told Barry, and he said, "Why shouldn't you win? You're a young pro; Colin or you would gain forty [contracts for] criteriums."

'[During the stage] suddenly Barry went from behind, Stablinski came crashing up and said, "Get him back, this is not what we want." I said [chasing him down] would be like fighting for someone's gold ring after they had died, and we would be the laughing stock of the press. "Let him get on with it." '

'Vin wasn't in a fit state to do it,' Arthur Metcalfe told me before his death in 2002. 'Barry was a young, ambitious pro, and obviously a win is a win whether it is given to you or whether you take it on your own merits.' Hoban's victory did not please what remained of the team. After the stage finish, there was what Lewis terms 'an argument' and

Metcalfe called 'a discussion with Barry', 'because the other guys in the team felt that he shouldn't have gone'.

In one way, however, it was only appropriate that Hoban should win the stage. His relationship with Simpson, which he described as 'constant rivalry', had played a key role in his career up to that day. The Simpson tragedy had an impact on all those present, but Hoban more than most. On a personal level, he married Simpson's widow Helen in December 1969; he also became the defender of his former role model's reputation.

Hoban and Simpson had much in common. Like Simpson, Hoban was a club cyclist who started out racing time trials and track pursuits, specialising in road racing only after moving to Europe. They had first competed against each other in 1956, and when Hoban turned eighteen the first senior road race he entered was won by Simpson. After Simpson's death, one journalist recalled Hoban showing him a photo 'that he took like a relic from his wallet': it showed the two of them sprinting for a £30 *prime* in a local road race in 1958.

Although he was only two years older, Simpson had four years' head start on Hoban. He raced for Great Britain at the Melbourne Olympics in 1956 and turned professional at the end of 1959; Hoban competed at the Rome Games of 1960, and was professional from the start of 1964 with the Mercier Cycles team. 'Barry rode the same way as Tom, relying on his basic speed,' said Arthur Metcalfe. 'In England, the style was for slow and hard racing, but Barry had lots of speed, so he'd go like hell from the start and you'd come across him later on. But he did it the right way round. You build the speed first and the stamina comes later. It was what gave him the speed to win all his stages.'

Hoban was the Simpsons' neighbour in Belgium from 1965 onwards, living in the village of Zomergem, ten kilometres from their base in Ghent. He would stay with Tom and Helen when he was racing in the city. 'When I was waiting for race contracts to arrive I would go to Tom's house two or three times a week. Most of the time, Tom wasn't there, but I would make myself at home on the sofa, and Helen would give me tea and sandwiches,' Hoban told the magazine *Miroir-Sprint* after Simpson's death. 'Tom would come back, pretend to glare at me and say, "You're here again, you idle so-and-so. Train a bit harder and see if that makes you better." Then we'd have a gossip and dinner.'

There were clearly undercurrents beneath the friendship, as might be expected between two ambitious sportsmen of the same nationality. 'There was a bit of friction, a bit of animosity, because Hoban wanted to make the grade as a star and it wasn't clicking at Mercier,' says Denson. Simpson clearly saw the ambitious young Hoban as a rival: when Hoban was outsprinted for the Tour stage finish at Bordeaux in 1964, Simpson approached the winner, André Darrigade, and thanked him for beating Hoban because he knew if another Englishman had won the stage, he himself would lose valuable criterium contracts.

There can be few sportsmen who have ended up married to their dead rival's widow, living in that former rival's house, helping to bring up his children and using some of his equipment. On the night Simpson died, Hoban had requested his friend's saddle be put on his own bike, according to the Great Britain team mechanic Harry Hall. 'Tom had an old handbag of Helen's which he cut up and put a bit of sponge underneath and he put it on a plastic saddle. I put it on to Barry's bike. All he wanted off the bike was the saddle. I was just doing the bikes and I remember him coming down and saying, "Will you put Tom's saddle on my bike?" '

When Simpson's stable of racing kit was disposed of, Hoban acquired some of the lightweight wheels and tyres. As we have seen in Chapter 4 a bowler hat and umbrella were Simpson's trademark; a few years after marrying

Helen, Hoban used them, he told me, in a photo shoot for a magazine feature entitled 'The Gent from Ghent'. In every way, Hoban stepped into Simpson's shoes: as he raced criteriums after the 1967 Tour, he felt aware that these were contracts that might have gone to his rival and friend had he lived. That, added to the stage win at Sète, gave him, he said, a sense of destiny: 'Now that they've let me win this stage I have got to uphold Tom's name. I've got to keep the flag flying for Britain. I've got to take over Tom's role as British cycling's ambassador on the Continent.'

Like Simpson, Hoban was born into a mining family, though he was from Wakefield in Yorkshire, while Simpson came from Nottinghamshire; unlike Simpson, Barry followed his father down the pit. The family were set slightly apart because they were Catholics, so young Barry was a loner. He enjoyed wandering the fields once his family had moved to Stanley, outside Wakefield, and he was always keen to make a few extra pennies, be it from selling conkers or from picking fruit.

Hoban's father Paddy had been an amateur racer on road and track before the war, and possessed a shed full of spare bikes and components with which his son used to tinker. Barry watched the 1954 Tour of Britain pass his garden gate, but had no aspirations beyond enjoying himself when he began riding with the local club Calder Clarion that year, at the height of the NCU v BLRC dispute. The Calder was NCU; Hoban used to see the Leaguers and think they were 'the ultimate' with their Continental style. He persuaded the club to put a panel of material on the front of their jerseys saying 'Calder', to look like a Continental sponsor's logo, and badgered his mother to embroider the name down their shorts.

By the age of seventeen, Hoban had begun to model himself on Simpson. His was a steady rise through the amateur ranks, including racing on the track at the Rome

Olympics and culminating with a move to northern France in 1962 at the age of twenty-two. He swapped one set of coalfields for another by moving to the mining village of Lapugnoy, between Isbergues and Béthune. The local club was sponsored by the Bertin cycle company, who had links with the British importer Ron Kitching, the biggest cycle trader in Yorkshire.

The village sat among hundreds of British soliders' graves from the First World War, and initially Hoban and the rider who had gone with him, Bernard Burns, were helped out with translation by an Englishman who had worked at a hospital in the village. They were not exactly innocents abroad, but neither were they seasoned travellers: Hoban had visited London for the first time at the age of nineteen, and had not gone abroad until he was twenty. Lapugnoy took some getting used to: Hoban said later he had spent his first two weeks in France eating omelettes, because it was all they recognised on the menu.

Like his fellow Yorkshireman Brian Robinson, Hoban was clear-headed. When he arrived at Lapugnoy, he set himself a deadline of two years in which he had to become good enough to turn professional. Later, when he achieved this, he would set himself the target of earning £1,000 for his first season, to prove he was worthy of remaining in the professional ranks.

The contract came after he had won over thirty-five races in his two years as an amateur in France; it was with the Mercier cycle company, which had sponsored the Bobet brothers as they watched Hercules disembark in the south of France, and which had offered Simpson a contract in 1959. Hoban had a rapid finishing sprint, but he was hired to race as a *domestique* for Raymond Poulidor by the team's *directeur sportif* Antonin Magne. Hoban would never have a close relationship with *'Tonin le sage'*, a legendary figure in French cycling, who had won the Tour in 1931 and 1934.

He liked to be addressed as 'Monsieur Magne' and decked himself out in a black beret and white smock to remind onlookers of his rural origins in central France.

Magne was not used to being questioned, and would be nonplussed when Hoban asked him to explain the instructions he was giving. At one team meeting, he was shocked when Hoban commented, *'Arrêtes ta connerie!'* – stop talking crap – although Hoban, who had learned cyclists' argot rather than perfect French, had not intended to be rude. Magne, on the other hand, knew only two words of English, according to Hoban, and they were very appropriate for professional cycling: 'good business'. Bizarrely, he called Hoban *le Gallois*, the Welshman.

Magne was a tight-fisted, conservative manager, who would buy his riders jerseys without zips to save a single franc and who was always last to accept technical innovations. Hoban, on the other hand, had a perfectionist side to him: 'His preparation was meticulous, his bike, his kit, everything had to be just so,' recalls one contemporary, Bob Addy. 'He would get special wheels if he thought he was going to do a good ride, twenty-eight-spoked wheels with special tyres. He was immaculate in the way he was turned out.'

Nowadays, a great fuss would be made of a new professional who managed what Hoban did in his first season, 1964: two stage wins in the Tour of Spain on successive days, and a near miss in a stage of the Tour de France. However, Magne never noticed that his British debutant was a strong sprinter, because, in Hoban's view at least, he had eyes only for Poulidor, whose rivalry with Jacques Anquetil was at its height. Hoban's autobiography lists numerous occasions when Magne overlooked him, but the day that stuck out was stage nineteen of that Tour.

This stage finished on the velodrome in Bordeaux, where Hoban had won a stage of the Tour de l'Avenir in 1963. The evening before, he asked the mechanics to put lightweight wheels and tyres on his bike, to give him a little extra turn of speed. Magne refused, affronted that his Briton was not content with the team-issue heavy tyres – 'the type that other teams would use for training', as Hoban describes them. The race ended with two laps of the velodrome; Hoban attacked at the bell, led for the entire final lap, but lost out by a couple of metres to the veteran French sprinter André Darrigade, who was illegally pushed by a teammate to enable him to gain the necessary speed. If Hoban had had the light tyres, it just might have made the difference.

Hoban was capable of winning major races, for example the Grand Prix of Frankfurt one-day classic in 1966, but that year he was not selected for the Tour. It was a situation familiar to other British riders employed by French teams: Poulidor was afraid that Hoban would team up against him with the German Rolf Wolfshohl, Hoban's room-mate and Poulidor's rival for leadership within the team.

By 1967, Hoban was aware that he could be a good Tour rider but was missing out because of his manager's policy. Moreover, he could not change trade teams, because the French team managers had an agreement that they would not poach each other's riders. The temporary reversion to national teams got him into the 1967 race, and if, as his former teammates claim, he was looking after himself on the stage to Sète, it would be understandable. Earlier that season, Mercier had cut his pay by half after a spell of six weeks when he was unable to race owing to an abcess the size of a goose egg inside his crotch.

Later in his career, Hoban was to be known as the Grey Fox, because he was old but wily. Hoban described himself as 'an assessor', the kind of rider who, if he were racing on a circuit as an amateur, would always go and look at the course beforehand. He had a photographic memory for races and roads, which helped, but his most important quality was the ability to think clearly in almost any situation. After four years of watching senior professionals 'use' him, by 1968, in his third Tour, he had acquired the ability to do a little using himself. As he put it: 'It's a question of sussing out what your assets are and how you can get the race to orientate to your way of thinking. Crafty riders make [the other] riders do what they want them to do.' Tactical acumen is the asset professional cyclists value above all others, but there is more to it than brainpower. Fatigue dulls the mind, meaning that only athletes who are physically in control, who are stronger than those around them, are capable of analysing a race situation to their benefit.

Important though it was, Hoban rightly considered his 1967 stage victory 'a gift'. His 1968 stage win at Sallanches, on the other hand, was a masterpiece of clear-headed racing through the Alps. He escaped the peloton early on in the stage, together with the Spaniard Andres Gandarias, who was placed fifth overall. Knowing that if Gandarias and he were to remain together the peloton would give chase, Hoban told the Spaniard that he was interested in winning a 'hot-spot' sprint rather than the stage. Gandarias duly 'sat up'; having taken the 'hot spot', Hoban's lead on the peloton was several minutes. There was no point in stopping, so he continued alone for seventy-five miles, over three mountain passes, to win. As well as the more mundane cash prizes, his winnings included a cow named Estelle (see plate section). Rather than taking her back to Ghent, he asked the local organisers to sell her and send him the money, but kept her collar and bell.

The following year, riding again for Mercier after the end of the brief return to national teams, Hoban laid to rest the ghost of his bitter defeat at Bordeaux in 1964. He had told his roommate Edouard Janssens six days before the stage that he would win here; unlike in 1964, though, 'Monsieur Magne' had let him fit light wheels and tyres.

Hoban's cunning and ability to make deals on the move helped to win him the day: the stage win was contested by a group of five, and having worked out the relative strength of the other four, Hoban decided he was the fastest. All that remained was to secure the win. '[Coming into the finish] I said to Francis Rigon, a friend of mine in another team: "Get to the track. Lead out, flat out. Don't let it stall, I will see you all right afterwards." He led out pretty fast, I knew the track, I swung up the track a little bit, used the banking, no problems whatsoever. I used Rigon, who was going to finish fifth anyway. He didn't have a cat in hell's chance. A little backhander, he helps you.'

A newspaper cartoon the following day showed him as 'Barril' Hoban with wine casks for wheels on his bike. What followed was that rare thing: a double of stage wins in two days. Again, it was his clear head that made the difference, but in this case the margin between winning and losing was far finer. The lead group on the road from Bordeaux to Brive was again five strong, but Hoban was not as fresh. He began to suffer on the hilly roads leading to the finish, and stopped contributing to the pacemaking in the group. This caught the attention of another of the quintet, the Belgian Jos Spruyt, a former teammate of Hoban's then riding with Merckx's Faëma team. He began telling Hoban to share the work. To get Spruyt on his side, Hoban told him: 'If you get away in the finish, I won't chase you.' Spruyt did indeed escape at the finish, but the other three cyclists in the lead group chased him down, and Hoban then won the sprint. He had gambled, correctly, that they would do the work for him, which in turn meant that Spruyt could not accuse him of double-dealing.

Winning two stages in two days is unusual in the Tour, even for greats such as Merckx, Hinault and Indurain. Hoban immediately felt the economic benefits, with nineteen contracts to race in criteriums in the seventeen days after the Tour finished. The double was not good enough for Magne, who refused to give Hoban a pay rise and sacked him at the end of the season after he rode a track meeting against the team's orders. For 1970 and 1971 he switched to a new team, backed by the Sonolor television company and managed by Stablinski, before returning to Mercier, where Magne had been replaced by the younger, more open-minded Louis Caput.

Stablinski had known Hoban from his days racing as an independent in northern France, and he remains deeply impressed with the Yorkshireman's ability. 'As an independent he was a stubborn rider, with a good sprint. He won some good races for me, and he was the kind of rider you need in a team, because he was willing to get in breaks so that we could race tactically. Not all cyclists have that character. You could rely on him in a sprint finish, and he was important for the team after the race as well. He had a good English sense of humour, and that was great for morale. He was a key part of the team.'

Hoban's race sense and intelligence would earn him four more stage victories. At Versailles in 1973, the difference between winning and losing came down to each rider's choice of gear for the finish, where a fast downhill into the final corner was followed by 250 metres uphill to the line. Hoban was the one who read it correctly. A year later in Montpellier, Hoban remembered winning a stage of the Midi Libre race in the city, and thought the finish line might well be in the same place. The race guide had said there was a corner 350 metres from the line, but he recalled that when he had won there the finish was only a hundred metres after the corner. Gambling that that would be the case, he went into that last corner with a small lead over the rest, and his stage was won, as there was no time for the other sprinters to catch him up.

The Grey Fox's final stage win in the Tour came in 1975, symbolically enough on the same velodrome in Bordeaux where he had subsided in bitter tears after losing the stage in 1964. This was one of the last occasions when the Tour used a banked track for a stage finish. They were popular with the public, who could see the field circling for the final sprint, and also with the organisers and stage towns, who could charge the public for entry. But they were more dangerous than a road finish, particularly if it rained, when the bankings would become dangerously slippery.

Having spent his youth track racing, and having ridden the occasional winter track event, Hoban had always been more comfortable than his rivals on such finishes. On a banked velodrome, riding high up the banking means a rider can stay out of trouble, and also enables him to use the force of gravity to assist his final acceleration down the banking, but few riders have the nerve to ride high. On that day in 1975, Hoban used his track craft to the full, and sped past all the top sprinters, some of whom were ten years his junior.

Hoban belongs in a special category of cyclists, those who seem to get stronger during the three weeks of the Tour. This quality is reflected in the fact that all his stage wins came in the second half of the race. 'I never finished a Tour where I was smashed completely,' he said. 'I was disappointed when it finished – if it had gone on for another week that would have been fine with me. Some stages I would be so smashed out of my mind I didn't know if I was coming or going. I'd flake out after my shower, be dead to the world for two hours, eat, be dead to the world until the next morning. I got better as the race got harder and the strength was sapped out of the other guys. I would get one range of mountains into my legs and I was stronger and faster.'

There is no scientific explanation for this: perhaps it was in part a legacy of long hours spent on the bike in his teens, when a typical weekend with his club might include riding ninety miles on the Saturday to a race venue, racing a twenty-five-mile time trial on Sunday morning, then riding home. He raced only one Tour in his first three professional seasons, which must have kept him fresh in mind and body; and, having ridden his first at twenty-four, he did not start another until twenty-seven when an athlete is generally considered to be physically mature. This probably enabled him to keep going long after most of his contemporaries had retired, finishing his last Tour at the age of thirty-eight.

Colleagues are effusive about Hoban's attitude towards his profession. Guy Caput, the son of the Mercier manager Louis, would accompany the team in training in the 1970s. 'Barry was exceptionally serious in his attitude to diet and training. I remember at one training camp in the south of France, the team was competing in little races, and I noticed that only three of the cyclists would ride back to the hotel after the race, rather than going in the car, because they wanted the extra mileage.' The trio were Joop Zoetemelk, who had a career that was even longer than Hoban's, including a win in the 1980 Tour, the late Gerrie Knetemann, world champion in 1978, and Hoban. 'For my father,' says Caput, 'Barry was the example for young riders to follow. He was professional from sunrise to sunset.'

Hoban's capacity to analyse a situation – what the French term *lucidité* – was as important when it was a matter of getting through the mountain stages to finish the Tour as it was in winning stages. The awareness of the time cut was a lesson learned in his first Tour, when Hoban was one of a group of cyclists in the backmarkers' group, nicknamed the *autobus*, who rode flat out through a Pyrenean stage, and finished inside the time cut by a single minute. 'He had incredible knowledge of a race,' says Caput. 'At Mercier he was far more than a sprinter. His judgement on everything that went on in the bunch could be relied on absolutely, so he was the team's *capitaine de route*.' This was the title given to a professional squad's senior rider, who would organise tactics on the road as a race unfolded.

His *lucidité* kept him in the 1977 race, on a baking Alpine stage when some thirty of the field – almost a third of the hundred who had started that year's Tour – finished outside the cut and were eliminated. The attacking had begun early; the race was split to pieces. Hoban was riding at his own pace up the first mountain, the Col de la Madeleine, with the Dutch sprinter Gerben Karstens, when the pair came up behind a group of some fifty cyclists, that day's *autobus*. Hoban had done the maths: a 185-kilometre stage would be covered in six hours, and 10 per cent of six hours would be the 'cut' of thirty-six minutes. It could be reckoned that when the climbers were racing hard, the non-climbers would lose a minute for every kilometre of the mountain; with three mountains totalling some forty kilometres that day, it was clear that every climb would have to be taken briskly.

'Karstens and I looked at one another, and I said, "Hey, Gerben, these guys are going home tonight." He said, "Yes, they are going too slow." "Come on, let's go," and next corner, away we went.' As Hoban and Karstens rode away, the Peugeot manager Maurice de Muer drove past and yelled to his rider Bernard Bourreau: 'Stay with the *Anglais* if you want to finish the Tour.' Hoban, Karstens and Bourreau finished well inside the limit; the *autobus* was twenty minutes too slow.

The fourteen years between Hoban's first Tour in 1964 and his final appearance in 1978 spanned the reigns of three of the greatest post-war Tour champions: Jacques Anquetil, who won Hoban's first Tour in the epic battle with Raymond Poulidor; Eddy Merckx, who dominated cycling in the 1970s; and France's Bernard Hinault, who took the first of his five Tours as Hoban contemplated retirement.

Hoban's run of successes also coincided with a period when the Tour's status within France altered subtly, with the race being recognised as the national institution it is today as well as the nation's greatest sports event. Two happenings symbolised that transition. In 1968 came the spring of nationwide student demonstrations, and France's two most important early-summer cycle races, the Midi Libre and Dauphiné Libéré, had to be cancelled. There were doubts whether the Tour would go ahead, but to emphasise that life would go on as normal, the government requested that the Tour be run. Summer without the race would have been unthinkable.

The definitive seal of official approval was given to the Tour in 1975 with the first finish on the Champs-Elysées, which hitherto had been closed only for the 14 July military parade. To underline the Tour's status, the final yellow jersey was awarded to Bernard Thévenet by the French President, Valéry Giscard d'Estaing. 'For the first time the battle took place in the place where victory should be fêted,' wrote Pierre Chany in *L'Equipe*. Bernard Thévenet's victory over Merckx was indeed fêted by a crowd estimated at between 500,000 and a million on the six-kilometre circuit taking in the Tuileries and Arc de Triomphe. A television camera was placed atop the Arc, and delicate negotiations were held to enable the helicopters used to transmit images to fly over the capital.

Taking the Tour to the heart of the capital was perhaps the most important development since the introduction of live television in the 1950s. Over thirty years on, it seems as if the great finale has always been part of the Tour, so integral is the backdrop of Arc and avenue now; however, from its inception in 1903 until 1967, the race had ended at the Parc des Princes, before switching to the Piste Municipale in Vincennes. The arrival on the Champs-Elysées emphasised that this was no sport on the margins. The Tour's accession to the status of national institution was all the more remarkable because the body that organised it was not a national sports federation or an international governing body, but a small private company run by two newspaper editors.

National institution the Tour may have been in its home country, but it was unable to make a success of its first visit to Britain in 1974, when Hoban was the only British racer in the pack. There was a certain logic to the race crossing the Channel. Goddet had retained his ideal of making his sport more international, and was as Anglophile as ever. There was nothing new about starting and finishing occasional stages outside France, which had happened on a regular basis since the 1950s. Moreover, the first air transfers between stages had occurred in 1971, and England was only a short flight away.

One of those who claimed credit – probably with tongue in cheek – for the Tour's trip over the Channel was the writer Les Woodland, who wrote a speculative article in *Cycling* about the Tour crossing to Dover, with a criterium in central London and a stage finish in Birmingham. A few days later, *L'Equipe* picked up on his article, running the banner headline: 'THE BRITISH WANT THE TOUR'. The impetus eventually came from the vegetable farmers in Brittany, inspired by the opening of a ferry link between Roscoff and Plymouth, and by Britain's entry to the Common Market two years previously. They put up £180,000, Plymouth £40,000.

Goddet was predictably bombastic about the race's mission: 'The Tour should set itself the task of broadening human relations by taking itself to countries where it is not known or which feel they have been neglected. The riders of the Tour and all the people who open the roads for them are a great warm current that spreads, fertilising the banks alongside it, bringing joy to those who immerse themselves in it.'

The warm current was spread along the Plymouth bypass between raw embankments of bare earth – which certainly needed 'fertilising' – and rows of tiny newly-planted trees.

Contrary to the Tour's unique selling point, which is that it goes out to the people, the race ran up and down the four-lane highway fourteen times. How, asked Woodland, can you get excited 'about a large bunch cruising effortlessly but unenthusiastically up and down a bleak bypass? The riders found no excitement in helping launch a ferry service, and rode sullenly all day.' The crowds were respectable rather than spectacular, while the stage itself was a bore, prompting the headline in the *Daily Mirror*: 'CAN 40 MILLION FRENCHMEN BE WRONG?' It would be another twenty years before the Tour returned, more sensibly crossing the narrow end of the Channel.

On the Tour, transfers between finish and start towns are always unpopular with the riders because of the disruption they cause to the daily routine of riding, eating, massage and sleeping (although in the twenty-first-century Tour they have become the norm rather than the exception). While the charter flights over the Channel from St-Pol-de-Léon to Exeter airport went smoothly, confusion over boarding passes on the return meant that the riders were herded from one place to another by customs, did not know which plane to get on and did not arrive at their hotels until late at night. No doubt overwhelmed by the urge to broaden human relations, Goddet left his passport in France and was escorted by police in and out of England.

For Hoban, it was a unique opportunity, but he failed to take it in spite of the presence of a crew from Yorkshire Television and even though his father Joe had ridden his bike down from Wakefield to watch him. As the only home rider in the field, Hoban, inevitably, was marked by the entire peloton, and could finish only ninth in the bunch sprint, which was won by an unknown Dutchman called Henk Poppe.

In fact, Hoban's trips to race in Britain were often unhappy. As the biggest British star on the world stage, he would occasionally be contracted to race high-profile events on the domestic professional calendar, but his relations with the British-based professionals were poor. In his autobiography he alleges dark deeds in finish sprints, with riders attempting to knock him off, and accuses the home-based cyclists of ganging up on him.

Bob Addy, a leading British professional of the time who rode alongside Hoban in the 1968 Tour, acknowledges that this was the case. 'His attitude would be "Eh, I'm from the Continent" and ours would be "OK, let's see what you can do." He'd sometimes get start money from the organiser which was more than the whole prize list, and that didn't help matters. He would always bring a couple of henchmen, a "posse", to help him perform well, and all of us would ride against him. It would be virtually a fifty-up team to do the bugger.'

In 1974, after a series of run-ins with the British professionals, Hoban vowed that he would never come and race again in his home country. He kept the vow until 1977, when the boxing promoter Mike Barrett ran a series of criteriums including Eddy Merckx in the field. In 1979, Hoban paid a flying visit for the Empire Stores marathon from London to Bradford, his last major win as a professional, by happy coincidence in front of his home Yorkshire crowd.

Ironically, in view of past events, when he left Mercier in 1979, Hoban ended up riding out his last season partly in Britain and partly from his base in Ghent. After retirement in 1980, he moved to Newtown in mid Wales to supervise production of bikes bearing his name at a newly built factory in the town. Lest anyone forget his close ties with Simpson, the first thing that visitors to the factory saw was a vast photo of the great man. The enterprise went the way of the rest of the British cycle industry; today, Hoban works as a sales representative for Yellow, one of the biggest cycle importers in the UK.

Partly because there were no high-profile events where he could be seen by the home crowd, partly because the British media did not give much space to his exploits, Hoban never achieved recognition among the wider public at home. Compared to Tom Simpson before him and Chris Boardman after him, he remains relatively obscure in Britain, which surprises contemporaries such as Stablinski and Guy Caput.

'My one big regret is not the question of money, although I could have made a lot of money today, but the fact that I am not known for what I did over there. No one knows who the hell Barry Hoban was. It would be nice to be known for what I did for the sport, and not pushed into oblivion as if it didn't count. When I go back to the Continent it's like the return of the prodigal son. I go to the Ghent Six and straight away everyone says, "Ah, Barry's here." It's a nice feeling. Over here, it's "So you rode the Tour de France a few years ago, so what?"'

In his final Tour, Hoban had another Briton for company in the *autobus*: a chirpy lad from Cheshire, seventeen years his junior, named Paul Sherwen. Sherwen recalls with affection that Hoban would come up to him in the *peloton* and whack him on the head with a newspaper when he considered he was poorly positioned. 'He taught me that every effort in the Tour has to pay,' says Sherwen. 'It's as if you have a bill, everything you do in the race adds up, and if you don't have enough money to pay at the end you're out of the Tour.'

One of the first copies of the French magazine *Miroir du Cyclisme* that I read illicitly at the back of science classes as a teenager included a picture of Hoban with an avuncular arm around Sherwen, close to the end of the 1978 race. 'Hoban passes the baton', read the caption. The symbolism was hard to miss: Sherwen was the next representative of British cycling in the Tour, after Hoban had taken over

The pioneer: Brian Robinson makes a lone break in the Alps during the 1960 Tour.

With more than twenty minutes in hand, Robinson wins the Tour stage at Chalon-sur-Saône in 1959.

The final stage of the 1955 Tour: Tony Hoar (*right*) and Henri Sitek (*left*), his 'rival' for last place, 'fight' over the *lanterne rouge* – a paper lantern provided by Hoar's team manager.

The Great Britain team at the start of the 1961 race.
Only the Irishman Shay Elliott (*fourth from left*), Ken Laidlaw (*sixth from left*) and
Brian Robinson (*second from right*) made it to Paris. Among those who failed to finish
were Stan Brittain (*left*), Vin Denson (*third from right*) and Tom Simpson (*right*).

Alan Ramsbottom (*left*) breaks away in 1963 with the 1959 Tour
winner Federico Bahamontes (*right*).

The glamour and the graft: (*inset*) Tom Simpson poses for the newspaper *L'Equipe* in bowler and yellow jersey; (*main picture*) alone in the Alps on a rainy day in 1965.

The tragedy: Doctor Dumas, in black shirt, pumps Simpson's chest
as he dies on the Ventoux.

The following morning in Carpentras, Simpson's passing is marked by (*left to right*)
Jacques Goddet, Félix Lévitan, the yellow jersey Roger Pingeon, Barry Hoban,
Vin Denson, Colin Lewis and Arthur Metcalfe (partially obscured).

The quick grey fox:
Barry Hoban wins his
eighth stage, outpacing stars
such as Francesco Moser
(in white), Bordeaux, 1975.

Hoban the seasoned pro in
1977, his penultimate Tour.

Hoban takes his solo victory
in the Alpine stage to Sallanches in
1968, where his winnings included
Estelle (*left*).

(*Right*) Belgian-Briton Michael Wright celebrates his third Tour stage win in eight years at Aubagne in 1973.

(*Below left*) Colin Lewis tackles the Portillon pass in 1967.

(*Below right*) A sodden Vin Denson in 1965.

from Tom Simpson as 'ambassador' for eleven years. However, Sherwen was more than just the new lone Englishman taking over from the old. His arrival marked the beginning of the march of the fabled 'foreign legion', an influx of English-speakers that would change the face of cycling and of the Tour.

CHAPTER SEVEN

The Foreign Legion

As a teenager, you don't select your sporting heroes according to any rational process. It is a matter of association and aspiration. In pictures of the Tour de France *peloton* in French cycling magazines, bought in Soho by my father along with items such as my first woollen racing jersey, I sought out the figure of Paul Sherwen: slick-haired, chin and elbows sticking out in a combative way, eyes shining with the light of battle. It was Sherwen whose results I underlined at the back of the magazines.

As a result, I could not argue about those results when confronted by a French friend, a top amateur racer. Sherwen never won, Alain pointed out, he was merely a *domestique*. I could not articulate then that my admiration for Sherwen had nothing to do with what he did or did not win. It was simply that he represented what I dreamed of doing. When we had the discussion I was nineteen, racing in France as an amateur, as Sherwen had done a few years before. I had got on the ferry with my bike and bag and had gone to live and race in unknown territory, as Sherwen had. From the age of fifteen, it was what I had wanted to do, and he was the role model, the man who had crossed the Channel, earned a pro contract and ridden the Tour. Simpson and Hoban had done the same thing, to far greater effect, but they were in the distant past. Sherwen was the here and now.

Sherwen's victories in the seven years he spent racing as a professional in Europe could be numbered on the fingers of one hand, and his impact on the Tour's results sheets was marginal. What mattered in the long term, however, was that he was the first of a steady flow of highly talented cyclists – English, Irish, Scottish, Australian – to pass through the Athlétique Club de Boulogne-Billancourt (ACBB), in the heart of Paris.

What made the ACBB riders remarkable was that they came through a single amateur club, one after the other, to open up cycling and the Tour, as documented in Rupert Guinness's 1993 account, *The Foreign Legion*. There were two other highly influential English-speakers, Sean Kelly of Ireland and the American Greg LeMond, but the ACBB legionnaires were a distinctive entity within professional cycling. Before Tour de France stage starts, they could be seen drinking their morning coffee together at the same table. The bond between them ran stronger than team loyalties, forged as it was by their shared apprenticeship and a common language, English, in a sport where the lingua franca is French. They shared flats, and cars en route to races; they shared expertise, and sought each other out in the peloton.

The existence of such a group, and the ideas they brought with them, opened minds in what was a conservative sport in Europe, to the extent that by the mid-1980s there was space for 'outsiders' in every team, and sponsors were actively seeking English-speakers. In Britain, the success of the 'foreign legion' brought cycling, and particularly the Tour de France, back into the public eye for the first time since the days of Tom Simpson. So began an era of increased media exposure – daily television coverage of the Tour, substantial space in the newspapers – that continues to this day. The 'legion' created a brief economic boom within British cycling, but their influence lasted far longer than that, going beyond their racing days into team management, media and race organisation. Paul Sherwen was where that process began.

'He reeks of psychological resilience,' wrote Guinness, and Sherwen's body language indeed has something of the boxer en route to weigh-in. His very confidence, most probably the result of a childhood well outside the European norm, made him the perfect candidate for ACBB. He was a rare cycling product of Britain's colonies: his early years were spent on the Kenya/Uganda border, where his father managed a factory producing fertiliser, paint and insecticide, and he has made his base since retirement in a large colonial-style house in Kampala.

Like most children of expatriates, Sherwen was sent to boarding school. Kaptagat Preparatory School was sixteen miles from the town of Eldoret, Kenya, 8,500 feet above sea level, in an area that produced talented distance runners such as Moses Kiptanui and Nelson Kipteker. This exposure to altitude at an early age may well have enhanced the capacity of Sherwen's body to produce oxygen-carrying red blood cells, vital in any endurance athlete.

The Sherwen family returned to Britain when Paul was fourteen, and his parents divorced almost immediately. He accepts that this disrupted childhood forced him to adapt rapidly, but it meant that when he went to Paris to join ACBB at the end of 1977, aged twenty, he found it easy to adjust. 'I had to grow up quickly. My background destined me to do that. Even now I can be in Africa, the next day New York, the next day Greece or the middle of the bush. It's all the same to me.' The call from ACBB had come after he won a British amateur classic, the Pernod Grand Prix in the Chilterns; the French club regularly sent a team over, and the management were duly impressed.

He is also that rarity in a traditionally blue-collar sport, a university graduate. Sherwen had taken a degree at Manchester, and was looking to a career in industry, probably managing a paper mill, when the invitation to ACBB came. He also possessed more traditional cycling qualities, leaving Britain with a reputation among his Cheshire cycling contemporaries as a hard man. One, John Herety, recalls early-morning winter training rides in sub-zero temperatures in which Sherwen never wore gloves.

In Paris, he settled in better than most of his successors. While other Britons found the management at the Paris club distant, Sherwen dined with the *directeur sportif*, Claude Escalon, and 'did the French thing', moving from dinner table to television to watch the evening's film. There was a total sense of purpose in his life: he lived two and a half miles from the Champs-Elysées but never went sightseeing. The self-analysis is typically sharp: 'I was a mercenary.'

Mercenaries from outside the European heartland had intrigued Micky Wiegant, the team manager at ACBB, since he had watched over the pioneering Irish professional Shay Elliott. Elliott had raced with the club as an amateur in 1955 before joining its professional arm, sponsored by Helyett, the following year. In 1959, Wiegant advertised in the British magazine *Sporting Cyclist* for Britons to join the team at their training camps, on condition they paid their own travelling expenses, and for board and lodging. Those training camps were held at Les Issambres, where Hercules 'disembarked' and where Wiegant had a holiday home. The camps would be held there until the 1980s, giving ACBB's English recruits a connection to predecessors such as Brian Robinson and Tony Hoar.

ACBB had been a hotbed of cycling talent for a quarter of a century. On the professional side, the club's team had been led by 1950s stars such Jacques Anquetil, André Darrigade and Jean Stablinski, which said much about Wiegant's ability to find and form future greats. In the 1960s, the club dropped its professional side, but the amateur team was still run by Wiegant. Sponsored by Peugeot Cycles, the production line kept rolling into the 1970s; its output included the world amateur champion Régis Ovion and the double Tour winner Bernard Thévenet. Wiegant also looked outside France for riders, in

1974 signing up the American Jonathan Boyer, who was to be the first cyclist from the USA to ride the Tour, and, in 1976, the South African Alain van Heerden.

As was often the case with top amateur clubs, ACBB fed its best riders into a professional team, in this case Cycles Peugeot. The club colours featured the same 'chequerboard' as Peugeot's, but were orange and grey: *ACBBéistes* were known as the *petits gris* – little greys. There was a presence about them: when they turned up at amateur races in their Peugeot team cars – handed down from the pros, naturally – their intimidated rivals would refer to the 'Armada' arriving.

This illustrious lineage was drummed into the cyclists who arrived at the ACBB headquarters at the basketball and handball complex in Boulogne-Billancourt, not far from the Parc des Princes. While Claude Escalon – nicknamed 'Claude Balls' – was smiling and shifty, Wiegant was an austere figure. He liked to be called '*monsieur*' and often referred to Elliott, but his main reference point was Anquetil. His protégés would frequently be told what the five-times Tour winner would have done in their place.

'You'd walk in and all the bikes were hanging up in a row,' recalled the 1979 ACBB 'graduate' Robert Millar. 'In the little office round the side there were all these photos of guys who'd been before you. There were some pretty famous names and you'd be thinking, "Jeez, am I good enough to do this?"' To make the point, the *petits gris* who had turned professional would occasionally turn up to pay their respects to Wiegant and Escalon, bringing with them a touch of the glamour and status to which the mere amateurs aspired.

As ACBB's best rider in 1977, Sherwen was offered a contract with Peugeot as a matter of course. However, he was aware that the team had a large stable of cyclists and that openings might be hard to find, so he opted instead for a new team sponsored by Fiat-La France, composed entirely of young professionals. It was managed by Raphaël Géminiani, who had been Anquetil's *directeur sportif* in the 1960s and had founded the St-Raphaël team for which Brian Robinson had ridden.

The '*grand fusil*' – big gun – was short-tempered, long-nosed and eccentric. He would threaten, light-heartedly, to knock his riders off their bikes if he saw them riding at the back of the bunch, and would refuse to let them wear racing capes when it rained, on the grounds that you couldn't race in a cape. Géminiani put Sherwen into his first Tour, in 1978, at the ripe old age of twenty-one. The team was leaderless; its best rider, Jean-Jacques Fussien, merely annoyed the 'heads' of the race each day by buzzing out of the peloton when they least expected it.

Sherwen made his mark on the third stage, infiltrating a ten-man leading group. His inexperience told; after putting more energy than the others into establishing the escape, he was left behind on the hills near the finish in St-Germain-en-Laye, north of Paris. He was, he admits, naively trying to ride the Tour as if it was an amateur race, assuming that strength and endeavour would win through, but omitting the need to marshal that strength. 'I had no idea.'

With the help and advice of Barry Hoban, he survived the three weeks, and returned in 1979 with Fiat, who again rode without a leader or a tactical plan. By now, Sherwen had figured out that his natural strength and ability to hold a place at the front of a fast-moving bunch meant he could pick up placings, if not wins, in mass sprint finishes. His best result in any Tour came that year: fifth on the Champs-Elysées at the end of a spectacular stage. Bernard Hinault and Joop Zoetemelk had fought tooth and nail for that Tour, and they ended up escaping together on the run-in to Paris, with the field splintered behind them. Sherwen was third in the group sprinting behind the pair for third place.

In 1980, he transferred to a new team, sponsored by the

La Redoute mail-order clothing company. He had by now accepted that he did not have the ability to win major races – an ability shown, for example, by the Irishman Sean Kelly, who had also ridden his first Tour in 1978, but won a stage and could have won another. Sherwen was clear-headed enough to realise that a good *domestique* has his value, although he was always a cut above the average water-carrier. In between team duty in the big events, he could figure strongly in the smaller stage races, and he was also capable of gaining valuable publicity for his team with epic lone escapes, such as one across the cobbles of northern France in the 1982 Tour.

Initially, Sherwen supported climbers such as the lanky, awkward Robert Alban and the compact, cunning Bernard Vallet, particularly on the flat, windy stages in the north that were his forte. By 1984, however, La Redoute had acquired another ACBB graduate, the Irishman Stephen Roche, as team leader. Like Kelly, Roche had made a rapid impression, and he arrived at La Redoute tipped as a future Tour winner. Sherwen is roughly the same height as the Irishman, so he was allotted the specific task of staying close to Roche on the run-in to each day's stage finish, in case he punctured or crashed and needed to swap bikes. In 1985, when Roche finished third in the Tour, much of Sherwen's time on hot days was spent dropping back to the team car to collect sponges soaked in eau de Cologne for the fair-skinned Irishman to put on the back of his neck.

Like Hoban, Sherwen became a master of calculating the pace needed to finish inside the time limit on mountain stages, so much so that he acquired the ironic nickname 'Climber'. That began in the 1984 Tour, on the stage from Bourg-d'Oisans to La Plagne, when Sherwen cracked at the foot of the Galibier pass, just after the sign telling riders that the summit was a mind-bending twenty-seven kilometres away. He drifted back through the bunch, past two other *ACBBéistes*, the Briton Sean Yates and the Australian

Allan Peiper. The latter was also in trouble, but Sherwen overheard Yates telling him, 'Don't worry, the climber is behind you.' Peiper and Sherwen finished ninety seconds inside the time limit – like all Tour cyclists, Sherwen can remember the exact margin between staying in the race and going home on days when it was touch and go.

Nothing did Sherwen quite so much credit as the way he completed his final Tour, in 1985. It is a telling illustration of the bloody-mindedness it takes to finish the race. A kilometre into the tenth leg through the Vosges from Epinal to Pontarlier, he was involved in a crash, and landed heavily against a metal crash barrier. He had a huge, swollen bruise on his back, but was told by the race doctor that nothing was broken. He continued, with two team-mates to assist him, knowing he would not make it within the time cut – and indeed he told his teammates to leave him, for fear that they too would be thrown out.

'I knew I would be eliminated, but I wasn't going to climb off because I knew it was my last Tour. My attitude was, "They can kick me out, but I'm not going to abandon." I abandoned in my head fifteen times. I was in a lot of pain, wanted to get off, told my teammates to fuck off. I was shouting at them up the hills, "Leave me, fuck off."' As he went up the finish hill in Pontarlier, his way was blocked by the crowds and by the team cars bringing the riders who had already finished back down to their hotels. His manager, Géminiani, and one of the race organisers, Albert Bouvet, successfully argued to the judges that they should waive the rules in his case. 'You must get to Paris now after what we have done for you,' said Bouvet that evening, and Sherwen duly lasted the remaining thirteen stages.

Paul Sherwen's Tours, between 1978 and 1985, coincided exactly with the era of Bernard Hinault, the combative, stocky Breton known as 'the Badger', who won five Tours in that time. Hinault bore no resemblance to the avuncular figure of *The Wind in the Willows*, but was given the name because of his fighting spirit, like that of a badger when cornered by dogs. In his first Tour, at the tender age of twenty-three, Hinault made it clear he was not a man to be trifled with when he led only the second riders' strike in the race's history. Sherwen had a ringside view as the field protested against the excessive demands the organisers had begun to make of them.

Even though, in the aftermath of Tom Simpson's death, there had been plans to make the Tour easier, in order to discourage drug-taking, that notion had been short-lived. By the late 1970s, Jacques Goddet and Félix Lévitan had introduced multiple daily stages, in which the riders would race two or three times on selected days, thus increasing the revenue the organisers received from the stage towns. Such days meant unhealthily early starts, at 7 to 7.30 a.m. In the 1978 Tour, one such day was preceded by a mountain stage in the Pyrenees at the end of which traffic jams meant the riders did not arrive in their hotels until as late as 11 p.m. They then had to get up at 4.30 a.m. to transfer to that morning's start. The day after that, they faced another early start, and a two-hour transfer to the stage start. The outcome was the first strike over working conditions in Tour history.

'Everyone was knackered,' says Sherwen, recalling the events as they approached the first stage finish at the little town of Valence d'Agen, just north-west of Toulouse. 'It was a hot day, and someone said, "Let's have a strike" and it just escalated. Everyone was too tired to race. The word came down from the "heads" that we would stop at two hundred metres to go and walk across the finish line. Coming into the town everyone waited for a long time, the big guys – Freddy Maertens, Michel Pollentier, Hinault, Gerrie Knetemann – got in the front line.'

Sherwen was prominent in the photos of the strike in my French cycling magazines, and I'd always wondered why. It had nothing to do with solidarity with his fellows, and in fact stemmed from an opportunist's willingness to seize his chance if it were presented. 'Sean Kelly and I didn't believe there would be a strike. We were in the second line because a lot of guys also didn't believe it would happen and thought they might have a chance to get the stage win. Kelly said, "If anyone moves we're going for it." We didn't take our straps off until the last minute.'

With Kelly and Sherwen and many others poised to sprint for the stage win if someone else broke the strike, the peloton rode slowly through the crowd and stopped. Sherwen remembers the disgusted spectators spitting at them. Hinault, clearly recognisable in the red, blue and white stripes of French champion, was a natural focus for the anger of those who had come to watch the race. He squared up to a group of spectators, then to the town's mayor, without backing down. The point had been made that there were limits to what the cyclists would tolerate.

The leadership Hinault showed on that day, at the age of twenty-three, in his first Tour, helped give him undisputed status as the last '*patron*' of professional cycling. The 'boss' of the bunch has to have the will power and the leg strength to force the rest to race just the way he wants, to curb the unruly elements, and in this Hinault succeeded Merckx, who had retired earlier that season.

Hinault's fifth Tour win came in spite of a crash at the stage finish in St-Étienne when the Breton broke his nose on his steel-rimmed Ray-Bans, finishing the stage with blood dripping off his face and two black eyes. Sherwen recalls: 'Everyone thought, that's it, he's finished. The next day a Colombian attacked from the start, the *Blaireau* put his riders on the front, pulled him back, looked round at everyone else and said, "I might have a broken nose, but I'm not finished just yet."'

The Colombians had arrived in 1983, the product of Jacques Goddet's snap decision to broaden the Tour's

horizons; he had been mightily struck by the truly international nature of the 1982 football World Cup, which took
place concurrently with that year's Tour. It was announced
that autumn that the 1983 Tour would be 'open', with half
a dozen amateur teams lining up alongside the professional
squads from Europe. The professional teams fought the
move, as they had the reversion to national teams in 1967
and 1968. They feared that sponsors might jump at the
chance to cut their involvement by backing an amateur
team in the Tour rather than a pro team all year round.

Their fears were groundless, because *mondialisation*, as
Goddet saw it, was a flop: the only amateurs to appear at
the Tour were the little Colombian climbers, sponsored by
the battery company Varta. And yet the Tour did become
truly international, though it had nothing to do with
Goddet's attempt to bring in amateurs. The change
happened gradually, as teams began looking outside Europe
for new talent. One turning point came in 1978, when Kelly
rode the Tour with Sherwen, and almost every year after
that a new nation was added.

The tide gathered strength in 1981. In that year Boyer
became the first American to finish the Tour, while the
Australian Phil Anderson reopened the race to the southern
hemisphere – fifty years after the last Australian had ridden
– by holding the yellow jersey for a day and scrapping
aggressively with Hinault. Outside the Tour, Roche made a
huge impression, with three stage-race wins in his first
season.

The transformation was rapid. In Sherwen's debut Tour,
in 1978, he, Kelly and Barry Hoban were the only
interlopers; in his final Tour, in 1985, six of the seventeen
teams not only included riders from America, Canada,
Colombia, Ireland, Australia or Britain, but were actually
led by cyclists from outside the European heartland. The
influx of talent revitalised the race, which Sherwen now
feels had been on its last legs. 'The Tour was nearly dead in

1978. They had trouble getting a field of 110, and there would be perhaps one Spanish or Italian team. They had tiny sponsors. It grew steadily up to 1985, then between 1985 and '90 it increased again. When I started, it was "Please come and ride the Tour"; by 1987 it had got to the point where they had to come up with a selection procedure because so many teams wanted to have entries.' It was a transformation as rapid as it was unexpected. The Tour had always been the centrepiece of the cycling calendar; in the years immediately following its *mondialisation*, it would grow to become the sporting behemoth it is today.

Sherwen does not seem a man who has regrets; even if he were, none would involve his cycling career. But his friend Graham Jones, with whom he shared a flat in Lille, has spent much of the last twenty years brooding over what might have been. 'They were inseparable for four years, but they were like chalk and cheese,' recalls John Herety, who followed his Cheshire neighbours to ACBB and into the professional ranks. 'Graham had all the sheer class, the way he sat on the bike and the way he pedalled. Paul had all the application, he was a bulldog mentally and he maximised what he had, took his physical ability to the limit. We never saw the best of Graham.'

Tall, slender and soft-spoken, with none of Sherwen's pugnacious body language, Jones bore more than a passing physical resemblance to Tom Simpson. Within a few months of Jones's arrival at ACBB in 1978, wearing the Peugeot jersey Simpson had made his own, French journalists were hailing the newcomer as the successor to the 'Major'. The connection was not totally fanciful: Jones's earliest cycling memory was the minute's silence at the Fallowfield velodrome near his home in Manchester following Simpson's death. His first sponsor was the bike shop owned by Harry Hall, who had been Simpson's mechanic on the fatal Tour.

Jones had seen the television pictures of Simpson at the time of his death, but what pulled him into cycling was a picture in the magazine *International Cycle Sport* of Eddy Merckx's bike, with its shiny Italian components drilled into a delicate fretwork to save weight. Jones was hooked. Like Simpson twenty years before him, he would sit drinking coffee with his clubmates at the meeting place and tell them he was going to race abroad. They would laugh and scoff: 'That's what they all say.' It merely made him more determined.

By the time he caught the bus from Manchester to join ACBB at the age of nineteen, living and racing abroad held no fears: he had ridden the junior world championships and had spent time racing in Holland and Belgium. So rapid was his progress in France, however, that he knew he was guaranteed a professional contract by late April, just two months after his arrival. He won six French amateur classic races, and led the Merlin Plage trophy, which denoted the best amateur in France, from start to finish. At the award dinner at the end of that season, the ACBB boss Micky Wiegant told his former protégé Jacques Anquetil: 'This guy is the nearest thing I've ever seen to you.'

Unlike Sherwen, Jones went straight to Peugeot, the oldest professional team in France, with a tradition going back to the very first Tour in 1903. The squad had won the 1905 race with Louis Troussellier; its past stars included Eddy Merckx and Simpson; it had just won the Tour twice in the space of three years with Bernard Thévenet. But the team had also been afflicted with drug scandals and had an ageing, conservative manager in Maurice de Muer, the same *directeur sportif* who had wrecked Alan Ramsbottom's career fifteen years earlier.

Whereas Sherwen had signed for a team with no structure and no stars, Peugeot was full of highly paid riders worried about keeping their place. From the start, Jones was used as a *domestique*. He fetched water bottles, waited

for his seniors when they punctured, let them pull themselves up hills by holding on to his thigh to save their
strength. For the older pros, it was all part of the mental
game to keep their status: grind the newcomer down, get
him into his place and hope he stays there. In this kind of
structure it was up to a rider to be selfish to prove himself a
winner. Jones now recognises he was too soft.

In March 1979, Jones had been a professional for all of
six weeks when he came fifth in the Criterium International
(a mini Tour de France over a single weekend) behind
Hinault, Zoetemelk and two of Peugeot's leaders, Michel
Laurent of France and Holland's Hennie Kuiper. He was
second on the race's mountain stage, attracting the attention of Jean-Marie Leblanc, a contemporary of Simpson's
as a racer and by 1979 writing for *L'Equipe*. Leblanc picked
out Jones as cycling's next big star. 'He made a huge
impression on me, he clearly had class, and I thought he
was a huge hope for the future. I was also writing for *Cycling
Weekly*, so I saw him a little and got to like him. I often
joked that he was my favourite rider.' Yet he was never
given the opportunity to prove himself. 'Nowadays a
manager would say, "He's a good time trialist and can
climb, let's manage him, pick a calendar that suits him,"'
says Jones. With de Muer, there was none of that.

Jones went to the 1980 Tour underprepared after
breaking his leg that January. He was the youngest rider in
one of the longest post-war Tours: twenty-three days on
the bike, with four or five seven- to eight-hour stages in the
first week. He came close to wearing the King of the
Mountains jersey and was placed eleventh overall when the
race left the Pyrenees and headed for the Alps. This was in
spite of the fact that de Muer had made him wait for Kuiper
on the key mountain stage, and in spite of the energy he
had wasted each day in his duties as a *domestique*.

When the Tour arrived at its rest day in Morzine after
the bulk of the Alpine stages, Jones was lying twelfth

overall, not far behind the leader of the best young rider's classification, Jean-René Bernaudeau. By now it had dawned on de Muer that his young *Anglais* might be worth protecting, but it was too late. Four or five of the team got a stomach bug, including Jones and his roommate Patrick Perret.

'I couldn't eat on the rest day, I had no breakfast the next day, I was tailed off on the first climb and rode most of the stage on my own,' recalls Jones. The Tour's doctor, Gérard Porte, nursed him through, holding out feeding bottles that Jones could pull to take the strain off his legs and providing a gentle push by putting a hand behind his head from time to time. Jones rode into the ski resort of Prapoutel-Les Sept Laux one minute inside the time limit. 'I don't know if I was happy or sad. I didn't know until dinner if I was in or out of the race. I assumed I was out when I crossed the line.' Now, he believes the illness cost him a place in the first ten overall and probably the white jersey of best young rider, as Bernaudeau was also ill and retired that day.

The following year, again riding as a *domestique*, Jones managed twentieth overall, the highest British placing since Simpson in 1964. Yet he raced the time trial at 80 per cent to save his strength for team duties, waited in the Pyrenees for Bernaudeau – who had joined Peugeot as one of their many team leaders and finished sixth – and waited in the Alps for the Australian Phil Anderson, who rode into tenth in his first Tour.

Nowadays, a rider who finishes twentieth in the Tour will claim he can do much better next year and have the rest of the season off. Instead, Jones was kept racing. By the end of that season, he had competed for between 130 and 140 days. A modern pro made to do ninety days' racing would argue he is overworked. 'It didn't occur to me that I'd had enough. Part of being a bike rider is character, the way you are. A lot of it is about confidence. No one thought to make me ease off, but I never had the urge to say, "Fuck you."'

Sherwen is adamant. 'Graham had the ability to get in the top five of the Tour if he had been nurtured, but he was over-raced.' Yet this was still a time when riders were routinely over-raced: it was not acknowledged for nearly another twenty years that rest was beneficial. In 1983, Sherwen rode ninety races before the Tour; two decades on, the biggest Tour stars would aim for between twenty-five and thirty. 'The problem Graham had was that he was unable to say no, but none of us did. We were always worried about the future. I never thought in terms of having a ten-year career: every year was a bonus.' Per racing kilometre at least, it was hardly a highly paid profession. Jones signed with Peugeot for a basic wage of 600 francs a month (about £800). In his best season, 1981, he banked about £25,000, but he had only one such year.

Jones finally escaped Peugeot in 1983; Bernaudeau was leaving to lead a new team sponsored by the Wolber tyre company, and he took the Englishman as his number two. But by then it was too late for Jones to turn his career round. 'At the time you always think there's next year, but after four years I had no interest in winning races. As an amateur, I could win any race I rode. Then, I probably had it too easy, and later it got knocked out of me. There is a knack to winning, a confidence thing. You get out of the habit, you start a race knowing you have no chance; it's almost the easy option for you to do your job and let the team leader get on with winning.'

At the end of 1984, after a year wrecked by an injury sustained when a car driver opened his door in front of him, Jones returned to race the British professional calendar and did not appear in the next two Tours. He made his final appearance in the Tour in 1987 with the ANC-Halfords team, whose adventures are described in detail in Chapter 9. It was not a happy farewell: he was nursing an illness and ran out of strength on stage six. The previous day he had been awarded the Tour's *Grand Prix d'Amabilité*, worth

£100, for the nicest guy in the race. Within twenty-four hours, Mr Nice Guy was Touring no more.

The award had echoes of an incident a few years earlier. 'I went for dinner with Roche at Wiegant's house in spring 1981,' recalls Jones. 'Roche had immense talent and everything went right for him in the first few weeks of his career. Wiegant was giving me a bollocking, saying, "Look, Stephen has won the Tour of Corsica and Paris–Nice." Roche looked at him and looked at me and said, "*Il est trop gentil.*"' In a sport where the very best have no option but to be selfish, to be just too nice is a fitting epitaph for many unfulfilled professional cyclists.

In 1985, Jones was followed back to England by his friend and former flatmate Sherwen. Sherwen had a back problem, felt the effort of racing full-time was no longer justified by the small returns, and wanted a season or two winding down with the Raleigh team, for whom he won the national championship in 1986. He had also begun working part-time at a financial consultant's, selling pensions. However, by happy chance Sherwen's retirement coincided with the decision of the British television station Channel 4 to begin covering the Tour with daily highlights.

Articulate, analytical and well known to those of his contemporaries who were still racing, Sherwen was the natural choice as a summariser alongside the commentator Phil Liggett on Four. As a working professional bike rider, though, he had to take time out each day during their first Tour together, in 1986, to train along part of the race route. Since then, their careers have blossomed in parallel with the successes of English-speakers in the Tour: from heading British coverage, the Phil and Paul show has expanded to provide packages to Australia, New Zealand, South Africa and the USA.

Sherwen also has his own genuine gold mine. This is a unique venture among retired cyclists, who tend to open motor dealerships or cafés, with a few stretching to a vineyard, while the British ex-pros usually run bike shops. Sherwen used to play on the spoil heaps of the abandoned workings at Busitema in eastern Uganda as a child. He snapped up the lease to reopen the mine from under the nose of Anglo-American when the Ugandan government begin reissuing permits following the collapse of the Idi Amin regime. Liggett is an investor, and so too is Lance Armstrong, a friend of Sherwen's since the early 1990s. 'He knew we were having a hard time at first but would still give me shit: "Hey, Sherwen, when are we going to get money out of this gold mine?"'

Jones also returned to the Tour, in 1989, as a driver of a press car, and he has since branched out into producing dry, incisive summaries for BBC Radio 5 Live. He has also played a key role in the organisation of the Tour of Britain since its relaunch in 2004. Like Sherwen and Liggett's television commentary empire, Radio 5's presence on the Tour since 1994 is yet another reminder of the event's rapid expansion between the mid-1980s and 1990s. By 2004, Jones had clocked up twenty Tours as a rider and media man, earning one of the gold medals that the Tour hands out for long service. Jones received his at l'Alpe d'Huez from Jean-Marie Leblanc, who took over as race organiser in 1989 and still jestingly calls him '*mon favori*' in tribute to the promise that was never fulfilled.

The might-have-beens haunt Jones as they did Derek Harrison and Alan Ramsbottom. 'I'm involved in cycle racing, I see guys winning. Never a week goes by without thinking back, particularly about that first Tour, where I possibly could have finished in the first ten, or worn the mountains jersey for ten days. It has kept me awake at night, thinking "what if, what if". One week I'm bitter about it, the next week I think, "I was twentieth and that's not bad: not many Britons even finish the Tour."'

*

An ACBB apprenticeship had certain similarities to the Hercules experiment of 1955. At ACBB, the best British and Irish cyclists were acquired, dropped in at the highest level of amateur cycling and left to fend for themselves, in much the same way that they might be in a professional team. Those who survived earned professional contracts. Hercules's season in Europe, culminating in the Tour de France, was a similar process, but one in which inexperienced riders were put into professional racing. In neither case was there any nurturing of delicate young minds and legs: the cyclists either survived or they didn't.

Initially, among the 'foreign legion' at ACBB, the dropout rate was low, because each year's English-speakers would nominate the best possible successors. By the mid-1980s, however, the number of English-speakers at ACBB increased, while the club displayed no interest in them if they did not perform like Sherwen, Jones, Millar and Roche. 'Australians, Brits, Americans, all were "warmly" welcomed, tried and then unceremoniously dumped,' wrote Paul Kimmage, another ACBB 'graduate', in his autobiography *Rough Ride*. 'It was like a factory production line.' The last Britons to go through the mill and come out with pro contracts were the Scot Brian Smith and the Mancunian Deno Davie in 1988.

The influx at professional level in the 1980s was followed by a flood of amateurs. It is impossible to estimate the numbers, but by 1984, when I went to race in Normandy, there were small communities of British and Irish cyclists across much of northern France and Flanders. They usually came in twos and threes, living, as Millar put it, 'in a cold-water flat, dreaming of being a pro', for a season or two before reality caught up. Some earned pro contracts, most – of whom I was one – merely enjoyed the process and discovered our natural (low) level. A few married local girls, founded businesses and stayed.

From a British perspective, there was a little more to it

than imitating Sherwen, Jones and company. France was becoming closer as twinning links were established between communities on different sides of the Channel and travel grew easier. School-exchange visits and the rise of the Continental holiday contributed to the sense of familiarity. The Thatcher revolution and a tightening of social security rules made life harder for British 'dole pros' – amateurs who raced full-time while claiming unemployment benefit. Prize money in British races had been outstripped by inflation; French prize money had kept up, and the weak pound made it attractive.

Small but ambitious French clubs knew that ex-pats were hungry for success. Britons and Irishmen, no matter how lowly, also brought a touch of glamour, meaning a few more pictures in the local newspapers to make the sponsor happy. In addition, the gradual decline of the French rural population had probably reduced the pool of home-bred cyclists coming through the ranks; hiring a few ambitious Britons who couldn't believe that they were actually being encouraged to race their bikes was a winning formula. Mistaken he may have been as to my ability, but the manager at ES Livarot who hired me was thinking along the same lines as Micky Wiegant at ACBB.

Unlike my *directeur sportif*, Wiegant had hit the jackpot. In autumn 1978, Jones wrote a letter recommending ACBB to Robert Millar, a diminutive Glaswegian who had won that year's British amateur road race championship. Millar duly chose the *petits gris* over the US Créteil, which had connections with Scottish cycling. The Scot was joined in Paris in spring 1979 by Phil Anderson, a long-haired Australian with the build of a rugby flank forward. Millar succeeded Jones as the 1979 Merlin Plage winner, and both he and Anderson joined Peugeot at the start of 1980. At the end of 1979, Millar recommended Stephen Roche to ACBB, and he would join them at Peugeot in 1981. At the end of 1980, it was Roche who approached Sean Yates, a powerful lad from Sussex, to succeed him at ACBB. He too became part of Peugeot from 1982, and would join Sherwen in a shared flat in Lille.

Millar, Anderson, Roche and Yates would make a massive impact on the Tour de France, and on cycling as a whole. Anderson was the first Australian to wear the yellow jersey in the Tour, while Roche would finish third in 1985 and win in 1987. Millar was to be the best British performer in the Tour, as well as in its counterparts in Italy and Spain. Yates would become a legendary *domestique*, Britain's most popular cyclist since Simpson. Together with Greg Le-Mond and Sean Kelly, Roche, Anderson, Yates and Millar would bring the Tour and cycling to English-speaking audiences worldwide. The number of English-speakers in professional cycling would explode: from four in 1978 to just under thirty a decade later. Sherwen and Jones had opened the floodgates.

CHAPTER EIGHT
The Small Yin

Each July, the Tour de France resembles a school reunion as former generations of cyclists return with handshakes and reminiscences to watch over their successors. They are there in every capacity: as team managers, press drivers, radio and television commentators, members of the organisation of the Tour, organisers of other races on jollies, PR men, agents. It is as if, having tasted the glory, they cannot keep away. After all, it is rare for a former pro to leave his sport behind. Those who don't come keep in touch in other ways: running bike shops, managing amateur teams, building cycle frames, attending the old boys' get-togethers.

Here, Robert Millar is an anomaly. The Glaswegian is Britain's best ever performer in the Tour, by a huge margin. A classic, bird-like climber, light and wiry in build, he was the best British cyclist, all round, since Simpson. Yet while Major Tom had built an unmatchable record in cycling's great one-day races, Millar's achievements in the major Tours and stage races far outstripped that of the glorious departed. His record in the Tour de France is immense: three mountain stage wins, the 1984 King of the Mountains jersey, fourth overall that year and five top-twenty overall finishes from eleven starts. His second-place finishes in the Tours of Spain (twice) and Italy are also British bests.

Incredibly for a man who has given so much of himself to a sport, Millar has simply disappeared, leaving not a trace behind him, limiting his links with the cycling world to the occasional email. Those who knew Millar and liked him now ponder his whereabouts and speak about him in the past tense. There are rumours that he has been seen in

Britain's West Country, in Spain, Australia. If he is not exactly on a par with Lord Lucan, there is perhaps a parallel with another cyclist who conquered the Tour's highest peaks then dropped out of the public eye: Brian Robinson's old team leader the late Charly Gaul, who became a recluse in a forest in Luxembourg.

To many observers, Millar has always seemed cynical, unapproachable or simply unfathomable. To me, though, he is one contradiction piled on another. He was marked down as an 'individualist' (his term) from the day he walked into the Glasgow Wheelers' club room in 1977. The Wheelers were the best cycling club in the city, numbering among their members Ian Steel, he of the abortive appearance for Hercules in the 1955 Tour, and Billy Bilsland, who had followed Steel and Ken Laidlaw to race in France. Another luminary was Bilsland's father-in-law, Arthur Campbell, then a vice-president of the International Amateur Cycling Federation. Millar never met Steel, but Bilsland and Campbell became his early mentors. 'Only Arthur and Billy knew anything about where I wanted to go as a bike rider. Everyone else was of the "you'll never do that" school of thought.' Millar had initially wanted merely to escape the city environment, 'see some countryside, get some fresh air', but at about the age of eighteen he decided he wanted to be a professional cyclist.

Campbell and Bilsland made the youth realise that 'becoming a pro was a long journey of progression . . . and each step needed to be taken seriously', says Millar. 'Scottish champion, British champion, race in France, start pro contract, average pro, good pro, great pro, each level requiring more work, and if I was lucky that extra work translated into extra performances.' Campbell recommended that he train in the Campsie Fells, north of Glasgow, and believes that is where he learned to be a climber, but in fact Millar was an all-round talent, winning the Scottish junior time trial championship and earning a reputation as a sprinter.

Both Bilsland and Campbell dismiss the myth that Millar was an impoverished child of the Gorbals as a fanciful invention. His family lived in Pollockshaws, a perfectly respectable working-class area of the city, and his father was a salesman. Of the story that he first saw the Tour de France on a television in a shop window, Millar says: 'I still find it insulting today. We had a television at home like most people did.'

As an adolescent, as later in life, Millar was not one to follow the crowd. When the Glasgow Wheelers went to Benidorm to train, the other riders kept their bikes in a common room. Millar took his to his bedroom. If, on a club ride, there was a character in the group whom he did not like, when they all went to 'drum up' (cook a meal over a campfire by the roadside during a ride) Millar would light his own fire, twenty-five yards from the rest. He was not antisocial; he simply did not want conflict. At ACBB, the Australian Phil Anderson formed a similar impression of Millar. 'He was quiet, an individual. We would train together all the time, but you'd barely know he was there. You could be out in wind or rain but he wouldn't say anything. He wouldn't even say if he was stopping for a slash.'

Millar was never one to shout about his ability, and Campbell recalls a curious incident that suggests Millar may not have opened up to his family either. 'He was riding the British championship and had a good chance of winning. I'd arranged accommodation for him, and called his mother to make sure he'd left. "Yes," she said, "but he hasn't told me where he is going." ' It is the behaviour of a youth who does not want fuss, either in the build-up or in the event of failure. It was not down to a lack of inner confidence. After the first of his British title wins in 1978, Millar had to ask his mother to alter the champion's jersey with its blue and red rings to fit his slight frame. The following year, when he travelled south again for the national championship, he took the altered jersey with him to wear on the podium, and duly won.

Millar's way was to play down emotion, to attempt to appear immune from feeling by hiding behind an ironic half-smile that would run up the right side of his face. When interviewed for the Granada television documentary *The High Life* in 1985, he spoke clearly only when he was discussing cycling; when he was asked about his family he mumbled and looked away from the camera. He admitted: 'I don't miss my family that much.' That might seem utterly bleak, but he could be as resolutely downbeat about other aspects of his life. Telephone conversations with him seemed to start with a set pattern. 'How are you?' I would ask. 'OK.' 'What have you been up to, what's new?' 'Nothing.' Then we would talk.

While Millar's emotional make-up is unfathomable, his utter determination to succeed has never been questioned. When Campbell offered to teach him French at the age of seventeen, he bought the tapes himself, came faithfully for a lesson every week, and 'always did his homework'. Within a year he could speak French. Later, he bought himself a cassette course and did three hours a day until he finished it. On one occasion during the winter, he pointed at his haircut and said it was deliberately 'brutal, in case I weaken and want to go to a disco'. Apart from a liking for Cadbury's Creme Eggs and car magazines, Millar permitted himself no indulgences. After retirement, when he guest-edited an edition of *Cycle Sport* devoted to his career, he did not want race placings under third to be included in his result list because 'if you didn't stand on the podium you didn't do anything worth remembering'.

Millar came to the Tour late compared to his fellow legionnaires Sherwen and Jones. His amateur career with

ACBB had included victory in the Route de France stage race and fourth place in the world championship, but he almost immediately fell foul of the team manager Maurice de Muer on arriving at Peugeot: 'I always felt he thought smaller riders were a poor excuse for people.' For his first three years as a professional, Millar was kept out of the big races. He was restricted to riding with the second string, which he termed Peugeot's 'Y team', Y being much further from A than B and thus a more accurate reflection of the team's status. It might also have been called the 'Why? team', as in 'Why have we been sent to this obscure race?'

When his fate is compared with that of Jones, in the long term Millar was probably fortunate that he rode his first Tour at the relatively mature age of twenty-four. He definitely made his own luck at the end of 1982 with a fine ride in that year's Tour de l'Avenir. The 'amateur Tour' created by Goddet in 1961 had just been opened to professionals under twenty-five, and Millar finished second overall to Greg LeMond, prompting Peugeot to renew his contract. He was also lucky that a younger and more sympathetic team manager than de Muer, the former professional Roland Berland, took over at Peugeot. Berland gave him his chance in the 1983 Tour, and Millar responded with Britain's first stage win in the Pyrenees. He broke new ground: Barry Hoban had managed a fine stage win over smaller climbs in the Alps in 1968, but no Briton had conquered the highest mountains in the Tour.

The mountaineering in that year's race opened with the classic set piece through the Pyrenees, starting in Pau and ending in the little spa town of Luchon after crossing four great passes: the Aubisque, Tourmalet, Aspin and Peyresourde. Millar escaped on the Tourmalet with the Colombian Patrocinio Jimenez, and sprinted away from him at the very top of the Peyresourde, where Simpson had ridden himself into the yellow jersey twenty-one years earlier. He had done well to recover after a hellish passage through the cobbles of northern France, then a fixture in the race route. In the space of an hour en route to Roubaix, Millar fell when the rider in front of him crashed, then punctured, then was brought down by another faller as he fought his way back through the convoy on the narrow lanes. Without the twelve minutes lost there, he might have finished in the top seven or eight overall, rather than fourteenth.

Millar's three mountain stage wins in the Tour all came in the Pyrenees, all in similar circumstances. In 1984, he again infiltrated the 'morning escape', and he had no doubt about the final outcome. When he led up the short, steep Col du Portet d'Aspet, none of his companions could share the pace, and he knew he was the strongest. His acceleration away from the Frenchman Jean-René Bernaudeau and the Dutchman Gerard Veldscholten on the final climb to the ski resort of Guzet-Neige was unstoppable, and he rode to the line alone, his back hunched and the mop of permed curls nodding with each stroke of the pedals.

This Tour, won by Laurent Fignon in dominating style, was one of the most mountainous post-war Tours, with four days of passes in the Alps. Millar took the lead in the King of the Mountains competition after riding in fourth at l'Alpe d'Huez. Overtaking the then four-times Tour winner Bernard Hinault on the upper hairpins of the fifteen-kilometre climb to the legendary finish remains one of Millar's most satisfying memories. Consistency through the Alps – fifth at La Plagne, ninth at Morzine, fourth at Crans-Montana – clinched his fourth place overall at the finish, which remains the best British result in the Tour. The King of the Mountains prize is one of the Tour's three major awards, along with the yellow jersey of overall winner and the green points jersey; Millar is the only Briton to have won one of the three.

Millar's achievements remained relatively unnoticed by the media in the UK, in spite of the *High Life* documentary, with a soundtrack by Steve Winwood. 'Robert never wanted to be famous, he just wanted to ride his bike, and the British media never understood the scale of his achievements,' says Neil Storey, who worked on the documentary and was involved in marketing Millar and the other English-speakers to UK audiences. 'Cycling was still a minority sport, there was a lack of television coverage, and I don't think the British media and public understood what the Tour was. That has changed in the last ten or fifteen years.'

From 1984 until 1990, Millar was in the top ten in one of the major Tours – Spain, Italy and France – every season. It makes him Britain's best stage-race rider by a very large margin. Tom Simpson, in contrast, was tipped as a Tour winner, but managed sixth, just once. However, the Scot was never able to repeat his achievement in the 1984 Tour de France. Millar knew after his first year of 'doubling up' that he was not physically robust enough to perform at the highest level in two major Tours in a single year, yet he was always made to ride the Vuelta or the Giro before the Tour de France, except in 1989.

In the 1980s, the Tour had not acquired the overwhelming importance it has now. Resting a rider specifically for the Tour remained unthinkable for another ten years. 'Despite the signs, the managers I worked with didn't seem to understand that I was capable of doing one Tour well each year,' he says. 'Maybe it was due to the fact that budgets got bigger every year, and they expected more and more. That was what it felt like. I tried to hide and take it easy in the Vuelta or Giro, but it's in my nature to compete when I can, so I'd find myself racing.'

In the eyes of many, Millar was the moral winner of the 1985 Tour of Spain. He was clearly the strongest in the race, but was robbed of victory when he was not told about a dangerous break until it was too late to repair the damage. Millar said later that it took him two years to stop 'feeling let down'. It was enough to make any athlete cynical. That defeat and Millar's subsequent poor form in the 1985 Tour de France (in relative terms: he was 'only' eleventh) poisoned the atmosphere at Peugeot. Millar was not willing or able to impose himself as the team leader. He was not performing to expectations, and he lacked the political skills to boss a team. As his Australian teammate Allan Peiper put it: 'Robert doesn't have the strength as a human being to control other people, it's not in his nature. He's more likely to say, "Let them do what they do and I'll do what I do."' The upshot was a culture clash with the French riders in Peugeot, who made it clear that they resented Millar, Peiper and Sean Yates talking English among themselves.

Millar spent 1986 and 1987 with the Dutch squad Panasonic, viewed at the time as the world's top team. Like de Muer, the manager Peter Post had a preference for large, strong cyclists, and he could not understand why Millar was unable to ride well in two major Tours each year. The Scot looked set for a high overall placing in the 1986 Tour after riding superbly on the first Pyrenean stage, where he finished second, but he fell ill in the Alps. Wearing the polka-dot jersey, as mountains leader, he had to ride up l'Alpe d'Huez in the back group of riders, the non-climbers. 'It didn't please parts of the crowd,' he recalls. No doubt the fact that Panasonic were Holland's top team and that the Alpe is the favoured spot for Dutch fans had much to do with it. The crowd mocked, yelled that he and the others were idle and overpaid. Some of his companions insulted the crowd back, but Millar was too ill to take any notice.

In 1987, having won the King of the Mountains, taken a stage and finished second in the Giro d'Italia, he was again below par in the Tour. The final straw, however, came one evening after the Tour, when the team were eating dinner and Post insisted the Scot finish his dessert: Millar refused

('I told him I didn't like crème caramel'), with the result that the manager did not speak to him for three days.

The following year, leading the chaotic Fagor team, he had a third disastrous Tour. The squad had been built around Stephen Roche, who had made history the previous year by winning the triple of Tour, Giro and world championship. The Irishman barely raced in the 1988 season, owing to a knee injury, and Millar had to take over as leader in the Tour of Spain, where he was sixth, and in the Tour de France. The team was riven with personality clashes and poor organisation, and he was utterly disillusioned. He had one chance to restore his fortunes when he forced his way into the day's escape on the Pyrenean stage to Guzet-Neige, where he had won in 1984. He was set for victory, ready to outsprint the Frenchman Philippe Bouvatier in the final three hundred metres, when Bouvatier was misdirected by a policeman and rode down the diversion intended for team cars and other race vehicles. Millar followed him, and by the time they had realised their mistake it was too late to prevent victory going to the Italian Massimo Ghirotto.

The incident epitomised his year at Fagor, and in 1989 Millar returned to his roots. The Z team was sponsored by a children's clothing company named after its founder, one Roger Zannier, and included many of the cyclists and personnel from Peugeot, who supplied the bikes. The manager was Roger Legeay, a former teammate of Millar's at Peugeot, with whom the Scot had shared a room until he objected to the Frenchman smoking. For the first time since 1984, Millar came to the Tour fresh, and the upshot was a stage win at the Superbagnères ski resort, where Simpson had lost his yellow jersey in 1962. The style was classic: an early escape over the Tourmalet, when the other man with Millar, Charly Mottet of France, repeatedly asked him why he was going so fast. The final sprint was a formality from Pedro Delgado of Spain, who had been the beneficiary of the home riders' coalition in the Vuelta five years earlier.

Millar left Z at the end of 1991 after two further Tours spent as what was termed a *domestique de luxe* - a rider capable of winning races on his own account who accepts worker status when the Tour comes around. Z had signed Greg LeMond at the end of 1989, which suited Millar: LeMond's focus on the Tour meant that Millar came under less pressure. This in turn meant that he could aim for the shorter, more mountainous stage races to which he was most suited, races such as the Dauphiné Libéré, which he won in 1990, and the Tour of Switzerland, where he took a stage in 1991. In the 1990 Tour, Millar was in fine form in the Alps, where he put in his finest climb ever up l'Alpe d'Huez, towing Ronan Pensec, a Z *domestique* who was wearing the yellow jersey. Illness forced him out in the Massif Central, which meant he was unable to ride up the Champs-Elysées alongside LeMond, Tour winner for the third time.

Millar's final two Tours, 1992 and 1993, looked like attempts to stave off advancing age, although the 1993 Tour – ridden as he approached the age of thirty-five – saw brief flurries of his old skill. He led the race over the vertiginous Alpine Col de Bonette-Restefond, at almost 9,000 feet the highest pass covered by the Tour. The race had tackled the mountain only once before; Millar noted with some satisfaction that his predecessor at the top of the climb was Federico Bahamontes of Spain, one of the greatest of Tour mountain climbers. Miguel Indurain chased him down as he attempted to win the stage at the Isola 2000 ski resort that day, and in the Pyrenees the Scot's attempt to win the stage at Pla d'Adet met a similar fate.

Millar's aim towards the end of his career was to match Barry Hoban's record of twelve Tour starts, but bad luck deprived him of what should have been two more Tours. In 1994, a knee injury left him unable to train in the two months before the race; a remedy was found a few weeks before the Tour, but it was too late. The end, when it came in 1995, was still more disillusioning. Millar was riding for a bizarre squad called Le Groupement, sponsored by a pyramid-selling company based in northern France. 'A gathering of people with little in common who happened to be in the wrong place at the wrong time,' he wrote. He rode himself into something approaching form in time for the Tour, and won the British national title on the Isle of Man six days before the Tour was due to start. Looking forward to riding the Tour in the national champion's jersey, he went to the team's headquarters to collect his kit only to find the squad had gone bust.

His career was over in circumstances that were completely beyond his control. 'I thought the governing bodies were appalling in the way they had no safeguards to stop such a thing happening. If a rider said, "I'm not working for you any more," it was a fate worse than death, but a team could just shut down and it was "too bad ... goodbye".' The effect must have been devastating: when a man has dedicated his life to one thing to the exclusion of all else, the least he can be permitted is to end it in his own way. The extent of the upheaval was reflected in the suddenness with which Millar threw his life in the air. In the next few months he left his French wife, Sylvie, and moved from his base near Troyes to the English Midlands, leaving France behind for good.

By the time I got to know Millar in the early 1990s, he was talking of cycling as fishermen talk of the sea, with passion and cynical detachment in equal measure. The cynicism, like the attitude, smacked of a defence mechanism against the advance of time. His career was approaching its end, he was fighting an unequal battle to race at his previous level, and the best way to deal with it was probably to affect not to take it seriously.

What sets Millar apart from every other cyclist I have spoken to is the peculiar eloquence with which he can take you inside his sport. This still comes as a surprise to many, because as a rider he was legendarily unapproachable, sometimes rude, always sarcastic. But it was clear to me, as it was to certain colleagues, that once you had worked your way through the protective carapace he was more informative than any of his fellows: uncannily observant, with unmatched ability to explain what it really felt like to race a bike in the Tour de France.

This first became apparent one evening in the 1990 Tour, when we started talking about the flat stages. These form a run-up of between seven and ten days before the mountains, and this early part of the race was, for Millar, a grim, stressful battle. The physical strain on the flat stages was more acute for the small men, the climbers, who could not see over the others and were buffeted by the wind. They would be exhausted when they arrived at the mountains.

Nerves would be frayed by the risk of crashing, legs flayed by constant sprints from one traffic island to the next. There was permanent pressure to keep in position near the front of the peloton – an obsession shared by the other 190-ish participants. And all the time Millar had to bear in mind that he had a job to do, together with the rest of Z, keeping their leader Greg LeMond out of trouble as he tried to win a third Tour.

Even at quiet moments when the riders were promenading at 30kph, the stress remained, because of the road 'furniture' – traffic islands, roundabouts and so on. Each time the vast bunch slowed to wind its way through an obstruction, there would be a corresponding acceleration, from near walking pace to 50kph, to regain position. 'On a normal flat stage with a bunch sprint you get a last drink forty kilometres before the finish and that's it,' he told me. 'The last forty kilometres are desperate. You're always listening for the crash, wondering which side it will be on. The back of your neck gets sore because you're [constantly resting your hands] on the bottom of the bars to get the brakes. A set of brake blocks lasts a day.'

There would be many more such conversations, and my colleagues and family would always know when they had taken place: it was impossible to avoid picking up a touch of Millar's unique accent, broad Glaswegian vowels mixed with French tonelessness, Anglo-Saxon profanity and the Australian-style question mark ending each sentence – you know? Millar was the obvious candidate a few years later, when we needed a monthly column for *Cycle Sport*. The Scot liked to vent his opinions; we liked content that was anything but bland. The handwritten fax was always on time, for Millar, I had discovered by then, was as punctilious as he was cynical.

In a sport where communication skills are far from common, Millar was almost unique. As well as being highly observant, he had a way with words. He wrote of being 'shot-blasted' by hailstorms, and the Alpine stage to Sestriere in 1992, one of the toughest in his eleven Tours, was 'the day the animals came in two by two'. His verdict on Sean Kelly – not an iron man, 'made of stainless steel'. A race ruined by crashes was 'another stamp in my Band-Aid Club book'. Miguel Indurain he nicknamed St Michael – 'You have to pray to St Michael when you want a rest or a [stop for a] pee.' Devising such phrases, says Millar, helped when racing or training was demanding physically but not mentally. 'I'd see things in a race and it would trigger a thought process, like seeing people standing on the top of hills we were about to climb. That always reminded me of when the Indians were waiting to ambush the cowboys in an old Western . . . waiting ominously silhouetted against the sky, arrows ready, waiting to pick off the stragglers.'

The depth to which Millar had been immersed in the minutiae of the Tour and his powers of observation were clear from his survival guide to riding the race, which was printed in *Cycle Sport* in September 1996, three years after his last Tour. Some of it is pure common sense: 'Read up each day's stage in the road book so you won't be surprised by a steep hill', for example. This item, however, is qualified by the heartfelt footnote: 'Don't do it last thing at night or you won't be able to sleep for worrying.'

Much of the survival guide has a degree of detail that only comes with experience. The item on shoes, for example: don't wear new shoes in the Tour, advises Millar, break them in first. Take a reserve pair in the team car in case one shoe gets broken in a crash. Any good training manual will say this, but the training manual won't recommend 'always, *always*' taking the shoes out of the car at night 'in case they get nicked'.

Some of it is pure politics; for example, the need for a Tour rider to make friends with the managers of other teams. This is so that when he is riding up through the convoy to regain the bunch after a stop they won't leave gaps, making it easier to use the slipstream of the cars to save energy. And there are items which make it easy to imagine Millar having a bad Tour and devising mental tricks to boost his morale: 'Before the stage start, look through your race food and eat the nicest thing before the flag drops, then you've had at least one good moment in your day.'

By the 1990s, Millar felt that the human face of the Tour was being lost. There was huge pressure to get results in the race, yet with twenty-two teams rather than a dozen as in the past there was a smaller chance of even winning a stage. Previously, a local rider might have been given dispensation to gain a couple of minutes' lead to greet his family. Now, the chances were that one of his colleagues would give chase. The increase in corporate guests meant that the Tour, he said, had become like the Derby – just a day out for a lot of people who knew nothing about the sport itself. He sounded like a whinger, but it was tempered with constant ironic humour. He had learned to swear in seven different languages, so that at least when another rider brought him down (more often than not a Colombian) he could abuse him in his own language.

Now, he reflects: 'I thought the first three Tours I did were not too commercialised, and I didn't feel like a disposable commodity. As the peloton's size got bigger, things changed, as if being a rider was some kind of secondary status. Staying in hostels and schools was not good enough; there were too many riders for the road layouts. The environment had changed, but the organisers were stuck in an age when they decided almost everything. The teams were becoming bigger, more organised and more professional, but most organisers' idea of change was to have more riders, longer stages and more transfers. After four Tours I knew it wasn't the best race in the world. It might be the most important, but there was a difference in the enjoyment level. I didn't love the Tour like some riders say they do. I respected it, its place in history, and I tried my best.'

The physical drudgery involved in the Tour is the same for any cyclist, but Millar could illustrate it in graphic terms. He told me that you could tell which week of the Tour you were in by the number of sleeping tablets you were taking: one in the first week, two in the second, three in the third. The fatigue, he said, kicked in after five days if he was in poor shape, ten if he was properly fit. If he struggled to finish a Tour, as he did in 1987, it might take until November before he stopped feeling tired.

The pure climber such as Millar makes ascending the great passes look effortless to the layman. He could scotch that one easily: 'Riding up one of the mountains in the Tour if you're bad is like being sick. The best way of describing how you feel is that it's as if you were a normal person doing a hard day's work, you've got flu and you can just about drive home and fall into bed. You can't divide the physical and mental suffering. You tend to let go mentally before you crack physically, with the constant noise all day – people yelling at you, the cars, the helicopters. If you're still physically strong you can block it out; if not, you never relax.'

Wherever he is now, his back will never be quite the same again, since the whiplash from a crash on a road through Normandy in 1999, where he flew over a Colombian and landed stunned in a heap on the tarmac, as if dropped from the sky. Two vertebrae in his back were displaced; one high up in his neck at the heart of the nerve centres was crushed. His team managers spent that evening scouring pharmacies for a neck brace, which he wore through the heat of Southern France and into the Alps. The grazing on his body meant he had to sleep on his face for two weeks. He accepted the price, as they all do. 'Being so focused on something isn't always good for you. I raced too much. There were times I overtrained. I accepted that the energy I was expending would probably mean I would not live as long a life later.'

When the Tour is seen in this way, the suffering involved puts the use of drugs into context. Millar tested positive for testosterone use after stage eighteen of the 1992 Tour of Spain. He swore the test result was incorrectly calibrated, but that is the usual defence. In an interview we did for the *Guardian* in 1998, Millar provided this perspective on doping: 'Given the real-life situation of drug use, I'd say [cycling] is no worse than in the real world where a million ecstasy tablets are sold every weekend. It's not an isolated cycling thing, it's just that people expect sport to be cleaner than real life.'

At the start of Millar's last Tour de France, I delivered to him a pair of custom-made lightweight wheels for the mountain stages from a builder in Liverpool, and light-weight componentry from a company in Southampton. By the 1990s, it was rare for professionals to go to such extremes, but Millar went further in his almost obsessive pursuit of excellence within his profession. Team-issue bikes are intended for racing and never have mudguard fittings for riding in the off-season. Professional cyclists put up with the discomfort, wet and dirt in winter, because the bikes are handed out free. Millar is the only professional I have known who went to the trouble and expense of getting a training bike custom-made so that he could have the comfort of riding with mudguards. He was among the first pros to use a mountain bike for winter training, also custom-built so that it had the same riding position as his road machine. He paid for his own blood tests, £100 a time, every six weeks, through a local doctor. Nothing suspicious, he said: it was so he could keep track of his mineral and blood-cell levels.

His knowledge of the Tour's great climbs made it clear that he did far, far more than simply get on his bike and ride. He could recall which side the wind blew from on the Col du Galibier and at what time (a headwind 'until about midday'), and what the road surfaces were at various places (on l'Alpe d'Huez, the tarmac was smoother from the village of La Garde, roughly halfway up).

His thinking was quirky, but rooted in common sense. By 1995, he had worked out just how many small fruit bars he needed to keep his energy reserves high in a stage of the Tour: he would start eating them after the first thirty kilometres, then take one every ten kilometres to the finish. For a 200-kilometre stage, for example, the total would be seventeen. When his knee gave out in 1994, he rationalised the injury by estimating that the joint had flexed over a pedal around 70 million times in his fourteen years as a professional.

Millar is a highly self-critical person, and his obsessive

attention to detail was born of insecurity, he says now. 'I could hide behind a very "couldn't care less" attitude, but I was very aware of the fact that I lived in a culture where your last result was the most important. I knew I could compete on the level just below the Tour de France winners (what I called "the animals"), but I don't think the managers knew how to take that talent to the next level. I dealt with it by trying harder, exploring different training regimes, changes to my calendar, different diets, but that just showed me I had reached my physical and mental limit.'

During the 1980s, with the arrival en masse of cyclists from other cultures, cycling became less conservative, and there was room for stars who looked and behaved differently. Millar had rapidly earned a reputation as a nonconformist. He acquired a tiny diamond ear stud early on in his career, and by 1990 he had adopted a ponytail – and this in a milieu where short back and sides were still the norm. Most radically, he had begun experimenting with vegetarianism in 1981, first by cutting out red meat before important races, then progressing to cutting out meat and fish altogether.

'It was a dietary choice, not an issue with animals. I did some research and discovered that we are not totally carnivore or herbivore so I figured out that whichever suited my intestines would help me get the best from myself. I had fewer upset stomachs.' It was hardly a step to be taken lightly by anyone living among the very carnivorous French, let alone a professional athlete who required large amounts of protein. On a practical level, it meant he had to compensate with protein powders and large amounts of dairy products.

When Millar lost form, team managers would inevitably mention his vegetarianism. Clearly, there was a lack of understanding, and it showed in another context: when he tested positive, his then manager Cees Priem said it was impossible, because he did not eat meat. However, the fact that he felt he could be a vegetarian, and that Sean Yates and Allan Peiper could eat muesli at breakfast rather than half-cooked steak, underlined the way cycling had moved on from Brian Robinson's 'eat what the French eat'. As Millar saw it, by the 1980s it was 'OK to be different as long as you ride OK'.

That Millar felt able to compete meat-free reflected a wider trend in the 1980s for English-speaking cyclists to take on cycling's sacred *idées reçues*. LeMond and Phil Anderson were the true radicals: it was Anderson who first took a lawyer with him to conduct contract negotiations (Barry Hoban had agreed terms with a handshake, as had Robinson). It was LeMond who brought wages, at the top end at least, towards those in other sports, with his contract of \$5.7m over three years at Millar's Z towards the end of 1989. The Americans changed mores in other ways. For ninety years, the world of cycle racing had excluded women, supposedly to avoid sexual temptation, but in the late 1980s the American team 7-Eleven brought with them a female masseur, Shelley Verses. Even wives and girl-friends had been shut out – to the extent that at Peugeot in the early 1980s riders would do midnight flits from hotels at training camps; yet by the end of the decade, LeMond's wife Kathy was a regular and accepted visitor at races.

At the 1992 Tour, the race numbers issued to the cyclists each day were sponsored by the European Union, and each had the twelve stars on it. Every morning before the start, in his hotel room, Millar would carefully scratch the stars out and inscribe a saltire with a blue biro. This was probably not so much an example of Braveheart patriotism as an expression of a wider *contra mundum* attitude. 'You have an attitude. It's like Billy Connolly says, a "stuff you" kind of look. You see someone like that, it feels like he hates you when he gets on a bike, rather than someone who says, "This is nice, isn't it?" You don't get anywhere being nice. Not in bike racing. You have to be a selfish person basically.' The Connolly comparison was apt: Millar is as observant as the Big Yin, and has a similarly detached, dark, occasionally vicious sense of humour that is not to everyone's taste.

Millar does not tolerate fools gladly, and he could sometimes disregard the niceties of human life. 'When he didn't like someone or something he'd let them know,' says his teammate at TVM, the Australian Scott Sunderland. 'I remember one night in a hotel the spaghetti was over-cooked, like glue, and he said to the waiter, "This would stick on anything," and threw it at the ceiling. It stuck, of course.' Journalists would often be greeted with a brusque answer or a brush-off, a screening process to weed out time-wasters. Fellow cyclists might receive similar treatment: Jamie McGahan, who had raced with him on various Scottish amateur teams, remembers meeting Millar in Troyes and being struck by his indifference. McGahan's verdict: 'As a human being he was a dead loss.' But other cyclists, such as Sunderland and his fellow Scot Brian Smith, found him 'helpful and open if you showed you respected him'. Sunderland believed he was 'one of the better guys I've shared a room with'.

Millar's own explanation was partly that the 'attitude' enabled him to hide his lack of confidence, but it also stemmed from his being totally focused on what he did: he had no interest in anything in a race outside himself. 'It gave me mental space to deal with stuff, pre-race, post-race.' It was also a way of ensuring he remained self-sufficient in an environment he regarded as akin to the jungle, where 'you had a few friends but they were still people who could take the bread out of your mouth'.

If the cynicism always seemed like a front, that was because there were plenty of signs that Millar was a man who did care. To start with, there was his obsessive devotion to the details of his profession. The photographs from his career were impeccably kept. When we visited him for interviews, he would come a little way towards the motorway with us, to make sure we didn't get lost. Most tellingly, in the early 1990s, there was no 'trophy room' in his home near Troyes, but there was a loft in the barn with a pile of Samsonite suitcases, each containing religiously folded team jerseys from every squad he'd ridden for, and all the race leaders' and King of the Mountains jerseys from every event he'd performed well in.

The barriers remained after retirement: Millar's answerphone specified that the caller would receive a reply 'if it's necessary'. But he did not view the entire world with a jaundiced eye. He would mock the affected and pretentious among his fellows, yet his tribute to Sean Kelly (*Cycle Sport*, January 1995) would have put most professional journalists to shame for its clarity and sincerity. Gilchrist, Bilsland, Sunderland and Smith make it clear that once a person had got through the barriers and earned his respect, Millar was a good man to know.

Millar has also taken a radically different attitude to retirement from that of his peers. Unlike Barry Hoban, he was actually given the chance to pass on his knowledge when he was appointed as national road-race trainer in 1997. In this capacity, he had the unconventional habit of racing his bike in the same events as the senior riders he was managing, to assess their progress. For all his experience, however, he did not seem to have the motivational skills to fire up his charges, and the post became redundant with the advent of National Lottery funding.

That disillusioned him as well. 'I tried to give something back, and the BCF job was a good example. I spent six months learning how to do the job, like admin, planning, what had and hadn't been done, then they appointed a performance director who told me I wouldn't be needed at the end of my contract, no explanation other than that the budget didn't allow it. I felt like my being there was to appease a movement of discontent ... it was as if my presence was some evidence of progress being made. I felt I'd been given a place that belonged to the establishment and it was only a matter of time before they got it back. I've moved on.'

He continued to coach one Scottish rider of promise, the son of a friend, for a while. He wrote bike tests for *Procycling* magazine, he learned tae kwon do, he rode his motorbike, he occasionally managed the Scotland amateur team. He did not want a career: his view was that he had spent most of his life having to do things and he wanted a break from obligation.

Millar denies that he has cut himself off from his sport. 'I don't go to cycle races because I have other interests, and I'd be jealous that I can't ride that fast any more.' Given his intensely competitive nature, that is easy to imagine. He adds: 'I don't seek to be involved, but I don't put it down. I'll cycle if I feel like it, but I have no desire to go far or fast, or hurt myself in the process. What I find is that people, public, fans, whatever you call them, they think they know you and they expect you to behave as you did when you were competing. It's as if you don't live in the real world.'

Be that as it may, Millar is inevitably missed. What he achieved is too significant simply to be forgotten. I wouldn't pretend to be among those who know him well, but I am one of those who wish he were around. He is fine company, with few airs and graces, and he is prepared to open himself up in a way that very few athletes do. To do so cannot be easy, revealing as it does something of the vulnerability that made him put up those barriers in the first place.

To understand his current absence, it is perhaps necessary to look back to his beginnings. From the days when he 'drummed up' at his own fire when out with the Glasgow

Wheelers, Millar has always approached cycling in his own way, rather than doing what anyone else might expect of him. Why should he do what is expected now? Those who ponder his whereabouts and feel he has turned his back should perhaps wonder whether they are asking for too much. As Millar told me in 1998: 'People want sport to be like life as it should be, without any of the bad sides, an ideal. Why should sport be different? In fact, it's just like life as it is.'

CHAPTER NINE

Innocents Abroad

'I don't think you should be riding. Get your team doctor to have a look at you.' This is not what any cyclist wants to hear before the Tour de France, but that was the prognosis on Paul Watson at the medical check the day before the *départ* of the 1987 race. Watson's reply spoke volumes about the readiness of ANC-Halfords, the first and to date the only British trade team to race the Tour: 'I don't think we have a team doctor,' said the twenty-five-year-old from Milton Keynes. 'We've got some paracetamol in a box somewhere . . .'

From the outside, ANC-Halfords' entry to the Tour encapsulated the romance of cycling and, in a wider sense, of sport as a whole. The team was founded in 1985 but within only two years it brought several of Britain's best cyclists to the start line of the greatest bike race in the world. Here was a zero-to-hero tale that matched the rags-to-riches saga of its sponsoring company, overnight-delivery specialists founded in the back of a taxi in Stoke in 1981, and worth a seven-figure sum five years later. For the first time since 1968 a British team was in the Tour – and ANC's kit bore the evocative Union Jack logo.

Yet behind the romance of the Britons pedalling off to fulfil their dreams and do battle with cycling's best, there was a hidden, disturbing story. The team ran out of money during the race. The riders and staff went through the toughest endurance event in cycling suspecting they were not being paid and returned home to find they were right. The episode was a reminder that underneath the glamour, professional cycling teams had often been poorly regulated and organised, and that professional cycling is a precarious existence.

Penniless ANC-Halfords may have been, but they were also colourful, with characters, tensions and sub-plots worthy of a two-wheeled sitcom. The team had even brought with them the perfect man to make sense of the script, the *Daily Star* journalist Jeff Connor, who travelled with them for the entire race. He could not believe the material on show before him and still gets nostalgic when he sees an ANC truck on the motorway. His daily presence in the team car would no longer be acceptable in the closed world of cycling: no team likes the press to get too close to the backbiting, double-dealing and bending of the rules that goes on behind the scenes. Connor was a fell runner, so his sports editor assumed that if he was sent to the Tour he would be able to ride a stage in the bunch, an error that perfectly expresses the level of knowledge of the race among mainstream British media at the time. His account, *Wide-eyed and Legless*, ranks alongside Paul Kimmage's *Rough Ride* as one of the finest accounts of cycle racing in the eighties written from the inside.

The rise and demise of ANC-Halfords had a wider significance. The group had emerged during a surge in the popularity and profile of cycling in the UK in the mid-1980s; this was largely due to the fact that the recently launched Channel 4 spotted cycling's potential as a televised sport. The success of Robert Millar, Stephen Roche and Sean Kelly had led Four to begin broadcasting a series of cycle races in British city centres in 1983, in which European-based stars such as Phil Anderson and Stephen Roche were brought over to compete against the British professionals. The arrival of even that small level of television coverage led to a rapid expansion in sponsorship of British cycling; Tony Capper, founder of the parcels company ANC, was riding that wave.

By 1987, the Tour de France was being covered nightly

on Channel 4. In that year they also began covering a highly successful British professional Tour sponsored by Kellogg's. Major companies were now deeply involved in sponsoring British domestic cycling, while the *Daily Star*'s involvement underlined that, for the first time, professional cycling had begun to get through to the British tabloid press. Connor's sports editor might not have understood the details of the Tour, but at least he wanted his journalist to cover it, which was progress.

The team's participation in the Tour was the high point of British cycling's renaissance in the 1980s. For one and a half seasons, ANC provided the final link in the British cycling chain: there was a professional Tour of Britain, substantial television coverage, about sixty home-based professionals and a British team racing the European circuit. After ANC went bust, there would be a slow but steady decline in the sport's profile and in the British domestic calendar, similar to the one that had followed the death of Tom Simpson twenty years earlier. A decade later there would be no Tour of Britain, and the home-based British professional class would be virtually extinct.

Tony Capper was a twenty-stone, chain-smoking ex-policeman. He had sold his parcels company and now ran the squad through a Stoke-based management company, Action Sports. 'A bit of a big gob, but ex-coppers often are,' according to the team leader, Malcolm Elliott. 'How he held together in that heat I don't know.' Capper was going bald, and never permitted the sunroof of the Peugeot team car to be opened for fear his head might burn. 'He was hellishly unhealthy. His diet was appalling.' Capper's favourite ploy while driving the team car was stopping for an ice cream late in the stage, then burning rubber to regain his place in the convoy. Connor wrote: 'As Capper put it as he scattered pedestrians or made a U-turn across the central reservation of a dual carriageway, being inside an official

Tour Peugeot was "as good as being in the presidential limousine".' 'He thought he was a team manager, that he could get in the car and give us whatever instructions we needed,' says Adrian Timmis. 'I remember him saying he'd been up one climb in the Milk Race in his Land-Rover and had only needed third gear, so we should find it easy.' Capper admitted to Connor that at one point during ANC's formative years he had had liabilities of around £200,000. On the Tour he never lost his nerve as the phone calls multiplied, the bailiffs raided the team's premises in England and the squad collapsed around him.

Cycling's sudden transformation into a truly international sport was clear from the blend of cultures and personalities within the team. The *directeurs sportifs* were a grumpy Belgian, Ward 'Muddy' Woutters, who worked for the water board, and a fast-talking former English international racer turned salesman, Phil Griffiths. As well as Watson, the British cyclists were the good-looking, impeccably tanned Sheffield 'playboy' Elliott, the 'foreign legion' veteran Graham Jones and Timmis, a reserved twenty-three-year-old from Stoke. There were two Frenchmen, the grizzled Guy Gallopin and Bernard Chesneau, who never made it to his native France; an ebullient Australian, Shane Sutton; and a Kiwi, Steven Swart. Most amusingly, given that the Tour started in West Berlin (its first and last start on the wrong side of the Iron Curtain), the ninth cyclist was a Czech defector, Kvetoslav Palov, who had turned up in Sheffield that April and ended up in the Tour three months later.

With the addition of four masseurs from four different countries, it was an eccentric mix, riddled with tension and sniping. Woutters and Jones did not get on; the rider had more experience than the *directeur sportif* and said so. Griffiths resented Capper, a non-cyclist, elbowing him out of the No. 1 team car, and the pair disagreed over tactics. Capper fell out with the head masseur, Angus Fraser, one evening over whether they were eating cod or turbot. Griffiths and the head mechanic, Steve Snowling, had a stand-up row over saddle heights before a time trial. Dinner-time, says Watson, 'was like the Mad Hatters' tea party'.

This bizarre mélange of languages and characters reflected the speed with which the ANC-Halfords squad had grown since its foundation in 1985, when it was a team of just three riders racing the British domestic professional circuit. A year later, there were three teams run by Capper's management company, Action Sports – ANC, Lycra-Halfords and Interrent – who raced separately in Britain to get round a ceiling on team numbers, and joined forces when racing in Europe.

The team's rapid growth led, inevitably, to ramshackle organisation. Elliott recalls finishing a major French stage race, the Midi Libre, then driving two hundred kilometres to the airport. There was nothing abnormal in that, except that the riders travelled in the team's bike van, sitting on bags in the back or on the wooden seats down the side, in forty-degree temperatures. En route to Watson's first race in 1986, in the south of France, the team failed to pick him up as arranged at Newport Pagnell services on the M1; he eventually arrived at their hotel at 3 a.m., only to find the clothing for the season had been handed out and he had been left with barely any kit.

'They were throwing us into everything, to get the world ranking to get in the Tour,' he says. They finished the Milk Race, two weeks around Britain, then headed for a race in Brittany the next day. 'I was begging not to go, but there were shouts and screams and threats down the phone, so I went. I got to the Tour and I was exhausted.' ANC had qualified for the Tour at almost the last minute, thanks to strong rides from Elliott and Watson in the 1987 spring classics (third in Amstel Gold and sixth in Flèche Wallonne respectively) and a stage win by Timmis in the Midi Libre.

From the outside, that most seasoned of Tour veterans, Barry Hoban, described ANC's entry to the Tour as 'premature', and within the team, privately, there was almost total agreement with that. 'None of us were ready' (Jones). 'The biggest mountain I'd seen was in Majorca' (Timmis). 'No one thought [the Tour] was what we were doing. It was kind of a distant, fifty-fifty thought' (Elliott). 'They had bitten off more than they could chew from day one [of the season]' (Watson). As Sutton said (well away from earshot of the management) at the launch of the Tour team: 'I'm knackered, I'm crook and we haven't even got to the start yet. We shouldn't be doing this, we're all half sick.'

Watson was tired out, Jones was ill when he started the Tour and 'was asked to ride because someone else pulled out', while Sutton had just recovered from illness. He too was asked to start instead of another rider who was injured, and was told merely to get as far as he could. 'There was all this talk about the Tour and I just went with the flow,' says Jones. 'I got carried away with it; I couldn't see myself not going as part of a British team. None of us were ready. We rode Paris–Nice in March and the Midi Libre in May, whereas you really need to spend the entire season building up.' Their longest event was the Milk Race, well short of Tour standard, 'two weeks' training and nice hotels'. As Elliott put it: 'There was a lack of enthusiasm when we were told we were going to the Tour. None of the riders were jumping up and down. That would have been like a turkey voting for Christmas. We all thought, "Shit, are you sure?" Graham had actually ridden it and was less than impressed, and we took our cue from him. Instead of five or six days like Paris–Nice it was going to be three weeks – thank you.'

The 1987 Tour was won by Ireland's Stephen Roche in a now-legendary duel with the Spaniard Pedro Delgado. Robert Millar highlighted that year as the point when he felt the Tour became 'too big, too important, [with] too many people and too stressful'. Millar had ridden his first Tour four years earlier, as one of just 140 cyclists, a number which would not have seemed out of place in the 1950s or 1960s. By 1986, however, the peloton had expanded by 50 per cent, to 210. In terms of the daily battle for road space, the figures speak for themselves: half as many men again trying to funnel off a wide *route nationale* on to a narrow back road; twenty-one team leaders and their *domestiques* fighting for 'position'; twenty-one teams rather than fourteen worrying about winning a stage to ensure that they went home with at least some prize money.

A closer look at the maths explains why the pressure on the riders increased another notch in 1987. A field of 207 was slightly smaller than the previous year; critically, however, there was the biggest ever number of teams, twenty-three, with nine rather than ten cyclists apiece. Whereas in a team of ten the chances were that one of the ten might be in there simply to make up the numbers, that was less likely in a team of nine, so the standard of racing was higher. There was also more of everything – forty-six team cars in the convoy rather than twenty-eight four years earlier, twenty-three teams and their vehicles squeezing into a town square for the start – while the one thing that had not changed was the size of the roads and the size of French town centres.

In one sense, ANC-Halfords was a product of its time. Cycling was expanding so rapidly that it could hardly be regulated. Team budgets were exploding. Wages for the stars were coming close to parity with sports such as tennis and motor racing, thanks to the demands of riders such as Greg LeMond and Phil Anderson and the well-lined pockets of sponsors such as the controversial French businessman Bernard Tapie. The rapidly growing number of teams on the circuit attracted multinational team sponsors such as Hitachi and Panasonic. The bigger teams were well run, but among the lesser lights ANC-Halfords was by no means the only outfit to overreach its budgets and leave riders and staff unpaid.

That year was when Tour followers began to worry about a phenomenon known as *gigantisme*. The fear was a straightforward one: that the scale of the event – vehicles, sponsors, fans, media, the organisation necessary to cater for them all – would overwhelm the sporting contest which was at its heart. The reason was simple enough: the event's sudden globalisation, and in particular its discovery by the American media and sponsors – Coca-Cola was the best example – following Greg LeMond's win in 1986. There were now some eight hundred media on the Tour, from countries as far from the cycling heartland as Kuwait and Japan.

The strain was making itself felt in 1987. Press photographers went on strike over working conditions owing to congestion within the race itself. The 500-mile transfer out of Berlin through the East German 'corridor' was nightmarish – but the Tour organisers received a £1m cheque from the city for the start, and gained several evocative backdrops for television pictures: the Reichstag, the Brandenburg Gate, the Kurfürstendamm, the Wall. Preventing the Tour from growing beyond its logistical means was to prove beyond Goddet – understandably, as he was by now in his eighties – not to mention the businessmen who replaced Lévitan.

The 1980s witnessed a subtle change in the Tour's support base on the roadside as well. To the French locals and holidaymakers, and hardcore European cycling fans, a new category could be added: what Connor describes with seventeen years' hindsight as 'generic sports fans' with no specific interest in cycling, who turn up to witness a national event. Roche's victory drew supporters who 'just follow anything Irish, anywhere around the world, dressed in green. Apart from one guy, Oliver MacQuaid, the ones I met at the end of the 1987 Tour had no idea about cycling: I found myself the expert. I've watched sport in Ireland – football at Lansdowne Road, Michelle de Bruin – and panning around the crowd I notice they are the same people. Even now I go to Lansdowne Road and see one or two familiar faces from that Tour.' Their Spanish equiva-lents would turn up in 1991 to greet Miguel Indurain in the town of Mâcon; 1996 would bring the Danes to hail Bjarne Riis. Not surprisingly, the first six Tours of the twenty-first century saw a vast influx of Americans swept along by the Lance Armstrong phenomenon.

For all that this was a new era in terms of numbers, it was a Tour that harked back to the past for its toughness: five consecutive days' climbing in the Alps, twenty-five days' racing. The event would never be as hard again. Added to that, Bernard Hinault had just retired: there was no senior pro to take control of the race and calm the unruly elements. With twenty-three teams fighting for the daily prizes, the speed of the 1987 Tour shocked even old hands. 'Robert Millar and Stephen Roche said it was not normal, how fast it was,' says Timmis. 'It went flat out from the gun and went faster and faster. I remember just one day when it was a promenade, during the final week.' Capper predicted before the start that stage wins and perhaps a brief spell in yellow were within ANC's reach. Like much associated with the team, it was fantasy.

Physically, Elliott was the only member of the team who was competitive. Chesneau was the first casualty, outside the time limit on stage three, while Jones and Watson abandoned on stage six, which included the race's first serious climbs in the Vosges. Watson was in negotiations with a Belgian team, Hitachi, for 1988, and saw no point in continuing. 'Carrying on just doing worse and worse was doing me no favours. I told them I wasn't riding the next day, and Capper took me aside for a pep talk, about how he had been in the SAS and you never pulled out, never let the team down. I looked at him, a twenty-stone blob, and thought, "You what?" ' Sutton battled on to the Pyrenees, while Swart lasted until the Alps, only giving in after an injury to his foot meant he could go no further. The only ones to make it to Paris were Elliott, Timmis, Palov and Gallopin.

'It got lonely at the dinner table,' says Elliott. 'At the time you'd be thinking, "They're at home doing whatever they want, I'm stuck on this Tour." ' But as the riders thinned out, the hangers-on increased in number. Capper had brought along a French translator, Donald Fisher; both their families appeared halfway through the race. There was Fisher's wife ('caustic and dripping with jewellery' as Connor recalls) and their poodle, which promptly died of the heat and was buried in a hotel garden. There was Mrs Capper and two teenage Capperlets, the younger of whom immediately announced that he was travelling in Griffiths's car. The presence of 'civilians' among the Tour men remains a taboo. 'It was a nightmare, you couldn't relax at the dinner table,' says Timmis. 'You can't have kids eating with you. It was like the more riders we lost, the more of Capper's family turned up.'

The back-up personnel, like the riders, thinned out, however. Woutters lasted a week. 'It really annoyed him that everyone wanted a free ride, everyone wanted an access-all-areas pass,' believes Watson. Capper disappeared into thin air four days before the finish. 'His excuse was that me and Malcolm had upset the kids,' says Timmis. 'The little brats were at the table one night and we were taking the piss.' That left only the head mechanic, Steve Snowling, to drive the second team car. Connor, as a spare pair of hands, ended up at the wheel of the team van, carrying all the bikes and spares, driving several thousand pounds' worth of equipment around France with no idea where he was going. 'That I was allowed to do that says volumes

about the team organisation,' he says. As does the fact that
the brakes failed on an Alpine descent.

Not that the standard of the Tour organisation was
impeccable either. In one hilarious episode, the team were
billeted in a school – Collège Marcel Aymard at Millau in
southern France – eating in the dining hall off plastic-
topped tables, with the staff watching them as if they had
dropped from another planet. The facilities were basic and
it was rapidly nicknamed 'Dachau'. 'It was like the sleeping
accommodation in a monastery or public school – two long
rows of beds facing each other with hardboard partitions,'
recalls Connor. 'It was horrendous, with people getting up
in the night and Capper snoring. I don't think many people
slept. Malcolm threw a little strop then calmed down.' 'I
always felt as an English team we got the short straw on
accommodation,' says Elliott. 'When you've had a day like
we had had' – six hours through the Massif Central – 'you
appreciate being able to put your stuff down, watch TV,
have a bit of privacy, but we were all in the same room from
the end of the stage to the start of the next.'

Hardboard partitions were not the only thing leading to
sleepless nights: rumours that the team had run out of
money and that pay cheques had not arrived had begun
circulating shortly before the race. Once in the Tour,
however, the riders were left with an invidious choice: quit
and face an uncertain future, or continue without pay in the
hope of attracting a backer for the next year. 'I've always
felt you're never treated as a normal person when you're a
bike rider. In a factory you'd go on strike, but as a bike rider
you have to ride even if you aren't being paid, in order to
stay in a job for the next year,' says Timmis. Amid
discussions among the riders about whether they should
continue, Sutton (who had bought a bigger house on the
strength of his ANC salary) kept calling home to find out if
the money had arrived in his bank account.

The consensus now is that the money paid from ANC to

Capper's company, Action Sports, had been used up in the rush to get the team to the Tour. The riders were paid up to the Tour start, and that was that. ANC was by no means an isolated case of a team overreaching itself: there have been numerous tales in a similar vein from France, Italy, Spain and Belgium. Britain had a repeat of the ANC fiasco in early 2001 with the Linda McCartney Foods team: 'sponsorship' by three major companies was a figment of the manager's imagination, and the squad went bust when the riders were assembled on the eve of their presentation to the press. It is only recently that the International Cycling Union has begun more stringent checks on the state of finances among leading cycling teams, to ensure that they are properly run.

With hindsight, Adrian Timmis acknowledges that far from being an opportunity, finishing seventieth in the 1987 Tour probably destroyed his cycling career. The slight, silent lad from Stoke had been a track pursuiter for Great Britain in the Los Angeles Olympics. Pursuits take about four minutes; within three years he was racing four to six hours a day for three weeks in the Tour. 'I wasn't ready. I'd just turned twenty-three and wasn't physically and mentally mature enough. Everyone at the time, guys like Sean Yates, Martin Earley and Graham Jones, were all saying it would finish me off. I was too young to know better.'

Timmis was tipped to be the next great British stage-race star. He was the kind of cyclist whose perfect style on the bike belies the suffering he is going through. That July, his sheer talent and ambition backfired on him. 'As a kid I thought, "The Tour de France, that's it." Today if a young rider does the Tour he will ride ten days to experience it, then get off. I won a stage of the Midi Libre and the team thought I was ready for the Tour. I was fit enough to get round, but it dug deep into what I had.' According to Connor's account, the 'almost painfully shy' Timmis 'changed almost visibly during the month in France, from a gawky young boy to a mature professional cyclist'.

Teammates noted that Timmis was completely self-contained, his emotions kept on a tight rein, whether he was scraping himself off the road after a heavy crash on the Pyrenean Col de Bagargui or watching the personnel snipe at each other around the dinner table. Similar things had been said of Brian Robinson in 1955. 'I'm a quiet person and I just got on with the job,' says Timmis. 'It was just survival, looking after yourself, always thinking about the next day. There was only one day when I didn't think I'd finish. It was the day after l'Alpe d'Huez. We started at Bourg-d'Oisans [in the valley below the Alpe]; it was fifty kilometres uphill to the Galibier. Stephen Roche had decided he had to do something and it was lined out from the gun. I cracked and swung out, assumed the *gruppetto* was going to form soon, but someone told me it was too early so I had to hang on. A little later the race did split up, but it happened so early that we still had to ride hard up the climbs and in the valleys.'

There would have been another way out, but Timmis was not prepared to take drugs. 'I didn't want to get involved in it, because I didn't want to have to face my mum, and my family, because they'd backed me all the way to be a bike rider. Perhaps that's one reason why the Tour did finish me off. Perhaps it was good that it did, because I never had to make the decision.'

Timmis signed a contract with Z-Peugeot – the team that had once fielded the 'foreign legion' of Jones, Yates, Millar, Roche and Anderson – for 1988 and 1989, but was released after a single year, because he never found form. Now, he believes he was suffering from chronic fatigue as a result of the ANC programme. 'I was so tired. I was up and down all the time. I was mentally tired because I would do a consistent training effort and it never translated into form. I'd have really good days and really bad days. In the Milk

Race in 1988, one day I'd be towing the bunch for ten miles, the next I'd do nothing. It took me a few years to get over it.' Eventually he turned to mountain-bike racing, and after retirement he became a *soigneur*, in which capacity he went through a rerun of the ANC nightmare of unpaid wages with the Linda McCartney team.

Like Robert Millar, Timmis was not drawn to cycling in search of celebrity. Nor was he driven by the money – he acknowledges that with ANC his wage was a pittance: £6,000. When I bumped into him in June 2003 at a very local road race, in a very anonymous village hall, you would not have known that sixteen years earlier this man in the plain jersey was rubbing shoulders with Stephen Roche and the greats. But he does now begin to accept the achievement. 'I put the video on last year and watched some of the 1987 race. It's an eye-opener. You forget what the climbs were like. In a way it was sad I never got to do it again. Perhaps it is a bit of an achievement, but to me it's not so very big. I just did it and was capable of doing it. I will be a Tour de France rider until the day I die.'

In the long term, the principal beneficiary of the ANC saga was Malcolm Elliott, who earned the bulk of the team's prize money for them in that Tour. He finished only ninety-fourth, but came close to winning stages in the bunch sprints at Bordeaux, where he was third, Avignon, where he came sixth, and Troyes, where he finished ninth, while he had the strength in the final week to take twentieth on the penultimate day's time trial. He was the only ANC survivor to ride the 1988 Tour, where he raced alongside Robert Millar in the Fagor team. That team, he recalls, was particularly badly organised and riven with internal conflicts, making ANC look positively benign.

A rapid sprinter and strong climber over short, steep hills, Elliott had been British cycling's brightest prospect since winning two gold medals at the Commonwealth

Games in 1982. Until the 1987 Tour, however, the talent of the 'Sheffield flyer' had always seemed to be greater than his ambition, which seemed limited to the Milk Race Tour of Britain, where he won seventeen stages in four years. He had a legendary reputation as a party animal, founded on his good looks and a succession of fast cars and motorbikes. Stories abound, particularly from the Milk Race, of Elliott drinking much of the night away and winning the following day's stage on a few hours' sleep. 'I'm not monastic, I did enjoy the trappings and was not particularly discreet about it. I don't know what the stories were but they were probably true.' Surprisingly quietly-spoken and attached to his Sheffield roots in spite of his playboy reputation, he was never certain he wanted to be a professional on the European circuit. He does not like being away from home. 'When I've been away for a long time I look forward to getting down the local with a few of my mates ... there's always the feeling in pro cycling of [being] always in transit.'

For all his talent, Elliott was not like Robert Millar or Tom Simpson, both of whom dreamed of the Tour from their teenage years. He is a man who takes life one day at a time. 'I live in the present, want to win the race at the weekend and the one after that. I never had a passion for the Tour. I get turned on by different races. I'm much more into one-day races, and the Milk Race used to get me going. The Tour is a three-week grind. I'm not that kind of rider.' Nor did he view the Tour as a stepping-stone to a lucrative career in Europe. 'I'm not really that analytical. I don't wonder, "Can I do it, can't I do it?" It was "What am I going to do next year, and the following year? Where could I ride and get well paid for it?" I had to ride for a team in Europe.'

Elliott has never imbued the Tour or any side of cycling with much mystique. 'I didn't consider the Tour to be the Everest of cycling achievement. I didn't think it was a massive peak with the other races in the foothills. It is a hard race and a long race, but just because I'd done it I didn't think I could take on anything. [Then] I still lacked a bit of confidence. Now when people talk about the Tour it has high, revered status. In 1987, the Tour was just the Tour, the Giro was the Giro and the Vuelta was the Vuelta. I've ridden all three; it's hard work in all of them – you start to suffer after ten or twelve days in all of them. The Tour gets a bit exaggerated in a lot of people's eyes. People diminish the quality of other races because they aren't the Tour.'

Elliott did not look forward to the Tour, and he did not particularly enjoy it when he was there. 'The first things that come to mind are the heat and the sheer duration of it. You're there at the start and you sit there and think, "In three weeks' time I'll still be doing this." It's best to try not to dwell on it. You can't comprehend how far it is and what you have got to go through.' He did, however, devise his own way of dealing with it. Elliott had learned early in his cycling career to tune out, to distance himself from what was going on. 'A lot of cyclists learn it when they're training. They can switch off, plod away for hour after hour, go somewhere else and roam around in their head.

'I could never think three weeks ahead; the most I'd think would be five days. I've often gone through a stage race promising myself I'll pack the next day. It's my way of getting through the day, a carrot. You'll see people on holiday and think that in a couple of days that'll be me, with the bucket and spade out building sandcastles. All of Europe seems to be on holiday in France in July. You'll be riding through idyllic villages with deep blue lakes, they are all at the roadside in shorts with a beer in their hand. I'd be thinking "I want to do that, I want to be on holiday." '

The one side of the Tour that he enjoyed was 'the whole last stage – general euphoria, silliness, people finally starting to relax'. That came as a sudden release after the tensions that had developed as the entire field grew steadily more and more tired. 'In the final week tempers fray easily because everyone is tired. If someone does something on the first day, like leaving gaps all the time, pushing in, thinking they can ride over you, you ignore it, but after twenty days you're going to say something.'

In the 1987 Tour, as later in his career, when he was a prolific winner for the Spanish team Teka, Elliott's speciality was the bunch sprint. To the outsider, this is the most fearsome side of cycle racing, more so than the 60mph descents in the mountains. There seems infinite potential for mayhem in the vast group of cyclists jockeying for position at 45mph, shimmying across the road, cutting each other up, barging their fellows out of the way in the rush for the line. Like most sprinters, Elliott found it best to act without thinking too much. Sprinting is, he says, a matter of 'going on instinct. It's like a mist comes down. When a sprint is over you don't recall it clearly. Part of the mist is fear, sheer adrenalin, a heightened sense of self-preservation, the instinct for survival. To get the most out of yourself, you have to feel that it's a matter of life or death that you win. Being a good sprinter is about getting in that frame of mind when you are fighting in the final kilometre.'

Elliott was one of the few ANC members to get any redress after the team's collapse, but it took a year's legal action and was actually due to an administrative oversight. His contract for 1986 had been signed with the delivery company, and he had kept a letter saying the company would employ him in 1987. That year, like the other riders, he was actually signed to Capper's management company, Action Sports, which ran the team, but the courts considered the letter equivalent to a contract of employment, so he got his cash. The other riders simply walked away; some turned up to ride the Tour of Ireland after being offered a symbolic cash sum by the co-sponsor, Halfords.

Post-ANC, Elliott plied his trade as team sprinter, first

with Roche's Fagor, then at the Spanish team Teka, with whom he won the points classification in the 1989 Tour of Spain and took eight major wins in 1990. After Spain, he spent five happy years racing on the US professional circuit, where the lifestyle and the racing were less demanding than in Europe. After retirement in 1997, he 'partied like it was going out of fashion, Friday, Saturday, Sunday, straight through, smoking forty a day. It was horrendous on my body, but it was what I wanted to do, and I finally got it out of my system.'

Eventually sobering up after the birth of his daughter Evie, he returned to cycling for the sake of his health and realised he still liked riding his bike. In 2004 he won the British Premier Calendar series, which denoted the strongest cyclist on the home circuit and in 2009 he was still capable of finishing in the top ten of stages in the Tour of Britain and Ireland against cyclists young enough to be his children. He only wishes that twenty years ago he had had his motivation of today. 'With hindsight I was too young for the [ANC] opportunity. I wasn't mature enough to make the most of it. I had focus but couldn't maintain it for long enough. I'd have a blow-out, have a week off the bike, self-destruct a bit and come back.' Now, the urge is partly to prove himself in spite of his age, but he confesses to being mystified by what drives him. 'Even now it's hard to put my finger on why I do it, why I want to go to the races at the weekend. It's a craving for competition, an urge to continue to prove myself. It's what I do. I'm good at it.'

Like Elliott, most of the various participants in the ANC saga are still involved in cycling. Timmis is now a trainer, while since his comeback Elliott has raced for a team sponsored by none other than Phil Griffiths, who runs a large cycle-component import-export business in Stoke (among his employees, coincidentally, is Barry Hoban). Watson turned to mountain-bike racing, spent time in the

US, ran a property management business in Milton Keynes and is now a television cameraman. Jones is now a key figure in running the Tour of Britain. Swart moved to the American circuit and returned to the Tour in 1994 for the Motorola squad. Sutton raced on the British circuit during the 1990s, then took a job as Welsh national coach, where the 2008 women's Olympic road race champion Nicole Cooke was one of his protégés. He then became a senior trainer in Britain's Olympic track cycling team, playing a key role in their success in Beijing and then assisting with the formation of the British professional squad Team Sky in 2009 and 2010.

As for Tony Capper, he was most recently rumoured to be in Cardiff, building another taxi business, but his last contact with one of his old protégés came in 1988. The year after the ANC experiment, Sutton signed a contract with the British-based squad Banana-Falcon. He and his new teammates were driving along a motorway in southern Spain en route to a race, when they were flagged down by a large, unhealthy-looking man in a big car. It was none other than Capper. 'He had been more than a sponsor,' says Sutton. 'He was an ally, a mate, he got close to us. He was the man on the street made good. Here he was asking all kinds of questions about how we all were and so on, but I wasn't impressed. I didn't feel I wanted to kiss and make up.'

The Tour's rapid *mondialisation* meant that ANC did not have the exotic novelty attached to the Britons in 1955 or even in the 1960s. Rightly so, as the 1987 field contained two Colombian teams and an American squad sponsored by 7-Eleven, while the nations represented in the race included Australians, Poles and Canadians. It was the 7-Eleven squad that Capper's ANC was aiming to emulate, and the Americans' progress is worth tracing, because it shows what might have been had the British team been a little more efficiently managed.

The 7-Eleven team began competing in Europe immediately after their formation in 1985. They won stages in the Giro d'Italia that year, then turned up at the Tour in 1986 and put their Canadian, Alex Stieda, in the yellow jersey on the first full day of racing. In 1988, they won the Giro d'Italia with Andy Hampsten. By the early 1990s, they had introduced a whole generation of American cyclists to the Tour, as well as millions of armchair fans. Then, in 1991, they pulled off a major coup by attracting the first mobile-phone company to sponsor cycling, Motorola.

With ANC defunct, British fans tended to follow the American team, but this was not solely because it was the only team on the circuit with English as its first language. There was a far more substantial reason: 7-Eleven and Motorola just happened to include the most popular cyclist Britain had produced since Tom Simpson, that legendary foreign legionnaire Sean Yates.

CHAPTER TEN

A Man Called Horse

The scene is a roadside store not far from the Californian town of Santa Rosa. The date is January 1992. The Motorola professional cycling team, at training camp in the area, stop off briefly during their six-hour training ride to stock up on food. An up-and-coming amateur star who has been invited to ride with the team – indeed he is contracted to turn professional with them after the Barcelona Olympics – begins to 'goof around'. A grizzled senior pro with the team growls: 'You won't be laughing when you're a pro, boy.' Our youngster is all of twenty years old and quite a legend in his own Dallas backyard, but he quails and says little for the rest of the time the team is in camp: two weeks.

Lance Armstrong admitted he was 'terrified, no, petrified' of Sean Yates and remained that way for some time. This is an intriguing thought, given their characters. Armstrong would become cycling's undisputed number one, an intimidating, prickly man respected and feared in equal measure by most within the sport. Yates is quiet, never one to blow his own trumpet, a man who communicates in understatements. If the brash youngster who would go on to dominate cycling in the early twenty-first century was running scared of Yates, that says much for the uncompromising aura that the silent man from Sussex had acquired by the early 1990s.

His reputation proves all the adages about actions speaking louder than words. By the time Armstrong made his acquaintance, Yates was legendary for several things. He had won a time-trial stage in the 1988 Tour de France at record speed, but that was now in the past. By the early 1990s, the big man specialised in dragging Motorola at colossal speed in the team time-trial stage of the Tour. This is a nightmarish leg for weaker elements, who have to maintain the pace set by the stronger men in the team. Yates's teammates would speculate beforehand how much pain he was going to give them, and ask him how hard he was going to ride. This was a mistake, as it merely motivated him to ride harder.

There were other celebrated Yates fetishes. He had learned to use his size where it was most appropriate, on the high-speed descents from mountain passes, where he would line the peloton out at 60mph, defying death – usually bareheaded – to set a pace that far outstripped any accompanying motorcycles and cars. Soon after Armstrong made his acquaintance, Yates began targeting the Paris –Roubaix classic, held over a network of cobbled lanes in northern France in April. It is the most feared race on the calendar. The cobbles, nicknamed the 'Hell of the North', are nightmarish to race on: slippery in the wet, throwing up clouds of dust in the dry. Many pros simply avoid the race, knowing that getting through the 160 miles without at least one crash is highly unlikely. Each year produces a crop of broken legs, splintered collarbones, shattered dreams and ruined seasons. Yates loved it: 'A man's race.'

By this time, there was no mistaking him. No other cyclist had a vast mass of varicose veins that looked as if a plate of spaghetti had been spilled on his lower right leg. No other pro rode his bike with his shorts pulled halfway up the thigh. So what if the sponsor's logo could not be read: that was how Yates wore them. His handlebars were pushed downwards at an uncomfortable, floppy angle, as if the strength of the man was forcing them towards the tarmac. His left heel pointed inwards, his right outwards. When he put on a crash hat, it was worn at a devil-may-care angle, implying, correctly, that he was wearing it merely to comply with the rules. His eyes always seemed to be narrowed; his tongue would protrude to one side when he made an effort. He rarely seemed to wear the gloves most cyclists put on to avoid skinning their hands when they crash.

His nicknames said it all: 'Tonk', 'the Beast', 'the Animal', 'Horse', although Robert Millar, never one to conform, christened him 'Captain' because of his roots in dinghy sailing. The names were coined by teammates rather than by supporters or press, which speaks volumes for his colleagues' affection. As for the fans, by the time he retired in 1996 Yates was probably the most popular British cyclist since Simpson, if signs brandished at the roadside and the decibel level at British races were any true measure.

The one thing Yates regretted was that he was never the teammate of a Tour winner, that he never had the chance to take part in the traditional ritual in which all the team get on the front and lead the peloton at high speed through Paris to the Champs-Elysées. 'I'd have loved to have been there, I'd have felt like ten men. I'd have gone at seventy kilometres an hour.' In 2005, he achieved the next best thing; the brash young man he growled at that day in Santa Rosa hired him as a team manager.

Lance Armstrong had not forgotten that when he came down with testicular cancer in 1996, Yates was often on the phone. When the Texan triumphed in his seventh and final Tour in 2005, Yates was at last part of a Tour-winning set-up. He was at Armstrong's side for the Texan's come back in 2009, but then came an intriguing twist: he was an early inclusion in the recruitment list when the British squad Team Sky was founded at the end of that year, and he was expected to be a key part of Great Britain's first assault on the Tour since the ANC days.

Yates has always been a larger-than-life character, not merely because he is built like a second-row forward rather than a cyclist. His flatmate John Herety believed he did 250 press-ups a day; Millar put it at five hundred, and added that Yates had to slit the sleeves in his racing jersey to accommodate his biceps. The press-ups were done in a variety of positions – legs on the bed, legs on the floor – to relieve the boredom. The legends were legion: Yates could almost break the ergometer used by trainers to measure physical power; Yates would wear out a chain a week in wet weather due to the strength of his legs; a teammate had cried at the end of one of Yates's 'special' team time trials; if he was trying to lose weight, he was capable of training for four hours, then going to bed in order to avoid eating.

Retirement after fifteen seasons as a professional did not calm Yates. If anything, the legends merely proliferated. He was said to have lost weight after giving up professional racing because he was training on top of long days spent gardening, and he certainly looks as thin now as he did in his prime. In the spring of 1997, six months after retirement, he returned to British time trialling, riding and winning events he had last ridden and won as an amateur almost two decades before. He made a brief return to racing for the 1998 PruTour of Britain, turning out for the Linda McCartney Foods team at two days' notice, on just one hour's training a day in between working as a gardener. In 1999 and 2000, he was the McCartney team's *directeur sportif*. When the team went bust, he was up on a roof working for his brother's building company the next day.

In the winter of 2004, while working as a *directeur sportif* at the CSC team, he was still training hard, putting in sessions in the mornings before breakfast, riding up the same mountains as the riders (between twelve and twenty years his junior) and doing the same interval training, in temperatures well below zero. This regime is even more surprising when you consider that in 2003 he had been hospitalised with a flutter of the heart. One chamber was beating at a different rate to the other. 'Normal people would have trouble walking, but I only had trouble on my bike,' he told me as if he was discussing the weather.

Yates is exceptional in having found the energy and motivation to practise a wide variety of other sports alongside bike racing: yacht sailing was his first love, along with rock climbing. He played in goal for the local soccer team, Forest Row, and feels he might have been good enough to play professionally. Motorcycle trials were a big interest in his early years as a professional cyclist; so too was skiing, and he later turned to ice climbing. In the early 1990s, he owned a high-powered Honda RC-30 motorbike, worth £10,000, as ridden at Le Mans. A decade earlier, bodybuilding had been another interest, when he was a fan of a then unknown Austrian called Arnold Schwarzenegger.

What fascinates Yates is the extreme element in sport, exploring how far men can drive themselves. Contemporaries recall that he used to tell stories of yachting in low temperatures, with fingers chilled to the bone, while John Herety explains his bodybuilding fetish: 'He liked the way they pushed themselves to extremes, the fact that if they mistimed their fluids they might die.' He is a big mountain-climbing fan – 'Joe Brown, Reinhold Messner, I've read all the books.' When we met in 2000, during his spell managing the Linda McCartney team, he had just finished Jon Krakauer's *Into Thin Air*, a harrowing account of climbers freezing to death on Everest. He confessed to an interest in polar explorers such as Robert Falcon Scott and Ernest Shackleton, for the way they drove themselves beyond normal human limits of endurance. 'I like to push myself. I'd like to go to Everest or Annapurna and see how hard it is, what it's like doing one footprint every ten minutes. I went with my brother to Ben Nevis in winter 1986, camped on the top, the tent blew away and we ended up sleeping in a river bed in minus twelve. I like the suffering.'

This is not, however, why he became the most popular British cyclist since Simpson. The reasons are rooted in British cycling culture, and one anecdote should suffice.

Yates had just been to race the North Road Hardriders, a classic British early-season time trial. He arrived in Hertfordshire at 9.30 p.m. the night before, could not find a place to stay, and slept in his Land-Rover on the coldest night of the year – 'Luckily I had my ski jacket and a couple of blankets for the dogs.' The race was cancelled, and he was 'gutted'. The Tourmen can seem remote figures, the more so now that few Britons ride the race. Yet British cyclists can identify with Yates, with the faith he has shown in his time-trialling roots, his devotion to duty and his total lack of pretension. And he speaks for every cyclist when he sums up his approach to life: 'Anything beats working for a living and I've been delaying the inevitable as long as possible.'

In the words of Robert Millar, Sean Yates was a professional cyclist despite himself. Yates had no long-term plan, no childhood dreams of racing the Tour like Millar or Graham Jones, merely a sense that he did not want a conventional nine-to-five job and would take cycling as far as he could. As he puts it: 'I had no qualifications, I hated school, I hated working inside.' Had he not ended up in the Tour de France, he says, he might well have been a builder or a gardener – he has done both trades since hanging up his wheels. He had a trial spell as an outward-bound instructor in Fort William, at the age of sixteen, but was too young and did not have the necessary qualifications.

Yates is the product of an unconventional upbringing on the edge of the Ashdown Forest in Sussex. His father was a teacher at the local Steiner college, Emerson, and Yates attended the local Steiner school. For all that he hated being in a classroom, he seems to have taken in the Steiner tenet that you do what makes you happy rather than giving your life a predetermined pattern. His philosophy is simple: 'I just get on with the day-to-day.' With the forest at his back door and no television in the house, Yates's was an outdoor childhood. He was 'constantly' on his bike among the bracken and pine trees from the age of six. One of the myths surrounding him has it that the young Sean would sleep in an unheated shed to toughen himself up, and that he would view it as a good night if the glass of water by his bed had frozen by the morning.

Yates's father, Roger, had worked as a sailmaker and made him a dinghy, which Sean began sailing on the local reservoir when he was twelve, but Yates senior was also a cycling fan. Sean still remembers his first long ride, from Forest Row to the coast, with his brother Christian, at the age of fifteen. A year later, Sean cashed in £100 of Premium Bonds and bought his first racing bike. He won his first road race, run as part of the local celebrations for the Queen's silver jubilee, from bottom to top of a local hill. He would put in seventy-five-mile rides over the South Downs with Christian and a few friends, with competitions for sprints along the way. Sean would win all the sprints, so he had to offer the others 2p a time to ensure they took part.

Like most British cyclists, Yates came to the sport through time trialling, initially with the local East Grinstead Cycling Club. Simpson and Hoban were just two of the greats who had started their careers in similar style: in a low-key, short-distance time trial organised by their club on a weekday evening. Like Simpson and Hoban, Yates began by combining these short-distance time trials with the track pursuit; unlike his illustrious predecessors he had no plans to race in Europe as a road professional. Time trials were what he did, chasing up and down the country in the car that his dad had specially adapted by taking out the front seat so that Sean could stretch out his long legs and sleep en route to the start. Early pictures show Yates in the full rig of the 1970s 'tester' – skin-tight hat, no socks and a bike tweaked with aerodynamic components. Yates's first cycling hero was a legendary exponent of this genre of time trialling, Alf Engers, holder at that time of the blue riband, the twenty-five-mile competition record. His first big rival was the local 'testing' king, Mick Ballard.

By the end of 1980, when he was aged just twenty, Yates had won the most prestigious title in British 'testing', the twenty-five, had broken the ten-mile record three times, and had ridden the individual pursuit at the Moscow Olympics. Stephen Roche then set him up at ACBB in Paris for 1981. His sights were not specifically set on a professional career, but he felt there was nothing more for him to achieve in the UK, and he owed it to his parents to take the next step, since 'my dad had run me all round the country'. While he had no particular ambitions, he had no fear either: 'I didn't go into cycling thinking I wasn't going to make it.'

ACBB contemporaries remember his time there with affection. John Herety, who lived with him at ACBB and in his early years as a professional, says: 'If he was into something he was into it in a big way.' Before he began taking weight loss seriously, the list of things Yates was 'into' at various times included fruit cake (he could eat a whole one), Mars bars (he could devour four on the ten-minute walk home from the supermarket), muesli (consumed from a vast yellow Pyrex bowl) and yogurt (eaten three tubs at a time, with Breton sponge cake chopped into it). Most celebrated of all was the garlic episode. 'He heard that it was good for warding off colds, so he didn't chop up one clove but a whole bunch and put it into his salad,' recalls Herety. 'I went into the room the next morning and it stank. It was seeping out of his pores for a week.' His Ford Granada made an impression as well: it had a vinyl roof, and exhaust pipes held on by leather toe straps, which burned through on the motorway. To cover the noise, the stereo was cranked up loud. The machine was christened 'Charger'.

After following the well-trodden route through ACBB to Peugeot, Yates's early professional years, 1982 and 1983 –

alongside the foreign legion of Graham Jones, Phil Anderson, Robert Millar and Stephen Roche – were largely a matter of survival. His wins were insignificant; Yates himself rather too substantial. 'He was way too fat to survive the climbs,' says Millar, who believes that Yates started each season overweight and spent the first few months shedding the surplus. At the end of 1983, he was told Peugeot did not want him any more, and he began looking for a deal in England. The team offered him a contract for 1984 at the last minute, thanks to the recommendation of the French riders, who appreciated his strong support riding on the flat. He was given a deal for 1986 solely because at the end of 1985 he turned up at a race he was not expected to be riding and met the right person.

Yates rode his first Tour in 1984, alongside Millar, and was struck by the extreme length of the stages. There were two days with stages over two hundred miles in the 1984 race, one down the west flank of France from Nantes to Bordeaux, the second out from the Alps to Burgundy. Twenty years on, the 2004 Tour had only seven 'long' stages over 125 miles, with the longest a mere 148 miles. 'We rode for ten hours into Bordeaux, in thirty-five-degree heat. I was going back to the team car to get bottles, and I'd finish them before I got back to the bunch. After the finish I went to the Perrier wagon and sat in the gutter pouring it over my head. Next day was my first mountain stage. I'm not the thinnest of guys. I was sweating like a dog, grabbing a bottle off the spectators every five hundred metres, emptying it over my head until it squelched out of my shoes. It was only because I didn't know any better that I was able to survive.' Getting to Paris was an obsession: he would pore over the route book, which had a race summary at the start with a square containing each stage's details. He crossed off each day's square when the stage had been completed.

For all that the team was part of a French institution dating back to the nineteenth century, Peugeot ceased to exist at the end of 1986, when the bike company ended sponsorship. Yates found another team, but it was down to a fluke, he says. He rode the 1986 Tour solely because a teammate, Jerome Simon, broke a leg the day before the start. He had just arrived home in Sussex from France when the call came, so he turned round at once and went back to Paris. During the Tour, he signed a contract with the Fagor team 'on a scrap of paper on top of a mountain somewhere'; in Paris, at the end of the Tour, Peugeot's withdrawal was announced. Had Simon not had his fall, Yates might well have been out of a job.

Fagor was the most chaotic and faction-ridden of teams, but it was where Yates turned his career round in 1987 and 1988. Most importantly, he realised he performed better when he was thin, and slimmed down his six-foot frame in dramatic style, going from eighty-three kilogrammes to around seventy-five and becoming as obsessive about keeping the kilos at bay as he had been about weight training earlier in the decade. 'The amount of power Sean could generate was amazing, but it was only when he lost ten kilos that it came through,' said Martin Earley, the Irishman who was his teammate at the time. In 1988, he moved to Nice at the instigation of another teammate, the Frenchman Charly Berard, and adopted a monastic lifestyle of training, resting and racing.

The changes culminated in his time-trial stage win in the 1988 Tour de France at Wasquehal, the northern town close to Lille where he had shared a flat with Paul Sherwen. He had given hints before that he could make the frame at the Tour – in his first start four years earlier he had managed fifth in the prologue time trial – but this was a shock result, at a record average speed of 30.77mph for the 32.5 miles. He knew he was in form, and 'badgered the mechanic' beforehand to fit his bike with a larger gear than usual. As for the race itself, Yates remembers the pain, in a matter-of-fact way – 'When you've got good legs it's not the kind of hurt you mind' – and taking every corner on the limit of his tyres' adhesion, looking at how far the police motorcycle outriders leaned over, and gambling on what his tyres would stand.

He had an early start time, being well down the overall standings – the start order in a Tour time trial is the reverse of the overall classification – and this gave him the luck of the wind: it was strong and on his back, but dropped for the favourites. There were several hours to wait before his win was confirmed, most of them spent sitting in Channel 4's commentary position alongside Sherwen and Phil Liggett. He could see the other riders come up the finish straight, and sensed that they were tending to weaken, where he had kept his rhythm to the line. As Sherwen and Liggett became steadily more excited, scenting history being made with Britain's first win in a Tour time trial, Yates remained predictably low-key. 'There was no panic. I knew I'd finished strongly and the other guys were dying.' In his quiet way, Yates is a proud man, and he reminds me that his ride is still the fastest in a Tour time trial before the arrival of aerodynamic 'triathlon' handlebars.

As well as the Tour win, Yates's two years at Fagor brought stage victories in the Tour of Ireland, Paris–Nice – where he had a spell in the leader's jersey – the Tour of Spain and Midi Libre. They underlined that Yates had turned the corner, from a strong *domestique* to a cyclist capable of winning big races, and it was on that basis that he was hired in 1989 by the American team 7-Eleven. Ironically, Yates had been among the Europeans who had viewed them with a sceptical eye when they arrived on the scene in 1985. 'Before I joined them it was like, "Here they are again." They were useless, like the Colombians. You would kill yourself hanging on over a climb, and they would let a gap go down the other side, just crack for no reason. You would try to steer clear of them.'

Yates gave 7-Eleven two of their biggest wins of 1989: the Tour of Belgium – never won by a Briton before or since – and the Grand Prix Eddy Merckx, sponsored by the former great, now a bike manufacturer, and by happy coincidence the team's bike supplier. He also experienced the toughest day of his twelve Tours on the stage from Briançon to l'Alpe d'Huez after coming down with food poisoning overnight from some frozen lasagne. 'I felt like crap from the start, did a mental descent down the Galibier, got back on the Croix de Fer. I was drinking water and puking up, drinking and puking. It was the kind of position where you can get eliminated – I was nervous: "Got to get there, got to get there." I collapsed when I got to the top at l'Alpe d'Huez, I was in agony, I was history. But I got it out of my system and came around for the next day.'

That he got through and managed the highest overall placing of his career, forty-fifth, speaks volumes for his iron constitution and resistance to panic, and for his descending ability, by now legendary, which enabled him to keep in contact with the race. It was precisely for days like this that he had acquired the skill. 'In the Tour the main thing is not to get eliminated. Going downhill fast means you can make up time, get back into the lead group after the first mountain, sit there for another sixty kilometres and then cruise up the last climb, while the guys who haven't got back on are in a small group, say twenty, with everyone shouting at everyone else. I realised I could save a bit of effort and just practised.'

In the 1990 Tour, after an early season spent 'suffering like a pig due to anaemia', he played an integral part in 7-Eleven's defence of their Canadian rider Steve Bauer's yellow jersey from Poitou to the Alps, a total of nine stages. There was a fresh incentive for the American team to ride eyeballs out to keep Bauer in the lead: Greg LeMond's dramatic last-stage success of 1989 had drawn American television to the race. The CBS crew were a distinctive presence, and the daily live coverage meant there was every incentive for the peloton's only American sponsor to milk the publicity. At the time Yates told me about controlling the race on Bauer's behalf, 'jumping on everything that moves, trying to keep it together'. If one rider attacked alone, they would let him get a healthy lead, then keep the pace steady behind. There were unexpected bonuses: on stage eight to Besançon, while hammering along with the peloton lined out behind, Yates was first to cross a roughly painted white line on the road, without noticing it. It marked a £300 prize put up by a village: he won the cash, but found out only when he arrived at his hotel that night. He still does not know exactly where the village was.

The flurry of victories in 1988 and 1989 did not change the Yates philosophy, that he was destined to be a *domestique* rather than a leader – following the example of Vin Denson, Paul Sherwen and Graham Jones – in spite of the immense horsepower his giant frame could generate. 'It's to do with your work ethic. I knew from the beginning that I wasn't going to be a big hitter, not every day. It's easier mentally to work for someone else than having someone work for you and having to come up with the goods. It's a bit of a cop-out really, but I thought, "I'm good at this, I can guarantee an income rather than pretend to be a leader and not have any fun."' The notion of working for a team, riding to his maximum for a purpose, appealed and he was shrewd enough to realise that although *domestiques* make up the bulk of the professional peloton, good ones are rare and highly valued. 'Most guys don't do it 100 per cent. It's like when you do a building job, there are so many cowboys that if you do it properly people think you're fantastic.'

Being a *domestique* fitted in with his attitude that you take life a day at a time, looking for what makes you happy, and it guaranteed him a contract with Motorola when the phone company took over sponsorship from 7-Eleven at the end of 1990. By this stage, which was when Lance Armstrong first met him, Yates was well known for his ability to tow the peloton for miles on end in pursuit of a break or to discourage hotheads from breaking away. 'It looks harder than it actually is to ride in front for a hundred kilometres; it's harder to win a race in the last five kilometres, because to win you have to be the best. You either have to be a fantastic sprinter or someone like Lance or Robert. Riding for a hundred kilometres on the front is more in the mind, you have to make yourself suffer, tell yourself it's what you're paid to do. A lot of guys take the easy route, sit in and finish twenty-second. I prefer to give it everything and be dropped twenty kilometres from the finish and know I've done a good job. The more of a reputation you get, the more people expect you to do it.' And he duly acquired the reputation. 'Sean was half the team,' said a 7-Eleven teammate, Dag Otto Lauritzen, of his efforts in the team time trials. Millar recalls Yates scowling when he came down the bunch to tow him up to the front, but that was merely the big man psyching himself up. 'He rarely got angry repairing other people's mistakes, chasing down breaks, and he'd never brag about how much work he had done. This was his role in the team. Riding in the wind was job satisfaction.'

Cycling is particularly cruel among sports in having a team structure in which the abnegation of the many secures the victory of a sole leader, who gets the glory and the serious money. It is said that an equivalent of cycling's system would be a soccer team in which only the centre forwards score the goals and central defenders receive a tenth of their wage. Most *domestiques* train as hard as their leaders and make similar sacrifices, but without the same reward. Cycling fans recognise this, which is why also-rans grovelling through the Tour's mountain stages are applauded as warmly as the leaders.

When Yates took the yellow jersey on 8 July 1994, it was a rare and magical occasion: recognition on the big stage for one of the sport's unsung heroes. At the start of the seven-hour, 169-mile stage from Cherbourg to Rennes, Yates was told by his *directeur sportif*, the Dutchman Hennie Kuiper, that he had a chance of taking the race lead. 'I just said, "Yeah, yeah, whatever," but as the day went on I just felt stronger and stronger.' Kuiper, who had finished second in the 1977 and 1980 Tours, was correct: Yates was well-placed in seventh overall after dragging Motorola to second place in the team time trial, and this was the longest stage of the Tour, north to south through Brittany, where the field were likely to tire. The Briton was one of four riders from the team in the first fifteen places overall; the plan was for them to infiltrate any late escapes and try to win the *maillot jaune* from the Italian Flavio Vanzella.

Both Yates and his American teammate Frankie Andreu were among the seven riders who sped away from the peloton on a back road some twelve miles outside Rennes. Their companions included the double points winner Djamolidine Abdoujaparov, a kamikaze from Uzbekistan with the longest name in cycling, and an Italian, Gianluca Bortolami, who had emerged that year – ephemerally – as a top one-day racer. The fine details of the stage finish underline the slenderness of the margin between glory and anonymity. Yates, the best-placed rider in the break, started the day thirty-eight seconds behind Vanzella, and the septet had just a fifty-five-second advantage with three miles to go. The picture became more complex when Bortolami sped away just over a mile from the finish; he was twenty-three seconds behind Yates overall, and there was a twenty-second bonus for the stage winner (meaning that twenty seconds would be deducted from the time he took to complete the stage). To deprive Yates of the yellow jersey, the Italian had to win the stage and finish three seconds ahead of the Briton.

Yates, however, did not know this: he only knew that he had to finish forty seconds ahead of Vanzella. On the line, Bortolami's advantage was just two seconds. 'We forgot about Bortolami and the time bonus. I wasn't aware how far behind me he was. My prime concern was to get time on Vanzella and get the yellow jersey. Afterwards, I was looking at the clock and someone said I was in yellow by one second from Bortolami, and I thought, "Christ, I'd forgotten about him."' Typically, he remained low-key as Paul Sherwen – by then Motorola PR man as well as Channel 4 commentator – interviewed him on the line, but his true feelings came out when he spotted his friend and teammate Dag Otto Lauritzen. 'Yellow,' he hissed through clenched teeth, punching the air with his fist.

'It was my eleventh Tour, and most people thought I deserved it. It's about your fifteen minutes of fame,' he said. The next day my paper, the *Guardian*, put the quiet, hard man on the front page alongside Jeffrey Archer and just above O.J. Simpson. What touched him most, however, were the congratulations from leading members of the bunch: the double world champion Gianni Bugno, the Belgian classics specialist Johan Museeuw and Miguel Indurain, on course for the fourth of his five Tours – all Yates's juniors by a fair margin. The *domestique* had just one day in the limelight: Museeuw relieved him of the lead as the race sped through Poitou the next day, but not without a little argy-bargy at the sprints – which also carried time bonuses – and an appeal from Motorola.

It mattered little: that year, Britain was more interested in the Tour than it had ever been. Even before Yates took the yellow jersey, Chris Boardman – of whom more in the next chapter – had become the first Briton since Simpson to wear the *maillot jaune*, and held the race lead for three days. Immediately after that, the Tour visited Britain for the first time in twenty years, and three million people watched the race pass through southern England. It was only reasonable to assume that after this high the return to France would be an anticlimax: instead, with Yates's accession to yellow, the British continued to live the dream.

Unlike the Tour's 1974 visit to Britain, when the Bretons instigated the stage in Plymouth to publicise their vegetables and the opening of the ferry link, *le Tour en Angleterre* – as the marketing men named it – was inspired by the British. The county and town councils involved put up the £500,000 necessary, and at the route launch Portsmouth's leader Syd Rapson made the point, somewhat bitterly, that central government had paid nothing. For the councils, said Rapson, it was 'an up-front investment', made in the hope of immediate cash from the race caravan and fans, as well as longer-term publicity.

For the Tour organisers, taking the race to Britain fitted in as well. Jean-Marie Leblanc, the former professional and cycling journalist who succeeded Goddet and Lévitan in 1989, is an Anglophile whose connections with British cyclists go back forty years, to the days of Tom Simpson. One of his central tenets is that the Tour should not become reliant on its heritage, but should reflect the events of its time, while respecting the past. The 1992 race, most radically, had been the 'Euro-Tour', celebrating European union with stages in every country bordering France. The visit to England was inspired by two events: the construction of the Channel Tunnel and the fiftieth anniversary of the D-Day landings. The caravan travelled through the tunnel, months before it actually opened, and returned to France by ferry, in what Leblanc saw as a tribute to the *débarquements* of 1944. Ironically, with Brittany Ferries providing a free bar on board, it was a rather drunken homage, and many of the caravan were in no shape for combat when they reached French soil.

In England, however, the experience was euphoric. From Dover to Brighton on day one, out and home from Portsmouth through Hampshire on day two, the crowds formed a virtually unbroken line for close on 250 miles. In august Canterbury, demure Tunbridge Wells and quiet country towns such as Overton, they were crammed ten deep on the main streets. Like all the riders, and all the Tour caravan, Yates was struck by the numbers and the warmth of the crowd, by the French-style picnics, by the old ladies sitting on garden chairs by their front doors, by the perfectly closed roads. 'What struck me was the amount of spectators, as many as anywhere else in Europe. Everyone had made a party out of it; there were banners everywhere. The place was packed. In Australia they take any excuse for a day off and get legless; the English are more conservative, they are not used to that, too caught up in going to work.' *L'Equipe's* senior writer Pierre Ballester was equally impressed: 'There were the crowds around the pubs, the schoolgirls in their blue skirts ... It was a time of stolid picnics on windy verges, of beer on pub terraces.'

Yates's accession to the yellow jersey was all the more emotional because he had provided one of the most telling images of the race's two days in Britain. It came when he rode ahead of the peloton to greet his family by the side of the road in the heart of what could be termed 'Sean Yates country'. This was the Ashdown Forest road on which Yates had won in Brighton–London in 1981 and which served as a final test at the end of five-hour training rides. 'In the old days it was traditional to stop and see the family, now it's less and less like that because the racing is more unpredictable. I knew it was possible: luckily there was a break up the road. I went to Johan Museeuw [who was wearing the yellow jersey] and said I was just going up; he said, "No problem."' The entire Yates extended family was there, together with many of the neighbours. There were brief hugs and kisses before he rode on. Like the yellow jersey that followed two days later, it was something he felt he had earned. 'I had been around so long by then I felt I deserved it. It was perfect.'

The contrast with Plymouth, twenty years earlier, could not have been greater, and that was a telling illustration of the wide-ranging impact made by Yates and the rest of the foreign legion. The achievements of Paul Sherwen, Graham Jones, Robert Millar and company had collectively bred both increased public and media awareness of the Tour in Britain, and a feeling among the Tour organisers that England deserved a second visit. Alan Rushton and Mick Bennett of Sport for Television, the promoters who organised the two English stages, also owed a debt to the foreign legion. Much of their experience had come from running televised criteriums and the professional Tour of Britain on the back of the legionnaires' success.

The vast public turnout was partly due to a campaign by Sport for Television to inform local residents, but it also reflected the steady growth in the Tour's profile in Britain. Coverage of the race in a prime-time evening slot on Channel 4 television had become an institution since its beginnings in 1986, because the race was sold in accessible half-hour packages that highlighted the cultural and scenic backdrop to the event as much as the pure racing action. It thus appealed to both racing cyclists and armchair viewers. That approach mirrored the way the British broadsheet newspapers now covered the event, pitching it at an audience of people who took regular holidays in France and enjoyed the country's culture, food and scenery.

Increased public interest in the Tour de France did not, however, mean that Britain was becoming a nation of cycling fans or that road cycling had become a mainstream sport. When the Tour visited in 1994, the British domestic professional class was on the point of extinction, as the televised criteriums that were its staple diet dried up and even the smallest team sponsors faded away. Simultaneously, the Milk Race and professional Tour of Britain disappeared – the latter temporarily – while there was a drastic contraction in the amateur calendar that catered for the sport's grass roots. Public and media interest was solely in the Tour de France.

In fact, this reflected a wider trend outside Britain: during the 1990s the Tour began to dominate the international cycling calendar to an extent that was positively harmful. The worldwide media profile of the Tour meant that teams' survival or disappearance depended solely on whether they rode the race and performed, while the biggest stars came to focus their entire seasons on only twenty-two days in July. The Tour had always been important: now it was almost all that mattered.

As Yates raced into Rennes to win the yellow jersey, Lance Armstrong was prominent in slowing down the bunch behind, working his way among the teams who were sharing the pace at the front and braking to shatter their rhythm. It was not popular, but it reflected the strength of the bond that had grown between the grizzled *domestique* and his brash young teammate, no longer a nervous youth but the world champion and Motorola's team leader. Paul Sherwen, working for Motorola as press officer, recalls watching Armstrong soaking up information from Yates 'like a sponge'.

When the Texan and the Briton shared a room together as pros at Motorola, Armstrong would sometimes get Yates to tell him rambling stories to send them both to sleep. 'It was "in my day", that kind of thing; I'd be racking my brains to tell him about some race I did way back when.' It was Armstrong who kept persuading Yates to do one more year, then another. The big man was not due to ride the 1994 Tour, but he was persuaded by the Texan, and after his spell in yellow he jokingly bet a year's salary that he would not be at the 1995 Tour. 'I told Lance and he wasn't too happy, so I told him maybe I would.'

After the highs of 1994, Yates's final Tour could only be an anticlimax, and it was ended by tendinitis, which forced him out on the thirteenth stage. With Robert Millar unable to ride after his sponsor had gone bust, Yates's withdrawal in the Massif Central closed the foreign legion era seventeen years after Sherwen's debut. From now on, British cycling would be represented by talented individuals such as Boardman and David Millar, flying the flag alone much as Barry Hoban had during the 1970s.

The injury that ended Yates's Tour career spoke volumes about his ability to drive his body beyond the norm and his relative indifference to what the long-term effects of doing so might be. It was born of a crash in Normandy during the 1991 Tour. In falling he had smashed his right thigh on to Phil Anderson's back wheel, so hard that it broke the rim. The bruise was agony. At the start of every stage the leg would be dead, and although the pain diminished as he rode, it was a relief when he was put out for good by a second crash in the south of France. This pile-up was more spectacular, as he punctured an artery in his arm and finished the stage covered in blood, but the previous one had more serious long-term effects.

'I noticed when I turned my left heel in it alleviated the pain, so I turned it more and more inwards.' His back twisted, and over the next few years he ended up sitting at an ever more acute angle across the bike, with one foot pointing inwards and the other outwards, the Velcro straps on his shoes worn very tight on the right and very loose on the left. In the end his pelvis was displaced almost on a daily basis. It was easily distinguishable, because at this stage in his career he was so thin that his hip-bones stuck out. 'I'd look down and it would be at a forty-five-degree angle.' Every day, the team physio would have to put all the bones back into place. By 1995, his legs were at such an extreme angle that he ended up with inflammation up the front of the shin, and when his Tour career ended that year it was because, in the tradition of the climbers and polar explorers he so admired, he could literally go no further.

CHAPTER ELEVEN

The Stranger

In autumn 1991, I sat down with Chris Boardman in a small, barely furnished terraced house at the top of the Wirral peninsula and asked him what he was going to do with his undoubted talent. The paradox was a simple one: in terms of horsepower on a bike, Boardman was clearly the best athlete in Britain, but he had no desire to follow the obvious route onwards and upwards. That route had been taken by every British Tour cyclist since Simpson: British amateur career, French amateur career – and by the 1990s that meant ACBB – professional contract, Tour de France. Boardman did not want to go there.

I could not figure Boardman out. Two years earlier I had followed him in a time trial in the Tour of Ireland, when he was a raw amateur of twenty-one competing with the best professionals in the world. He had been in line for fifth or sixth place until he punctured. He had won the Grand Prix de France amateur time trial. Clearly, he could ride a bike over a short distance as quickly as the likes of Sean Kelly. The problem was that his focus was time trialling, British style, which would take him nowhere on the international stage. What was not clear to either of us was where it *would* take him.

Fast-forward nine years to a balmy early October night in southern Brittany. The champagne flowed as Boardman, his team manager Roger Legeay, the *soigneur* Michel Decock – universally known as *le barbu*, the bearded one – the former foreign legionnaire John Herety – by now the British road-racing team manager – and I celebrated after the rider had taken fourth place in the world time-trial championships.

The fourth place was the least of it. What we were

toasting was the final European race in a remarkable career. In just seven years as a professional, Boardman had worn the yellow jersey of the Tour for six days, more than any other Briton, and had taken three wins in the race's prologue time trial, a record he held jointly with another specialist, Thierry Marie, and with the great Eddy Merckx, who snapped up one prologue after another en route to his five overall wins. All I could do that night was sit in, enjoy the conversation, cast my mind back nine years and say to myself: oh ye of little faith.

What I had failed to take into account was that Boardman was unique, driven to race a bike for fundamentally different reasons to those of his peers. Pleasure in the act of cycling is what draws most cyclists into competition and what keeps them there. They start riding a bike as a means of escape, it turns into a social act through riding with friends and family and the cycling club, and they are drawn into competition as a social act as well. Once competing, even at the highest level, most retain the pleasure they originally felt in cycling for its own sake; it remains physically and sensually satisfying, and can be done from the front door. 'I just like riding my bike,' is the refrain. There are usually underlying reasons why they need that escape or why they are driven to compete, but the pleasure is common.

Even though Boardman comes from a cycling family – his father Keith was shortlisted for the Tokyo Olympics – he has always maintained that he never felt that pleasure. He got on his bike at the age of thirteen, found he liked competing, and that was that. His parents tried to discourage him from racing. They felt he should enjoy his cycling, but he was determined to race, and once he began to ride time trials he was hooked, going on to win a series of British titles. 'At school I was the kind of kid who faded into the background. I didn't have a great time, wasn't popular, and with sport I found something I could do which made me stand out from the crowd: it was something other people wanted to do. I was gutted whenever I lost, but I would come back. I got beaten regularly, but I was the one that stuck at it. Other people would go off and get a life.'

As he sees it, he was not a natural cyclist but a person with a competitive streak who happened to find that bike racing was the best area to express that. It might have been running, it might have been clay-pigeon shooting. He just sat on the bike first. He had no interest in its social side. He is almost wistful in his regret that he could not be something he was not, no matter how much people like me might have wanted him to be it. 'I'm different because I'm not a cyclist. I rode bikes. Ninety per cent of me said, "I don't believe I'm here," 10 per cent said I had to do it. It was a medium to get what I wanted. I was a visitor, which was very sad because it's such a lovely sport.'

Boardman's relentlessly analytical approach stems from mild dyslexia. 'He has a very unusual memory, he's organised, but that is because he has to write everything down,' says his wife Sally. Boardman jokes that he cannot remember the dates of his children's birthdays but can clearly recall every time trial he has ever ridden, down to the position of the drain covers, which is vital when it comes to cornering. 'I get the most stressed out when I don't know what the answer to something is. Order makes me comfortable, and I put passion and creativity into creating that order,' he says. Cycling was, he says, 'an exercise in problem-solving'; this is something all of us do, but where Boardman differs is that analysis is a habit. 'I have to make notes about everything, which means I am already analysing everything around me.'

Time trialling is in itself a series of problems to be solved – how to become more aerodynamic, how to start faster, how to avoid 'dying' at the end of a race. It lends itself to analysis more readily than road racing: the man with the best figures – primarily power output and drag coefficient – will win nine times out of ten, provided he is prepared to make the effort. Work in training and bike development will be met with a measurable result in terms of time gained. Road racing, on the other hand, has infinite tactical nuances and offers none of the same certainties. The image that Boardman came up with for this side of the sport was that of the lottery: you might attack a hundred times in ten road races, but only draw the winning ticket once. That Boardman had to present an analogy to explain this to himself says much about his need to systemise the world around him: for most road racers, the uncertainty is taken as a given.

As was said of Sean Yates, Boardman became a professional cyclist 'despite himself'. Unlike Yates, who initially was not bothered about being professional or not, Boardman did not want to take that route, but he took it because there was nowhere else to go. In 1987, Boardman had met his mentor, Peter Keen, a schoolboy time-trial champion turned physiology graduate. 'Pete could apply the science to the real world,' explains Boardman. 'He would say, "The figures are x, y, z and here is what it means, so if you do this you will be better."' They were close in age, and had the same systematic approach. 'We grew up together.' By August 1993, the double act of scientist and cyclist had taken racing 'alone and unpaced' to the absolute limit of what it could offer.

Boardman had already become a household name in Britain by winning the gold medal in the individual pursuit – in essence, a series of four-minute time trials – in the Barcelona Olympics, riding the dramatically aerodynamic Lotus bike, with its single front fork and futuristic carbon-fibre frame. In July 1993, he went further – literally and, in the eyes of the cycling world, metaphorically – in taking the world one-hour distance record. The 'hour' is a 60-minute time trial on a velodrome. It is relentless in its intensity, because there is nothing to break the rhythm. It is merciless in another way as well: the hourman is alone on the velodrome, and if he fails to meet the standard that failure is brutally exposed.

Boardman deliberately scheduled his bid on the Bordeaux velodrome for the evening the Tour visited the city. It was an audacious decision, given the record's pedigree. The hour had just been broken by the Scottish amateur Graeme Obree, using a revolutionary aerodynamic position, but it had been held previously by two of cycling's greatest road champions, Fausto Coppi and Eddy Merckx (who famously had almost to be lifted off his bike afterwards). Bernard Hinault and Greg LeMond were deterred by the risk of failure and possible loss of prestige and never tried it. The European cycling media are fully aware of the record's history, and making the bid in such a high-profile fashion meant Boardman could not afford to fail.

A distance of 53.331km gave Boardman the record, and afterwards he sat down with his manager, a genial computer specialist named Peter Woodworth, and debated his next step. 'Pete presented me with this paradox: "You can stay where you are and get knocked down eventually, or turn professional and move forwards." It was not something I ever wanted to do. I never wanted to turn pro – it's hard and dangerous, so you don't want to do that. But if I didn't do that, then what else was I to do?'

Boardman's choice of Roger Legeay's GAN team – sponsored by *Groupe Assurances Nationale*, a French insurance company – was thought through. There was no question of signing merely to the highest bidder. Legeay spoke English and had a predilection for English-speakers. He had rubbed shoulders with the foreign legionnaires Graham Jones, Sean Yates and Robert Millar in his time as a rider at Peugeot. He had hired that most demanding of

English-speakers, Greg LeMond, who had won him the Tour in 1990 and was still leading the team, even though his best years were behind him. There was another important factor: Legeay would permit Boardman to continue living in the Wirral, commuting to races by air, a break with the tradition that to race as a professional in Europe a Briton had to move across the Channel.

The Tour de France did not initially come into Boardman, Legeay and Keen's plan for 1994. It was assumed that Boardman would win European time trials – such as his first victory, the Grand Prix Eddy Merckx, a few days after he signed his contract with GAN – and bid for time-trial prologues in stage races while gradually adapting to professional road racing, and perhaps taking on the Tour de France in 1995. The transition was tough: the road races Boardman had won in England bore no comparison. 'For the first couple of months I was getting my head kicked in every day.' But when he won two time-trial stages and a road-race stage in the Dauphiné Libéré race, Legeay could not resist putting him in the Tour. Ten years after *mondialisation* began, the Tour's television audience was estimated at 100 million in 160 countries. Hence, if Boardman won the prologue time trial in Lille and consequently wore the yellow jersey, even for a single day, that justified GAN sponsoring the team for the whole year.

Boardman trained as if for the Olympic pursuit race, everything he did geared to speed. He raced a club ten-mile time trial between Chester and Wrexham, winning at around 32mph. He moved out of his house temporarily, because of the risk that he might catch a bug off one of his two children. Before the four-and-a-half-mile stage through the heart of Lille, he went round the circuit on the Lotus bike, slipstreaming his team car at speeds up to 40mph before the corners, when the car would move over, to let him experiment with how fast he could go round each bend. Eventually, he decided not to use the brakes at all.

He did not believe he could win, but on that early evening in Lille it was all too easy, Boardman now feels. In the Tour prologue, the teams seed their fastest riders, who become the final twenty-two starters. Boardman left the start ramp tenth from last in the 189-man field, and on the finishing straight on the plane-tree-lined Boulevard de la Liberté he sped past the man who had started a minute before him, France's Luc Leblanc. All he had to do was wait and see whether his time would be beaten by either of the two overwhelming favourites, Miguel Indurain and the Swiss Tony Rominger. Indurain – at the height of his power, and on the way to his fourth consecutive overall win – was fifteen seconds slower; Rominger nineteen seconds. These are huge margins in an effort lasting less than eight minutes, but this was probably Boardman's finest Tour moment: his average speed, 55.152kph, remains the fastest accomplished on any stage of the Tour.

It was a moment of transformation. Boardman had suffered from a lack of confidence when riding in a bunch. On seeing the risks his fellow professionals took, he initially thought they were crazy, before rationalising that as they rarely crashed they probably knew what they were doing. Suddenly, he realised, winning the yellow jersey had earned him respect, and road space. He had crossed 'the invisible line that allows you to race at the front. In an echelon of twenty riders, who are you going to push out of the way? The new pro gets it every time. With the yellow jersey, people think twice about it.' Moreover, on the first road-race stage from Lille to the grim little town of Armentières, he managed something that Simpson had failed to do thirty-two years earlier: he defended the jersey.

There were three stages through northern France to complete before the Tour took the Channel Tunnel for England. Boardman wore yellow in all three, losing the lead at the mouth of the tunnel, in the team time-trial stage that finished in the terminal after a wind-lashed loop over Cap

Gris-Nez. GAN had done little special training for this exercise in skill and cohesion. They were a shambles, unable to stick together owing to a welter of mechanical problems and the unfortunate fact that Boardman was far stronger than anyone else. Boardman plummeted to twentieth overall and realised that he would have to take on the leader's role in the team, where LeMond was a spent force.

The roadsides that day were lined with British club cyclists, giving a foretaste of what awaited over the next two days on the other side of the Channel. It made losing the yellow jersey all the more bitter. When Boardman rode out of Dover Castle the next morning, he realised what he had missed. 'I was absolutely gutted, because people were so enthusiastic. I could just imagine what it would have been like coming to England with the yellow jersey.' It was an emotional homecoming, even without the *maillot jaune*; to celebrate, Boardman made a strong attack on the finishing circuit in Brighton and experienced a 'total, complete ego trip' going up the climb of Wilson Avenue to take fourth place, crossing the line with his hands in the air as if he had won. The scenes were euphoric; on the following day, after the stage in Portsmouth, he had no time to get a shower, because of the crowds. He travelled the half-mile from the finish line to the camping car without pedalling, powered only by people slapping him on the back.

By 1994 team managers were prepared to save young riders from exhaustion by limiting them to ten days' racing in their first outing in the Tour. Boardman did not make it to the Pyrenees, but instead agreed with Legeay that he would pull out on the stage that took the riders to the Hautacam ski resort. That did not stop the press becoming over-optimistic about his chances of winning the Tour in the future, although there were no reasonable grounds for believing he could. Unwittingly, and somewhat naively, he fed the speculation. Asked whether he thought he could win the Tour, he answered that he had 'two arms and two legs the same as everyone else and would love to give it a go'.

Inevitably, that was translated into 'I can win'. Because Boardman had acquired a reputation for doing what he said he thought he could do – the hour record, the Olympic title, the prologue – the bubble of expectation grew, and when he finished second to Indurain in the 1995 Dauphiné Libéré, it grew further.

When the 1995 Tour started in the Breton port of St-Brieuc – by coincidence Tom Simpson's home before turning professional in 1959 – Boardman was in the form of his life, and under pressure. 'When you've won something, you either do the same again or you fail. People were expecting me to win. The team had had a slack year, they were anxious. I knew I couldn't just ride round. I knew my form was spot on.' His objective was a high overall placing, but the prologue was what he termed 'insurance': it was a stage he knew he could win, and winning would mean the rest of the Tour could be ridden more peacefully. Unfortunately, neither Boardman nor his team took the weather into account. The pattern for that week had been rain showers every night, and the organisers had timed the prologue start for late in the evening, as dark fell. That was partly in recognition of the 'nocturne' tradition of Breton racing, but was also an example of the way television was dictating terms. This was prime-time, Saturday night.

As the rain lashed on the GAN camping car before the start, Boardman's teammates told him he could win. 'My judgement was impaired. I was up for it. I remember the first few corners, my wheels were starting to skip and I thought, "I can't believe I just got round that."'

He made his way through the corners, his back wheel skittering on the sodden tarmac, then began the descent to the river. On a right-hand bend, at 50mph, the road surface suddenly changed from damp to wet. It was dark, so he could not read the road, both wheels slipped, and he slid for several yards across the surface, landing with his left foot in the crowd barrier. The team car, driven by Legeay, was close behind, but skidded to a halt as it hit him, breaking his nose. Incredibly, he got back on the bike, before realising he could not move his ankle.

The margin between disaster and triumph was minute: this was the last corner, with only an uphill section to the finish remaining. 'I needed to get those twenty yards, I was two seconds down [on the leader, Jacky Durand] and it was a done deal that I would have won. If I'd got through people would have said "what skill", instead it was "how reckless".' Rather than reliving the previous year, he flew home on the Tour's private jet from the airport in Dinard, pumped full of morphine and wearing only his underpants; his right wrist was broken and his ankle was fractured in six places, held together with two two-inch screws put in with a Black & Decker drill.

With Boardman in hospital, the only British success story in that Tour was not particularly British. Max Sciandri was christened Massimiliano, but was born in Derby and brought up in Bournemouth, Tuscany and Los Angeles, where his father owned a restaurant. By 1995, he was an accomplished one-day racer, but competition for places in the Italian team to ride the world championship being tight, he took out an English licence that year. It was a similar flag of convenience to that flown by Michael Wright in the 1960s and 1970s.

A cosmopolitan character who speaks English well, with an American accent, Sciandri was a natural acquisition for the Motorola team, alongside Sean Yates. He provided them with the next best thing to a home win in the Tour of Britain in 1992, and was within a few yards of taking the stage at Chalons-sur-Marne in that year's Tour de France when he was pipped by the cunning Dane, Bjarne Riis. From then on the suspicion lingered that for all his talent,

Lean, mean and moody: Robert Millar climbs in the 1986 Tour.

The foreign legion: (*clockwise from top left*) Paul Sherwen, fresh faced in 1978;
Graham Jones sizes up the next hairpin in 1980; a bulky, youthful Sean Yates climbs
to Crans-Montana in 1984; Millar attacks in the polka-dot jersey, 1984.

From the back streets to the big time: ANC-Halfords pose in 1986 with Tony Capper (*left*); (*below*) a year later they finish the Tour's team time trial, led by Adrian Timmis, with Graham Jones close behind, Malcolm Elliott (*far right*) and Shane Sutton (*second right*).

Robert Millar faces another
day among the 'Indians',
Serre Chevalier, 1986.

Yellow jersey and rainbow jersey: Yates leads a youthful Lance Armstrong in 1994.

Chris Boardman on Tour: (*below right*) speeding to the yellow jersey on the Lotus bike in 1994; (*above*) k-o on the road to Cork, 1994; (*main picture*) mauled at Montgenèvre, 1996.

David Millar outsprints David Extebarria and Michael Boogerd in Beziers, 2002; and *(below)* looks enigmatic in the Tour, in 2003.

Mark Cavendish holds his arms aloft as he becomes the first Briton to win on the Champs-Elysées in 2009.

Bradley Wiggins secures a first British win in the Tour de France as he crosses the line to win the final time trial at Chartres in 2012.

Le Tour en Angleterre: Crowds pack the streets in Winchester in 1994. Scenes like these have been repeated each time the Tour has come to Britain.

and in spite of the fact that he had won a brace of stages in the Giro d'Italia, when it came to the biggest occasions he was a rider who would freeze under pressure.

By 1995, he was back among the Italians, riding for a team sponsored by the MG clothing company, with his sights set on the 'transitional' stages between the Alps and the Pyrenees, which are too tough for the sprinters but not tough enough for the overall contenders to take an interest. The first of his targets was the stage from Bourg-d'Oisans, at the foot of l'Alpe d'Huez, to St-Étienne, where he and the Colombian Hernan Buenahora were the only survivors of an eight-man escape. The sprint was never going to be a contest, but Sciandri was still nervous enough to look back as he crossed the line, just to make sure Buenahora was beaten.

The nationality question meant that no one was sure whether Italian television or Channel 4 had first claim on the stage winner, but the Tour's press officer was in no doubt as to which nation Sciandri belonged to. 'French or Italian' was the order at the press conference, to the disgust of those of the British press who spoke neither language. Aware of the issues, Sciandri was totally diplomatic when asked which country should be celebrating the win. 'It's a victory for me and my team,' he said.

After retirement, Sciandri returned to Great Britain colours, initially by acting as a link-man between the Lottery-funded GB team and professional squads interested in signing promising youngsters. From 2009 he took over the running of the under-23 road racing academy which was based in his home town of Quarrata. This little furniture-making centre in turn became a base for British riders who had been through the academy before turning pro.

Crashing was very much on Boardman's mind when it turned out wet again for the 1996 Tour's opening time trial, in the Dutch town of Den Bosch. 'I knew if I crashed again everyone would have a field day. I went so slow, and couldn't believe I'd lost by two seconds. I was gutted.' What followed in that Tour was even more painful. Boardman rode well as far as the first mountain stage through the Alps to Les Arcs, run off in horrendous conditions of chilly rain and fog. There he cracked, losing twenty-nine minutes. He was in good company: both Miguel Indurain and the man tipped as his big rival, Laurent Jalabert of France, were in trouble as well.

Mentally, Boardman was still riding like a Tour contender. He raced hard for eighth in the time trial to Val-d'Isère and infiltrated the stage-winning escape on the stage to Super-Besse, in the Massif Central, finishing seventh. With hindsight, he realised that all he was doing was wasting energy; by the time the race reached the Pyrenees, he was spent, and as a result the seventeenth stage over 160 miles and seven mountain passes between Argelès-Gazost and Pamplona turned into an eight-hour nightmare. 'After five kilometres I was out on my own. I was going up the [first] climb thinking, "No way can I do this." I could not imagine doing another ten kilometres, let alone 260.' But he could not quit, because Paris was 'just around the corner'. He oscillated between the two states of mind for the whole eight hours, counting every ten metres as they ticked over on the little computer screen on his handlebars. 'It was horrific, probably the kind of thing you can do once in your career.'

Bizarrely, two or three days later, his form started to pick up, as if his body had adjusted to the unprecedented workload, and by the finish Boardman believed he 'could have gone on for another three weeks'. The resultant spell of form was, he believes, 'the pinnacle of my physical career'. On the back of that Tour, he rode to an Olympic bronze medal in Atlanta, a world pursuit title in record time, a second hour record and the silver medal in the world time-trial championship.

The suspicion remained, however, that Boardman was not a man of the Tour, and confirmation came the following year. He took a second prologue win, in Rouen, and had a single day in the yellow jersey, but his race was ruined by a crash on the descent from the Col de l'Aubisque in the Pyrenees. That left him riding with displaced vertebrae and pain 'like someone stubbing out a cigarette on my back', not to mention the fear of crashing again because the pain was affecting his ability to handle the bike. His abandon in tears thirty-four miles into the stage between St-Étienne and l'Alpe d'Huez had an inevitable feel about it. The bitterness was because he knew the expectations British fans had of him: he was driven up the Alpe in a team car, at walking pace, and could see the fans' faces fall when they realised it was him sitting in the back seat. 'Horrendous,' he says. And the race had greater significance. 'I realised at that moment that I had plateaued, and that was when it became a job. It was not a matter of how to move forward but how to do the same things again. A big chunk of the passion disappeared.'

That passion – 'healthy naivety', as Keen puts it – had led Boardman and his trainer into a search for new solutions, which challenged many of the accepted ideas of professional cycling. He trained less, looking for speed not stamina. Legeay, his *directeur sportif*, could never believe he won the races he did on only fifteen hours' training a week, where the average pro will do twenty-five. Keen and Boardman threw out the received wisdom that a cyclist's ideal position on the bike depends on measurements, beginning instead with how the rider felt and looked, using a mirror and a video. To adopt the most aerodynamic position, Boardman designed his own handlebars. They came up with the idea of using a gym treadmill to replicate climbing up l'Alpe d'Huez. Those who feel Boardman is a mere number-cruncher – and I was once among them – should reflect on the creative energy he and Keen put into those attempts to see how far he could get in the Tour. 'I would just tell people the facts, but behind it there was so much heartache, so much deliberation, so much angst.'

Boardman never made any bones about his dislike of his speciality, the prologue time trial. He hated the stress born of the level of expectation, the waiting 'in an intense state of paranoia, analysing every sensation'. In 1998, he turned up at the race start in Dublin depressed, short on form and lacking in confidence after a poor early season. He put in half a dozen laps' warm-up in the sea of noise made by British fans who had travelled across the Irish Sea, and was demoralised because he knew he could not give them the victory they wanted. He told Legeay that he could not win then came the turning point. 'About ten minutes before the start I began thinking, "Sod it, they can't hang me, they can't put me in jail."' He decided not to worry about the result, and 'be as good as I can be'.

He rode the course through the heart of the Irish capital, from the start outside Trinity College, through the Georgian squares, across the River Liffey and up O'Connell Street to the finish outside the GPO in six minutes twelve seconds. The final five hundred metres, slightly uphill from a dead turn by the River Liffey, were where the stage was lost and won, but he calculated it perfectly, according to his principle that in the perfect prologue he would 'die' only in the final metres. It was, he believed, his best win 'because it was so unexpected. It made so many people so happy. I really enjoyed it.'

He never made it to France. Having defended the jersey through the Wicklow hills on the first stage, he crashed out of the race, for the third time in five Tours, on the day the race headed through Sean Kelly country en route to Cork. As the peloton were winding up the pace for the sprint in the little yachting town of Youghal, he momentarily let his front wheel come into contact with the rear wheel of the rider ahead, and lost control. He fell on the left of the road, slid into a wall and was stretchered away in a neck brace, covered in dust and blood from a cut on his head, the twelfth rider to quit the Tour in the yellow jersey.

It was also Boardman's third serious crash in five Tour starts. This is more than most professionals would experience, and it arose because he did not have the usual grounding in amateur road racing. Time trials do nothing for a cyclist's ability to ride in close proximity to his fellows: Boardman was still a more than acceptable bike handler when he turned professional, but the difference between crashing and staying up is minimal, and the lack of 'flying hours' early in his career still told. After that pile-up, he would never again know success in the Tour.

It was also a turning point for the race organisers, who had taken their event to Ireland to pay tribute to Sean Kelly and Stephen Roche, and also to avoid the risk of being overshadowed on home turf by the football World Cup. But Jean-Marie Leblanc and his team were conscious of the risks of *gigantisme* that had arisen during the 1980s, and were put off further foreign excursions of any distance by the massive logistics. The riders and the vast caravan of vehicles got to the start under their own steam, but bringing them back to France involved three chartered ferries and three chartered jets. A project to start the race in the French West Indies was hastily shelved. The idea of starting the Tour on the eastern seaboard of America, bandied around since the emergence of Greg LeMond in the 1980s, was not raised again for five years. When Quebec offered to host the *départ* in 2008, the city was turned down.

The Tour was on a cusp in another sense. En route to the start in Dublin, the Festina masseur Willy Voet was arrested by French police on the Franco-Belgian border. In his car, one of the official vehicles loaned to the Tour by its car sponsor, Fiat, Voet was carrying the team's supply of drugs for the Tour, 235 doses of the blood booster erythropoietin (EPO), 82 doses of growth hormone and 62 doses of testosterone, not to mention two capsules of a mixture known as 'Belgian pot': a cocktail of amphetamine, morphine, heroin and cocaine. The evening before the race started, a young, ambitious investigating judge, Patrick Keil, opened an investigation into drug trafficking, with Voet as the main source. Voet was, however, not just any masseur. He was the confidant of Richard Virenque, the Tour's most popular cyclist, tipped to win the 1998 race after his second place in 1997. Festina were ranked top in the world and included another favourite, the Swiss Alex Zülle, and the world champion, Laurent Brochard.

When Boardman won the prologue and rode across the Wicklow hills in the yellow jersey, all that was known at the Tour was that Voet was missing and that police had seized a consignment of drugs. But when the Tour returned to France, each day seemed to bring a new twist in the tale. It was a surreal picture: in the north-east corner of France, in Lille, Keil and his team were conducting interrogations and planning arrests, while on the other side of the country, the Tour headed down through Brittany and Poitou into the Dordogne, with the caravan waiting nervously for Keil's next move.

The first crisis came in Brive, late in the night after stage six had finished, when Festina were thrown off the race after their manager, Bruno Roussel, admitted that EPO and growth hormone had been administered to the riders, under medical supervision. By the Pyrenees, another team were under investigation: Robert Millar's old squad, TVM. Their management were arrested on the first rest day. The first riders' strike came the next day, in the Midi. In the Alps, the stage from Albertville to Aix-les-Bains was cancelled after the riders refused to race, and five more teams left the race in protest after the police interrogated six TVM riders late into the night. For a national institution frequented by presidents of the Republic, welcomed by mayors of great cities and followed by most of the French people, this was a public-relations disaster of epic proportions, and there were calls – notably from the establishment newspaper *Le Monde* – for the race to be stopped on the grounds that it was terminally tainted.

With hindsight, the Festina débacle was the logical culmination of a century of drug-taking on the Tour. It had always gone on, and the police inquiry painted a picture of a sport in which doping was more than a subculture. Senior riders, team managers and masseurs perpetuated the use of drugs; this reached a grotesque level when teams were organising the communal fund used for drug-taking before they were sorting out racing programmes. The Simpson tragedy in 1967 had marked the point where the cycling authorities had had to do something about the massive use of amphetamines on a daily basis, but after that the problem had gone underground.

Most of the drugs and techniques used during the 1970s and 1980s were undetectable, such as hormonal 're-equilibration' with testosterone, in which the hormone was injected to 'keep the natural balance'. The naturally occurring anaesthetic cortisone was taken to dull pain and induce euphoria. Steroids were used as training aids, while Paul Kimmage's *Rough Ride* highlighted the fact that amphetamines were still taken in races with no drug controls. There were still a good many of these. The drug was used both socially and in training, as was Belgian pot, which could be acquired on a barter basis – for a set of team kit, for example. On the Tour, there had been major drug scandals in 1978 and 1988. In the first, the *maillot jaune* Michel Pollentier had been found cheating the doping control; in the second, the eventual winner Pedro Delgado tested positive for a diuretic, but was let off as the product had not been put on the UCI's banned list.

By the mid-1990s, the drug of choice was erythropoietin, the hormone that stimulates the body's bone marrow to produce red blood cells. The arrival of EPO changed the doping equation completely. If it was administered wrongly, there was a risk of blood clotting, thrombosis and death, so it needed to be taken under close medical supervision, which meant that teams had to hire doctors. This gave an advantage to teams who hired the best, or most reckless, medical help. On the road, the hormone's effects were far less random than those of any other drugs. By boosting a cyclist's red cells, the oxygen-carrying capacity of the blood was enhanced, and with it endurance and climbing ability. The Festina case came to court in 2000, with Virenque in the dock, and revealed widespread use of the drug. So too did other court cases, particularly in Italy, and various confessional books by cyclists and team personnel, headed by Voet's best-selling *Massacre à la chaine*.

Boardman made it known he did not want to go down that road, and was recognised as a 'clean' rider. Analytical as ever, he drew an analogy with robbing a bank. You know it will make you rich, but you don't do it because you might get caught. In cycling, using EPO might make you rich, but the risk of getting caught was low, so people did it. 'Everything has a price and you need to decide if you are able to pay it. If I had done something and got caught, everything I did would have been called into question, my kids would have had a hard time at school, there would have been the papers.'

Now he says drug-taking 'was not something I witnessed, and the team's performances reflected that. I remember that in 1994 Roger got everyone in the team van and said, "Look, the shit is going to hit the fan over doping. I don't want anyone near it. I know you're doing your best, and I support you." He basically told us to plug away and get the results through hard work. I would refuse to speculate in public.' In private, he formed his own opinions based on what went on around him. 'Everyone disappears up the climbs and you're maxing out on the flat sections, and at first you think it's a one-off. There are no facts to go on, apart from anecdotal stuff. But you look at a big bloke, one year he is finishing two groups behind you, the next year he's four minutes ahead. If it looks too good to be true, it generally is.'

Boardman could never know how many of the cyclists he was racing against were using drugs, and the only way he could deal with this was to look inwards and concentrate on what he did himself. What the others were or were not up to was a hazard of the trade, in the same way as a rainstorm might be. 'It doesn't do to dwell on things that you cannot change. How I dealt with it was by doing my little ride. I concentrated more and more on how I could perform, not on how I could beat other people, because I couldn't control that.' He was probably helped by the fact that he was commuting, never getting any closer to cycling's drug culture than sharing road space.

He is rational enough to realise the issues involved. 'If you believe it's black and white it's simple to judge, but it's not that clear-cut. You can take this, earn £100,000 a year and have financial security. The likes of the riders at Festina made the choice and now have to live with it. I was very fortunate that there was something I could do, something I could use and that had value. When you see someone like [former teammate] Nicolas Aubier driving a taxi with his morals intact, you realise it's a shitty choice for guys who did not have a speciality as I did.'

By 1998, Boardman had got to the bottom of his failure to stay the pace for the full distance in the 1996 and 1997 Tours. Routine blood tests had always shown that he was low in testosterone; he puts this down to heredity, compounded by the workload of training and racing, which suppresses the body's production of the hormone. In 1998, tests revealed osteopoenia, the precursor to osteoporosis, which is caused by a deficiency in the hormones that tell calcium to bind to the bones. The thickness of his bones was that which might be seen in a sixty-year-old woman. If he did not get treatment, he was told, he would be suffering from stress fractures in ten years.

The simplest and most effective treatment involved hormone replacement therapy, in other words boosting his testosterone levels. Boardman obtained verbal clearance from the sport's governing body, the UCI, to have the treatment and even went as far as buying the medicine, but his application was rejected at the end of 1998. 'I presented two dossiers from individual specialists and a bone scan. They said it was no problem. I got it organised and they turned me down. They said if I wanted the treatment I would have to stop cycling. "We're going to sanction somebody doing testosterone? No!"'

It was cruelly ironic, in view of the widespread hormone abuse that had been revealed in the sport that year, that Boardman was turned down for fear that it would open a loophole for less scrupulous colleagues. Testosterone boosting was already commonly practised and undetectable if done in a restrained way. Boardman accepts he could have simply injected the drug, not had osteoporosis, and probably had a better career. 'I could have ignored the UCI, taken something, enough to recover, and had a career as a stage-race rider.' Never a man to waste emotion, he has worked it out and says he can see their viewpoint; it seems almost too reasonable.

By that evening in Brittany in 2000, Boardman had told me he would have been more healthy if he had been taking drugs throughout his career, and he certainly looked that way. Every year, it seemed, he had sounded more jaded, while the bags under his eyes had grown from thin sickle moons to vast saucers with bags on the bags. He had faced a dilemma: quit racing, or continue in the knowledge that he was damaging his health. There was an alternative form of treatment: infusions of a medicine called pamidronate, which was legal but which lowered the level at which he could perform, so that the doses had to be timed to come after major events.

In 1999, he finished the Tour for the second time, taking fifth in the prologue time trial and fifteenth in the final time trial at Futuroscope, a space-age theme park in Poitou, as Lance Armstrong wrapped up the first of what was to be a record-breaking run of six victories. Boardman noted 'a lull in the pace' as the use of EPO became less widespread, although the Festina scandal had led, inevitably, to a change of climate. In the past, it had been hopefully assumed that riders were not using drugs unless it was proven otherwise, now, 'the speculation got very wearing. It got very witch-hunty. As soon as anyone was going well the fingers would be pointed.'

Boardman rode through the 1999 Tour in the knowledge that he was damaging his health. 'There was no soul-searching. I decided to manage it, for financial stability and to finish my career properly. It's easier to make the decision when you can't see or feel something, and it's something that's going to happen in ten years.' This was not the only fallout from his intense drive to succeed. In 1997, as he built up to what he hoped would be a definitive perform-ance in the Tour, which would show whether or not he could compete, he began losing weight and found that it became an objective in itself. That summer, he was proud of his lack of body fat, but he now reflects: 'What I had was an eating disorder. It was something I could control, that I could do and see a physiological result. You have to be obsessive, because you're starving yourself, but if you're not careful it becomes a goal in itself. I'd be aiming to be five hundred calories under what I needed each day, Pete would tell me I could eat normally, and I would think, "Well, that's a day wasted."'

Boardman had always put his competition before his personal life. He points to an episode when his and Sally's second child, Harriet, was born. 'I took Sal to the hospital at 1.30 a.m. on Friday night, called up that morning, was told she had some time to go, so I just drove past the hospital on my way to Hull.' It was the national twenty-five-mile championship, and he felt he had to go to look at the course. 'I was about the fourth person to find out I had a daughter. What was I doing?'

Sally and Chris were married when they were both twenty, and started their large family early. She describes herself as laid-back, and points out that both her father and brother were cyclists, 'so Chris chose the right person'. If she had had a different character, she says, they might not still be married. 'Chris was not doing it for himself, he was doing it because he hates to let people down. He had the weight of everyone else's fears on his shoulders. Things were not going as well as they should have been. He was trying harder and harder, but it didn't work. He was training himself into the ground, everyone else was progressing around him, and he couldn't work out why he was not able to recover. When the testosterone thing was diagnosed, and he realised it was not his fault, he relaxed a lot.'

By 1998, he had recognised that his obsession with competing was putting the marriage under severe strain. 'It's a real wake-up call, a massive shock, a defining moment in your life. I had stretched it to the limit. I had to make a choice about what were the most important things. It was not a question of Sal saying I had to quit. She was actively encouraging me to be selfish [but] . . . you look at someone and see they've gone and realise "I want this." There are a lot of psychological things which you prize, and when you become aware that you are at home physically but not mentally, and when it's going to cost you your marriage as well, you realise it's not worth it.'

*

In terms of influence on British sport, and British cycling, over the longer term, Boardman is perhaps the most important cyclist this country has produced. His results on the road do not match those of Simpson, and his Tour de France record does not stand comparison with that of Robert Millar, but he has shaped the sport in a way few would have thought possible. Boardman's high profile in the British media was enough to clinch Prudential's decision to invest several million pounds in a short-lived professional Tour of Britain in the late 1990s. Boardman's late attack on the Tour de France stage into Brighton kicked off a passion for cycling in an immensely talented teenager named David Millar, who was to maintain the British connection with the Tour after Boardman rode for the last time in 1999.

Most vitally, however, Boardman's gold medal in the pursuit at the 1992 Olympic Games was instrumental in the decision to build a velodrome for Manchester's Olympic bid. The velodrome became the base of the all-conquering Great Britain Olympic track squad, the 'medal factory' that produced eight golds in Beijing in 2008.

But none of those medals would have been won had Boardman not kicked off the whole process sixteen years earlier.

His gold in Barcelona was followed by a bronze in the time trial in 1996 at Atlanta, where Sciandri landed the bronze in the road race. This was a proven track record of success that led to UK Sport's decision in 1998 to invest millions of National Lottery pounds in potential Olympic cycling medallists. Keen was the man who sold UK Sport the idea, and Keen it was who, on the back of his work with Boardman, founded the coaching system that won the British team seven Olympic medals at Sydney and Athens.

'Chris had a massive role in making cycling a credible sport worthy of significant funding,' says the coach. 'He ended a psychology of failure in British cycling. It would be a different landscape now if he had not done what he did. He was the key pioneer.'

Retirement seemed to come as a relief to Boardman, who often had something of a tortured soul about him as he raced. He has kept in touch with the milieu, but it has nothing to do with pleasure or leisure. He commentates for television and played a key role in the GB team's success in Beijing as head of the 'secret squirrels', the research and development team who came up with the aerodynamic clothing and bikes that helped win the medals. He was also one of the team's quartet of senior managers; he mentored medallists such as Bradley Wiggins and their coaches and overhauled the talent-spotting and development structure.

'Sometimes I find myself wondering what I was doing spending so much of my life, and my family's life, trying to go fast on a bike. But then something would happen. I'd get fan mail, for example. Someone would say they had been to the velodrome and were smiling when they went away after seeing me beat the hour record, or something. It's not about sporting results per se, but about riding for one hour' – or in the case of his Tour de France prologue wins, a few minutes – 'and sending everyone home happy. I could have kept doing it if I'd enjoyed it, but I couldn't justify the sacrifice just to go to work. It's sad that I was never really part of it. I don't miss it in the slightest.'

CHAPTER TWELVE

The Lost Boy

We met the day after the 2004 Tour de France finished, in a bar in Fulham. David Millar had always had a cool, grunge-kid aura, had always looked elegantly wasted, rock-star style; now he looked like a man who had not slept for a month. His eyes were red-rimmed, as if he had been crying or rubbing them time and again. It was hard to know what to say: what can you say to someone who has self-destructed as spectacularly and disastrously as Millar had done?

A year earlier, the Scot had stepped onto the Tour's prize-giving podium after winning the final time trial of the centenary race ahead of Lance Armstrong and Jan Ullrich. It was Millar's third Tour stage win in four years, confirmation that he was the most talented British cyclist in at least a generation. The victory came at the end of a Tour in which the twenty-six-year-old had suffered from a chest infection and been within an ace of pulling out; not surprisingly, he looked like a man who could not believe his luck, for all that his designer-label underpants were sticking out over the front of his tracksuit bottoms.

Millar's downfall was shockingly sudden. On the evening of Tuesday 22 June 2004, he was a world champion earning half a million pounds a year, heading for Tour de France and Olympic glory, a leading representative of the clean new generation in cycling. Two days later he was a self-confessed drugs cheat, a pariah with his life and reputation in shreds, without a job or a future.

In that Fulham bar a month later, the conventional courtesies did not seem adequate. All I could do was listen. Gradually I became aware that there were two stories here. For the last five years I had described Millar's colourful, dramatic rise to the top of world cycling; running in parallel, but only occasionally breaking the surface, was the story of a susceptible, fragile man lurching from one crisis to another.

Putting the two strands together, it was clear that this was not a straightforward affair. This was not the story of a man who had cynically set out to cheat and lie, nor that of an innocent unaware that he was being led into cheating. Nor was he an athlete stuck in a system where drug-taking was endemic to the point of being almost obligatory. Millar's tale was complex and ambiguous – and important. There were far-reaching questions here about professional cycling's attempts to clean up its act in the difficult years since the Festina scandal. To combat a phenomenon you have to understand it: with Millar, it was possible to travel into the mind of an athlete who felt driven to dope.

In autumn 1996, when he ended his single season as an amateur at the Vélo Club St-Quentin in northern France, Millar was that rare thing: a highly talented Briton being fought over by several professional teams. There were five squads trying to sign up the nineteen-year-old, who had been racing for all of eighteen months. No British cyclist had risen in such meteoric style; Tom Simpson, for example, had had several seasons competing in England before a brief sojourn in Brittany landed him his pro contract in 1959. The winner in the war for Millar's signature was a newly formed team sponsored by a loan agency called Cofidis.

Millar had not wanted to delay, even though nineteen is an extremely young age to start a professional cycling career, the norm being between twenty-two and twenty-four. He had seen the Tour in Britain in 1994 and from then on knew what he wanted to do. In the UK he had raced for an amateur team managed by Bob Addy, who had ridden the 1968 Tour. 'We said, "Why not wait for a year in the UK, ride with the seniors?" but he said, "No, I'm going to get a pro contract." We were like "Whoa, wait a bit" but he just went ahead and did it.' Initially, Millar's agreement with Cofidis was that he would race for an amateur team in 1997 to gain experience while being paid by the professional team, but he wanted to race at the highest level as soon as possible.

A year before the Festina scandal, cycling was drug-ridden, but at nineteen Millar had had no time to get into bad habits. He was shocked by what he found. 'I came to professional cycling incredibly naive,' he told me in 2002. 'Even in my year as an amateur I was very protected. They saw I was very young, sacrificing everything, very talented, winning some of the biggest races in France on rice pudding and pasta. I was left alone and came to professional racing thinking it would be the same. Some of the big riders were very open with me, told me the bottom line, and I was shocked. It scarred me pretty badly.'

He was actually relieved when the Festina affair happened. He was in only his second year as a professional, but already he was sick and tired of racing against colleagues who he knew had lesser ability but who were clearly using drugs. At the start of 2000, with his first Tour on the horizon, he made his position clear. 'I think you have to make a conscious decision about whether to enter into [doping] or not. I've decided I'm not going to enter into that. I don't know why – it's nothing like being a "really decent guy" – but it just defeats the purpose for me. I'm a professional, but there are lines that have to be drawn.'

Like Chris Boardman, Millar won the opening stage of his first Tour. It was impossible to avoid being caught up in the symbolism and excitement of 1 July 2000. The venue was the Futuroscope theme park near Poitiers; Millar was the man of the future. His mother Avril had bet £100 on him to win the Tour before the end of 2006. She drove down from London, and was at the heart of a little knot of spectators in black T-shirts proclaiming 'It's Millar time'. Having set the fastest time, Millar had to wait for the favourite, Lance Armstrong, to finish before knowing he had won. On hearing Armstrong's time was slower, his tears and jubilation were genuine. As cycling awaited the Festina trial that autumn, this rising star was clean, and was open about it.

Millar also had a feeling for the sport's history. In the second half of the Tour, he kept with him a limestone pebble from Mont Ventoux, where Tom Simpson had died thirty-three years earlier. One of Simpson's daughters, Joanne, had picked it up next to the memorial to her father, and gave it to Millar the following day. He was holding it in his hand in the start village that morning, and he kept it in the pocket of his racing jersey. 'It's moving every time you go up the mountain,' he said. He was gloriously, youthfully uninhibited and it was inevitable that British journalists would call him 'Boy Dave'.

Millar defended the yellow jersey for two days, surviving a high-speed crash into hay bales in one stage finale, but he finally ceded the *maillot jaune* in the team time trial, as Boardman had in 1994. A more serious crash on the run-up to Mont Ventoux left him with a dislocated collarbone and compressed ribs, meaning that he spent the last ten days of the Tour racing with 'permanent stitch', and a massive burn on his neck where it had been skinned by a tyre in the pile-up. He earned an apology from the Tour organisers after blowing his top when a vast traffic jam prevented Cofidis from getting to their hotel after the marathon Alpine stage to Briançon. 'Sadomasochism on the grand scale,' he rightly called it. But he remained strong enough to ride well through the Alps, and on the Champs-Elysées he looked among the fittest riders in the race.

By the late 1990s, there were few charismatic personalities in professional cycling. The demands of the sport were so great and the stakes so high that the riders saw less of the world outside. The way that the Tour had grown meant it was harder to see a human face among the athletes, who seemed to spend most of their time cloistered in hotel rooms or team buses. The doping scandals had soured the relationship between the press and the riders, who were edgier, more reticent. Against this more anodyne, homogenous background, Millar was truly colourful. His flamboyance earned him the nickname '*le dandy*' in French newspapers. He wore his emotions on his sleeve and was highly articulate. It was easy to empathise with him when he displayed anger, vulnerability, or excitement.

He had written a humorous, no-holds-barred column in the magazine *Cycle Sport* for several years. He had a yellow open-top Land Rover and a Subaru Impreza. He was passionately into his music and books. At eighteen he had told his mother: 'I can be a great artist, Mum, or a professional cyclist.' His namesake Robert, who was no relation, was duly impressed. 'He's a surfing dude. You can see he has natural talent [and] he's putting up with the inconvenience of training and turning up with clean socks at the start of the race. He's slightly fragile, like a good racehorse. He's probably got more talent than I had, or Chris Boardman had.'

The mental fragility noted by Robert Millar may well have had something to do with David's nomadic, unstable childhood. His parents divorced when he was in his early teens, and he divided his time between London and Hong Kong. His volatile nature had been evident during his first Tour and after the race finished, and during the run-up to the Olympic Games in Sydney in August 2000, he went through a personal crisis. 'I had been making a lot of sacrifices, living a life I didn't enjoy, not hanging out with people I normally hang out with,' he told me. 'I got the [yellow] jersey, got back to Biarritz and realised nothing had changed. I had thought that if I was good at cycling my life would be better, and I realised it hadn't changed anything.' Instead of going to that year's world championship, he said that he 'disappeared. My parents were worried, they could see I was changing. I was becoming unstable.'

I ask Millar to describe the margin between taking drugs and staying clean. 'It's that,' he says, and holds up finger and thumb in front of me. The gap between them is half an inch. 'I was 100 per cent sure I would never dope, 100 per cent, then all of a sudden it was out of control. Cycling had become my life, the only thing that defined me, and I resented that. It was "fuck it". It was like flipping a coin. I didn't think about it. There was no twiddling my thumbs, no sleepless nights. You don't stop and think. If you think about it, it's game over.

'There was no clear-cut explanation. In 2001 I doped for one race, the Tour of Spain. The other seven I won were on water [i.e. clean]. I ended the year sixteenth in the world, which for a twenty-four-year-old is huge, and 90 per cent of it was done clean. I was loving it, winning, racing, but that wasn't what pushed me to doping that year.'

The key was the 2001 Tour de France. Millar started as favourite for the prologue time trial held on Cofidis's home turf in Dunkirk, but as with Boardman six years earlier at St-Brieuc the pressure proved too much for him. His form was not perfect, so he overcooked a bend in search of extra speed, and slid across the road on his left side. There were no broken bones, just a variety of nasty cuts and grazes, and for the following morning's start in St-Omer he was swaddled up like a mummy. It seemed like fate was getting its own back on him for having the temerity, before the race had even started, to issue invitations – glossy, highly designed – to his post-Tour party in Paris.

What followed was what the French term *un calvaire* – a journey through pain, a daily struggle to hang on to the bunch. On one day, he trailed into the finish far behind the front-runners, struggling to get inside the time limit with one or two fellow sufferers. On another day, Bastille Day, he attacked and broke away from the peloton in a fruitless bid to raise his morale and that of his team. He spoke lightly of witnessing life at both ends of the Tour – in the yellow jersey the previous year, the *lanterne rouge* twelve months later. He tried to sound convincing when he said he was certain he could ride through the bad spell. The true picture came when I met him after the stage finish at Verdun, five days into the Tour; there was a note of hysteria in his voice and he had the haunted eyes of a man on the edge of breaking down. 'I was so sick and pissed off,' he says. 'I was thinking, "Let me go home." By day nine or ten I was starting to go mental. The team were, like, "David, don't give up, you are the only guy can win a stage, hang on, you can win one in the last week." '

The consensus in cycling circles is that fighting to stay in the Tour this way strengthens character. 'He's had a bad week, but it will be of service in future,' one Cofidis team manager, Bernard Quilfen, told me. 'When you've experienced what David has you come out of it a stronger person.' What followed suggests the opposite was the case. It wasn't that his managers were unconcerned or negligent. They simply could not read his mind. Another *directeur sportif*, Alain Bondue, asked Millar if he wanted his girlfriend to come to the race to boost his morale. She was unable to get there. It was the final straw, although Millar is surely exaggerating when he claims: 'No other team in the world would have pushed me through what I went through in that year's Tour. I was going bananas and they pushed me through.'

Millar left the Tour, did not touch his bike for a week, and partied in Biarritz. Before the Tour of Spain he left France for two weeks, and spent the time training hard with motor-paced rides. During those two weeks he bought EPO at £250 a capsule, and injected it into his shoulder. On the back of this training regime he won the prologue of the

Tour of Spain, took a road-race stage in convincing style, and was within a few seconds of winning the world time trial championship in Portugal. There was no risk of testing positive: the EPO was purely to help him train, and there were no out-of-competition tests.

Before every major race, the Union Cycliste Internationale carries out blood tests intended to weed out those who may be abusing EPO to the point where it is damaging to their health. A rider's blood thickness (haematocrit) is measured; those over the limit of 50 per cent are made to rest. Millar had no fear of failing the tests. He was using only small quantities, so his haematocrit count was 46 or 47 per cent, well below the limit.

He believes that his doping began partly as an act of adolescent rebellion in the face of his increasing resentment towards the demands of his sport and his team. It could, in fact, be considered a form of self-harm, in his eyes the worst act that he could be driven to do. 'It was like a way of getting back at the team. "Look what you've pushed me to." It was like, "I'll show the fuckers." ' Thirty-four years before, on the eve of Tom Simpson's death, doping had been something to joke about, that could be done relatively openly. In 2001, doping was something that could take you to a police station or a court.

However, for a rider who had doubts about the extent to which he should be 'profi', as he would put it, doping was also the ultimate professional act. The day after we met, he explained to Jeremy Whittle of *The Times*: 'This is the paradox. When you boost your performance you become ten times more serious than you have ever been.' He realised that in 2001, when he did not ride well in the Tour, those around him also did badly. 'There are forty or fifty people involved in the team, and I'm like, "I've got a lot of responsibility here." The only reason Cofidis was invited to the Tour of Spain was if I started. I felt I was letting them down if I was not performing. I assumed the role given to me of being a professional.' Doping was 'mental insurance' for Millar. By going against what he knew to be ethical and sensible, he could prove to himself that he had left no stone unturned in his preparation.

For some cyclists, the sacrifices the sport demands are automatic, routine; in fact, they provide a framework to life. It was not so for Millar. At times he would fluctuate between living the life of a professional cyclist and living like any young man. He seemed torn between the need to do something he loved and the limitations his sport demanded of his life. In 2002, Millar explained to me: 'It's hard to decide what I want from cycling. I'm not prepared to take eight years of my life, be a rich young man at thirty-one or thirty-two and find I've missed a whole part of my life. I don't want to be a lonely recluse forced to go back to cycling because it's all I have. I could walk away from it, but there is nothing else I could do in life that I can do as well as cycling. Very few people find what they are made to do. [But] I miss intelligent conversation, having a beer with someone, [talking] about books you can recommend, music.'

His dilemma would have seemed self-indulgent to professional cyclists of the past, who had the option of working in the fields or the factory or sitting on a bike. It may also seem self-indulgent when set against the hundreds of thousands of pounds he was able to earn. But it was deeply felt. He went further in an interview with Richard Moore in *Scotland on Sunday* that June: 'You have to realise that you have to be horrible to people. You have to tell them not to come to races, because there's no point. I'm not going to see them. I don't want to be thinking I have to go and see people. It sounds like I'm a selfish bastard, and it is kind of lonely at times. I don't think any more. I've stopped thinking, stopped reading, stopped writing.'

Millar had become engaged in 2001, and he was devastated

when the relationship suddenly finished towards the end of the year. 'I was madly in love, it all went wrong, I wasn't right in the head and I partied like mad.' He returned to Europe with glandular fever, in such a state that he turned up at the team's training camp without a bike. He got through the illness by the spring of 2002 with the help of a doctor in the neighbouring Basque country. His stage win in that year's Tour de France, at Béziers, was masterly, and, he insists, it was taken clean.

En route to Béziers, Millar infiltrated the stage-long break, then won the sprint from the remnants, who included the Spaniard David Etxebarria, who already had two stage wins in the Tour to his name. Six months later, he continued to talk about it with the enthusiasm of a nineteen-year-old amateur. 'I still get goose bumps thinking about being in [that] break with Laurent Jalabert, with someone every two hundred metres waving a sign saying *"Merci, Jaja"*. I love racing like that. Jalabert made a conscious decision to please the public, to give something back to the sport; he was visibly enjoying himself, and that's the most beautiful way to race. There's not another sport like it. There's a whole romantic side to cycling.'

There was another side, unfortunately. 'I'm away for 180 days a year and when I come home I'm a mental milkshake,' he said before that Tour. He estimated that in the four months running up to the world championship in 2001, he returned to his base in Biarritz for all of six days. 'Hong Kong is where I would call home; England never felt like home, nor did France. I created a very nomadic lifestyle, and it's not good as a professional athlete having no base.'

The following season marked Millar's final descent. He was angry inside because he had missed out on a performance bonus despite winning his stage in the Tour. That was, he acknowledges, his own fault for failing to read the contract correctly, but it was another source of frustration. In 2003, he had one conflict after another with Cofidis. He criticised the team's pay structure, based partly on winning world ranking points, and said it bred selfishness within the squad. The team bosses accused him of a lack of commitment, and by June that year he had decided to assert himself. 'I thought, "I'll fuck you over. I'll make them pay me a shitload of money and run this team." I had to show I could get over the climbs and get on the podium at the Dauphiné Libéré, I wanted to ensure it, so I went to Spain and prepped for it.' What that meant, he explained, was 'training fucking hard and doing a certain amount of EPO over ten days so I could keep doing the training. I was on the programme well, EPO and testosterone patches' – the latter to avoid depleting his levels of the male hormone – 'which was big shit for me.'

At the Tour, he was again favourite to win the prologue time trial, but once more disaster struck. He was clearly in the lead until his chain came off, and he had to slow down to put it back on the chain ring. In spite of the time he lost doing this, he finished second by a mere 0.08 seconds to the Australian Brad McGee. There followed a showdown with his team manager, Alain Bondue, whom he blamed for the mishap – although Bondue claimed Millar also bore a share of responsibility – and who was eventually demoted. To make the point that Cofidis was poorly organised, Millar threw his bike down in front of the team staff, grabbed the sponsor, François Migraine, by the shoulders and took him to where another team, the Spanish squad ONCE, had their bikes. 'Look at the passion and commitment they put in,' he said. 'I've been saying for a long time we lack that.'

He was fit enough to try to win the Bastille Day stage in the Alps, but by the Pyrenees he was on his knees, coughing heavily from a chest infection. He spent seventy-five miles chasing the backmarkers through the first Pyrenean stage, then suffered desperately the following day on the stage into Bayonne, just over the river from his adopted home town, Biarritz. Soon afterwards he lashed out at his team doctor: 'I yelled at him, "When are you going to let me go home? Will someone tell me to stop?"' A day and a half later, he won the time trial into Nantes, equalling Robert Millar and Chris Boardman's tally of three stage wins. Jan Ullrich might have won had he not fallen off, while Armstrong might have triumphed had he not been solely interested in gaining time on the German. However, Millar's victory was no fluke: this was the second fastest time trial in Tour history, at 33.97mph for the 30.5 miles, and he too had fallen off on the sodden roads leading into the city.

His world-time-trial title that autumn was won with the same 'preparation' as before, and he says now that he felt 'emotionless: I knew I'd won after fifteen kilometres and was just going through the motions'. He still did not understand why he was cheating. 'I couldn't explain to myself why I was doing it and it all became very confusing. I wasn't good with myself. I changed slowly as a person. Going through such a big ethical change from one day to the next is going to affect you on a deeper level. I became unstable. My self-esteem started evaporating. I was living a lie and it wasn't good for anyone.'

The police net closed over that winter. The French drugs squad were keeping a close eye on two Cofidis team members, both from Poland: a masseur named Bogdan Madejak and a young rider, Marek Rutkiewicz. Both were taken into custody in January 2004, and other arrests prompted journalists to refer to 'a Cofidis affair'. According to Millar and the team management, there was no 'Cofidis affair'; it was merely a matter of a few individuals taking drugs without the team's knowledge. During the spring, however, the number of 'individuals' grew, and gradually Millar entered the frame. François Migraine conspicuously failed to endorse him as clean in an interview; he was named by a teammate, Philippe Gaumont, who was taken in and interrogated by police.

The police came for him at 8.25 in the evening of 22 June, as he was ordering dinner in a restaurant in the town of Bidart, just down the coast from Biarritz. There were three gendarmes in plain clothes, a little pumped up with the adrenalin of the occasion. Millar had just finished his final event before the Tour and had driven home with Dave Brailsford, who runs Britain's lottery-funded cycling programme. Brailsford was keeping tabs on Millar's progress as a potential Olympic medallist, and had been to watch him race in the Route du Sud; he was escorted back to Millar's flat with the rider and the police, and had to look on as the gendarmes systematically took it apart. Brailsford was also questioned for five hours before being released once the police had ascertained he had no knowledge of Millar's drug-taking.

Having been duly intimidated – the first gendarme to enter his flat was holding a gun – Millar was thrown into the cells for twelve hours before interrogation began. He cracked in the forty-seventh of the statutory forty-eight hours of questioning, admitted doping on three occasions and was released late in the evening of 24 June.

When searching his flat in Biarritz, the police had found two empty capsules which had contained the final doses of EPO that he had taken before the world championships. They had travelled in his suitcase to Manchester, Hamilton – where the world championships were held – Las Vegas and back to Biarritz, where Millar had found them on unpacking, thought, 'What the fuck has my life come to?' and put them on the bookcase in his bedroom, 'the one place nobody goes, nobody touches'.

Presented with the evidence, he initially invented an unlikely story for the police, then finally thought, 'Fuck this, I can't live with this. It's not 100 per cent my fault, but I'm not going to live like this. I could have kept fighting, fighting, fighting, but I'm fundamentally not a good liar.' Millar kept the empty capsules, he says, as visual evidence to remind himself of where he had been. Perhaps, he agrees, he wanted to be exposed, subconsciously at least. Perhaps it was his equivalent of the mark where a mixed-up teenager might have cut himself. 'It had scarred me. I didn't give it much thought, but I knew what I was doing.'

Brailsford, who was aware that Millar would be traumatised by the experience, took him out for dinner, and together they watched England's defeat at the hands of Portugal in Euro 2004. It was, Brailsford said, as if the man he had driven home from the Route du Sud that Monday and the man sitting with him that night were twin brothers who looked the same but were completely different people.

The following morning, Millar's confession was leaked to the press. On 1 July he travelled to Paris, and confirmed his statements to Judge Richard Pallain, who was in charge of the inquiry. Immediately, Brailsford, who was also acting chief executive of the British Cycling Federation, banned him provisionally. On 4 August a disciplinary commission formalised the ban; David Millar would not race for two years.

There is a twist in the Millar tale. He is adamant that in 2004 he was racing 'clean' and was determined to turn his back on doping. The turnaround came when he realised that Brailsford's World Class programme could give him the back-up and guidance which he had not found at Cofidis. In early 2004, he began working with Chris Boardman's former trainer Peter Keen, and even now Brailsford and Keen remain convinced that from then on he was not using drugs.

'I will go to my grave with the belief that he was doing it clean as of the start of that year,' says Brailsford. 'There was a strong working relationship, and he saw there was a solution, that he could do it differently. It was the way he bought into it that convinced me: he was training more regularly than previously, looking after his nutrition, giving us feedback.' 'I wanted to win the Olympics clean for myself,' says Millar.

The close relationship that Brailsford and Keen built with Millar did, however, bring its own perils. By doping in 2003 for an event which he was riding as part of Brailsford's British team, Millar was putting in jeopardy the millions of pounds of lottery funding that had flooded into British cycling since 1998. Brailsford says that after Millar's confession there was no question of the funding being withdrawn, since he was not receiving cash from the lottery-backed programme. Had Millar ridden the 2004 Olympics and won a medal before the truth emerged, the outcome might have been different.

Whatever its effects in Britain, the Millar scandal said far more about European professional cycling of the time. Cofidis, for example, was against doping, but there were ambiguities. The team could point to a zero-tolerance policy when a rider tested positive or was charged by police, yet riders with poor doping records had been put on the roster.

In 1999, the culture inside Cofidis had been worrying enough for the sponsors to commission a psychiatrist's report, which was first published in a French medical journal without mentioning the team's name, then leaked to *L'Equipe* during the police investigation. The psychiatrist, Jean-Christophe Seznec, concluded that some of the riders were abusing Stilnox, a sleeping pill, for recreational purposes, and that there were initiation rites involving drugs. The lack of a coherent anti-doping policy was shown when, in the wake of the scandal, the team stopped racing, then returned to the sport with a far stricter philosophy.

Millar's downfall showed why drug-taking had not ceased within cycling after the Festina scandal, even though that event had been considered a watershed. While the rewards in cycling are higher than ever, the demands remain colossal. Millar himself is adamant that he was over-raced.

He told police that on occasion he had to feign illness in order to get a rest, and he told me that within days of a serious crash in spring 2002 he was being asked to compete again.

Cyclists need sympathetic support from their teams, and the most successful create their own networks of specialists to cater for their needs. By the end of his career, Chris Boardman had his own trainer, Peter Keen, a personal manager, Peter Woodworth, a sports psychologist, John Syer, and a cycle-maker, Terry Dolan; the ex-legionnaire John Herety would also assist him on occasion.

Post-Festina, the authorities had beefed-up drug testing. There were ethical charters and zero-tolerance policies. But if a rider who had not wanted to take drugs had then embraced them, that indicated the measures were not sufficient. If a cyclist could dope with impunity in order to train harder for the Tour de France, then out-of-competition testing needed to be made stricter to close that loophole. Millar said he had had to 'stop thinking' in order to dope; Boardman's experience confirmed that if a cyclist could take a step back and ponder the pros and cons, he was less likely to dope. Driven athletes lack perspective – that is part of their make-up – so the case for educating riders about the implications of drugs was convincing: make them think.

The culture of cycling was also called into question. It could not be said that his team and his sport had made Millar take drugs. That was his decision alone, and he is an adult. But had enough been done to discourage him? Consider the approach of Boardman's team, who told riders that winning mattered but not at any price. Millar was told not to dope, but had to race in a way he felt was unreasonable. The team may have felt it was reasonable, but he did not, and between the two parties, it was not addressed. Millar felt the only person he could turn to during his crisis in 2001 was Massimiliano Lelli, a member of what he termed 'the fucked up generation'.

Like most of the British cycling world, I did not want to believe that Millar took drugs. He had told me in June 2002: 'I don't need to dope. I don't have to live with myself doing that.' By then, of course, he had already used EPO, although he may have believed that he was not going to do so again. There were other reasons for believing he was 'clean'. He was a bright middle-class boy who raced his bike because he wanted to do so and understood the issues. His results had never included the curious highs and lows that arouse suspicion.

But there were grounds for doubt. The Festina case had highlighted what we all knew, that an absence of positive drug tests did not mean drugs were not taken. When figuring out whether or not to trust a cyclist, it was better to study peripheral signs: the clarity, or lack of it, in the way a cyclist spoke about drugs, the people with whom he associated. That evidence could never be conclusive, but it enabled one to keep an open mind, and the ambiguities about Millar had been there for a while. From 2002, he had been working with a doctor in Spain without the knowledge of his team. During the time I had known him he had ceased to be open about drugs and begun attacking the notion that journalists might write about the subject. Yet I did not ask the direct question: do you take drugs? To do so in sport is akin to asking a neighbour whether or not he beats his wife.

The stance of the magazine *Cycling Weekly* was uncompromising. Its editorials on Millar included phrases such as 'no shame', 'trying it on' and 'how do we know we can trust him?' That mattered, because the magazine is still the voice of life on two wheels in Britain as it was in the Hercules days, and its editor Robert Garbutt explained: 'We normally try to be detached but because he was "Our Dave" we felt personally let down. The magazine had no option. You cannot defend someone who has confessed to taking drugs on three separate occasions. You can't say someone has to be let off the hook. After all, it is not as if he volunteered the information.' The magazine received a large volume of letters, and the letters page, perhaps the best guide to the way the average British cyclist was feeling, ran the full gamut of emotion, although Garbutt admitted he was 'surprised by the level of public support' for Millar.

Others were a little more forgiving. 'I thought "for God's sake, not Dave as well",' said the man then tipped as Britain's next big road star, Londoner Bradley Wiggins. 'I'd always looked up at Dave as a person with similar build, similar physical power to me, and I'd thought, I can do what Dave's doing one day on the road. I got a bit pissed off about it all, a bit embittered towards the professional scene.'

To some extent, Millar's exposure came as a relief to me. Anything is better than doubt and suspicion. At least I knew. But I was angry. I felt I had been betrayed. Millar had not actually lied to me, but he had answered my questions about doping in a manner that he admitted was 'ambiguous' if not actually dishonest. Even so, I could not avoid feeling sympathy, given the dire straits in which Millar had ended up. I was angry at the stupidity and self-destruction of the act, not the man, even though he had cheated and deceived. Condemning drug-taking and disowning the drug-taker were two different things.

The sympathy towards Millar shown by many cycling fans reflects my own ambivalence about the doping issue. We admire what the men do on their bikes; we would prefer not to know the lengths to which some of them go. We can empathise with the temptation to seek moral or physical support at the chemist's even if we are adamant it should not be sought. Professional cyclists do these things for themselves – they are driven to win or they merely want the money – but we feel a certain responsibility for what they do, if only for the delight we take in watching a spectacular sprint or descent, or a climber in flight up a great mountain.

With Millar banned, the 2004 Tour started without a single Briton in the field. It was only the second time this had happened since Brian Robinson and company had turned up at the start in Le Havre. The 2005 race was also fallow, but in 2006 Millar returned, having appealed against the length of the suspension, leading the Court of Arbitration in Sport to rule that it should be dated from the date on which he had been arrested, rather than the date of his hearing. That meant that the Scot could return to racing just in time for the 2006 Tour, not a simple proposition, as conventional wisdom has it that a cyclist needs at least some competitive miles in his legs before taking on the Tour.

By the start of 2006 Millar was ensconced in Derbyshire and training hard to a programme that had been devised by Simon Jones, one of the British Olympic team coaches, to take him through the twelve months leading up to the Tour. Indeed, British cycling played a key part in his comeback. Brailsford said, 'When he started thinking about it, we had discussions. He wanted to optimise his training, the psychological approach, his nutrition, his lifestyle.' Millar had begun his personal rehabilitation by offering his services to the Olympic team as an anti-doping mentor for the younger riders. He had a contract with the Spanish team Saunier Duval in his pocket, and had met the Tour's director Jean-Marie Leblanc to apologise for his conduct – he had also written a lengthy letter to Leblanc – and he had been told he would be welcome back at the race. Millar had built his own support network, stretching from Brailsford and Jones through to his old mentor Mike Taylor, the 1995 Tour stage-winner Max Sciandri, and his fiancé Nicole, whom he married in October 2009.

In July 2006, there he was at the Tour's *Grand Départ* in

Strasbourg, just in from a training camp in the Pyrenees with John Herety, and lean-faced from a starvation diet in which he had shed two kilos of fat in five days. Millar was making a fresh start on what he termed his 'second career', but cycling had not changed in his absence. The climate of mistrust in the sport had worsened, and was summed up by the grilling Millar was given by former Tour rider Paul Kimmage in his pre-race press conference. The race itself was rocked by the biggest drugs scandal in its history, with a long list of favourites eliminated just before the start due to their apparent involvement in the Operación Puerto blood doping inquiry. The first man to Paris, Floyd Landis, was disqualified due to testing positive for testosterone.

The atmosphere on the race was poisonous, but Millar was still glad to be there, having experienced what life was like when he was deprived of the passion that was at the core of his existence. 'Hanging out in the real world I realised not many people can do something where they can achieve excellence, something they love doing. It's having something that does take over your life, which I used to think was shit – it sucked, it was a burden – but now I realise I'm lucky to have something I'm so passionate about. It does take over your life twenty-four hours a day, seven days a week, so now I think, shit, what am I going to do in six or seven years when I stop doing it?'

Against all expectations, Millar finished that Tour, in the company of a British debutant, the Olympic pursuit champion Bradley Wiggins, who had been so shocked by the scandal two years earlier, but ironically enough was now riding in the colours of Millar's old team Cofidis. They were under new management, and one of the places the new Cofidis bosses had looked for advice on staying drug-free was the Great Britain team. In January 2007 Millar's personal history with Cofidis came to an end, when the case involving the team finally came to court and he was acquitted of drugs charges on the grounds that it could not be proven he had used banned substances on French soil.

From being briefly a pariah, Millar turned gradually and gracefully into an elder statesman and respected anti-doping campaigner. He returned to the Great Britain team as early as autumn 2006, and was the team's main focus in the world road championships for the next three years, but he opted not to appeal against his ban from the Olympic squad after seeing the controversy that erupted when the sprinter Dwain Chambers attempted to have his ban overturned. By 2008 Millar was wearing the national champion's jersey and he had won over two of his most vehement critics, the former professional Paul Kimmage, who had launched a vitriolic attack on him on his return to racing, and that august publication *Cycling Weekly*.

A key element in his rehabilitation was the part he played in the foundation of the American team Slipstream in 2007. It was, Millar said after that year's Tour, an idea that had emerged from discussions with Lance Armstrong's former teammate Jonathan Vaughters. 'We [both] wanted to do the same thing, which is to create the first of the next generation of cycling teams.' Slipstream, said Millar, would be different from other teams in that 'the baseline is purely ethical. [The sponsor] Doug Ellis wants a cycling team but he wants one that doesn't win at all costs. He feels he can only be proud of it, if he has no doubts about it. He needs guarantees, even for a rider like me, he needs hard copy to prove I am clean.' It was in essence an answer to the problems that had dogged him at Cofidis, using the solutions that had become apparent through his work with the British Olympic team.

About 30 per cent of the team budget, between US-$300–400k was devoted to setting up a medical profiling system for the team's cyclists. The team worked with an independent ethics group and consulted the World Anti-Doping Agency. The profiling system included a blood volume test, the only reliable way of detecting whether a cyclist has used a blood transfusion. An independent body was to monitor whether or not the riders were fit to race. In a new departure for professional cycling, the bulk of the team was based in Gerona, Spain, where the ambition was to build a support network that will prevent riders becoming 'just hired guns who turn up at races', as Millar put it. 'We've taken that idea from what Dave Brailsford and British Cycling do and put it into a top-level professional team.

'There are no 100 per cent guarantees but we are trying to create a group of guys who trust each other, who won't fuck each other over, and don't want to win at all costs. If we don't win a race in year one, that's not the thing. We want to have fun, enjoy racing, give it 100 per cent and race well.' The final seal of approval for the Slipstream project came when they pulled in a big-name sponsor in Garmin in 2008. In that year's Tour, Millar came close to pulling on the yellow jersey with a strong ride in an early time-trial stage at Cholet, where he took third to the German Stefan Schumacher, who would subsequently test positive. Millar's Tour de France of 2009 was spent largely on team duty for Bradley Wiggins as the Londoner raced to a shock fourth overall.

There were further triumphs in Millar's career, but they were isolated instances. At the end of 2010 he won a gold medal in the time trial at the Commonwealth Games for Scotland; in 2011 he achieved more, leading the Giro d'Italia to become the first Briton to wear the leader's jersey in all three major Tours. Later that year, he helped Garmin-Slipstream ride to victory in the team time trial stage at the Tour de France. Shortly before that, his autobiography *Racing Through the Dark*, a frank account of his fall and rise, was published to critical acclaim. At the end of the season his and Nicole's first child Archie was born, and shortly afterwards he played a vital role in Mark Cavendish's sprint victory at the world championships.

The Tour wheel turned full circle the following July. By then, Millar had been selected for the Great Britain team for the London Olympics – the BOA's life ban on athletes who had tested positive having been rescinded by the Court of Arbitration in Sport – but against that happy background, his Garmin team were having a nightmare, with one rider after another falling victim to a crash. Stage twelve of the Tour ran out of the Alps to Annonay, a classic transition day. Millar was in the thick of the action early on, and was among the final survivors of the large breakaway group that dominated the stage. At the finish, Millar's sprint victory from the Frenchman Jean-Christophe Peraud was a formality, but what counted was the date, and what he said. July 13 was the date, the 45th anniversary of Tom Simpson's death, and at Millar's winner's press conference he spoke eloquently of the meaning of his victory: a former drug taker, now rehabilitated, winning on the anniversary of the Tour's most chilling drugs episode.

As retirement beckoned, Millar looked unlikely to achieve what he had told me would be his ambition for his 'second career': 'to become the best British cyclist ever, and to do it clean'. He had been overtaken by Wiggins, Tour winner and multiple Olympic gold medallist. But it could be argued that in the wider context of his sport as a whole he had achieved far more than mere results. He had earned redemption in a manner denied to almost all the other riders entangled in the lengthy series of doping scandals that scarred cycling between 1998 and 2008. No cyclist apart from Millar made such a high-profile confession to doping and then managed a complete comeback at the highest level, with his credibility completely regained. In doing so, Millar showed it was possible to race clean. By being willing to act as a spokesman when doping returned to the agenda, he helped the sport break with the old code of silence. In the Garmin-Slipstream project, Millar helped to create a model for the sport's future. From the broken youth I met that day in July 2004, the rider we had called 'the boy' grew up, had become a father himself, and he had much to be proud of in adulthood.

CHAPTER THIRTEEN

The Fastest Man in the World

'*Guardian* man wins Tour de France stage' proclaimed the banner headline on the front page on 10 July 2008, above the picture of Mark Cavendish punching the air as he took his first stage win in the Tour, at Châteauroux. It was a relatively quiet day on the news beat, admittedly – but even so, my paper gave the young Manxman's ghosted column star treatment. The opening anecdote was pure Cavendish. He had dropped back early in the stage into the convoy of team cars to talk to Brian Holm, his *directeur sportif* at the Columbia-High Road squad, and told him to call a bookmaker. 'Why?' Holm replied. 'Because you need to put a thousand euros on me to win the stage,' replied Cavendish.

Fast forward four years. By then Cavendish had gone from a newcomer on the block to one of the biggest stars in world cycling. In the 2012 Tour he wore the rainbow jersey of world champion – the only Briton to wear the stripes since Simpson – and won three stages to take his personal tally to twenty-three. That left him ahead of Lance Armstrong in the record books and, more importantly, perhaps, one in front of the great French sprinter André Darrigade. Cavendish was the best sprinter in the history of the Tour de France, and was voted the best sprinter of all time by *l'Equipe*.

Like Tom Simpson, Cavendish is a larger-than-life figure who inspires one anecdote after another. Another good story emerged in 2005 from the former Foreign Legion member John Herety, not long after Cav won the world Madison championship on the track at the tender age of nineteen. Cav would go training on the Isle of Man with fellow amateurs, always ending the ride with a full-on sprint for the town sign at the island capital Douglas. As they rode towards the sign one day, one innocent asked, 'Who are you going to be today?' adding, 'I'm going to be Mario Cipollini.' Cavendish's answer spoke volumes: 'I'm going to be me.' Those five words sum up his approach to life and cycling.

The quote on the cover of a French cycling magazine at the start of 2010 was in a similar vein: 'I am the best.' In any other sportsman this might have been bravado or simply bullshit – Cipollini said such things, for example – but that didn't apply to Cavendish. You had to agree when he said: 'Other people have a big mouth just to be famous. I just happen to have a big mouth.' He exudes absolute confidence in a way that no British cyclist ever has, and few British sports stars ever do. His utter belief in his own ability has more than an element of Muhammad Ali's willingness to predict in which round he would knock out his opponent. As Cav has said over and over again, he is not talking himself up, merely stating what he views as fact. And the facts bear him out.

In 2009, at the tender age of twenty-four, Cavendish achieved a feat that had eluded every other sprinter in cycling: six bunch sprint wins in a single Tour de France. The Belgian Freddy Maertens had won a total of eight stages in the 1976 Tour, but only five of these were sprints, the rest time trials. Maertens also won five in 1981. The British record of eight Tour stages that had taken Barry Hoban nine years to accomplish had fallen with the ease of a ripe plum, just after Cav reached halfway in his third Tour. There was more. He took a narrow sprint win in Milan–San Remo in the spring, the kind of victory that can take some specialists a decade or more to pull off. By the end of the year, Cavendish had managed to win at least once in every stage race he had started since March 2008, an astonishing record of consistency.

That amply qualified Cav as the fastest man in cycling by the start of 2010, but he was also one of the most charismatic – second only to Lance Armstrong, perhaps – and probably the most outspoken. In the space of two seasons he had turned into the biggest star British cycling had ever produced, on the world stage at least. Whereas Tom Simpson had been one of half a dozen big names of his era, Cavendish was firmly in the top three, along with Armstrong and the 2007 and 2009 Tour de France winner Alberto Contador.

Like Simpson, Cavendish initially emerged as a track racer, but there is a little more to the comparison than that. He exudes the intense appetite for life that was the hallmark of the 1965 world champion, be it his superfast Audi, his love of Italian design classics such as Alessi kitchenware and vintage Vespas or his ambitions: to have a book written about him, to own a boat, and have a house with a spiral staircase (Simpson dreamed of having a tree growing through the heart of his home). Cavendish seems to live every moment to the full, with passion unrestrained, tears welling up after the big wins, the great defeats. Without a second thought he can shout 'I love you' at a teammate who has just led him out to a bunch sprint win (Roger Hammond, Tour of Britain, 2007), mouth off about a rival team, tear a strip off team personnel if the wheels he needs are not in the car, or wax lyrical about experiences such as his first Tour de France when his personal refrain was 'I'm fucking loving it.' Rightly he has been called the Wayne Rooney of British cycling.

On top of his speed, the physical staying power and mental strength that took him to Milan–San Remo means he may eventually match, or overtake, Simpson in winning major one-day races such as the world title and Paris–Roubaix. But Cavendish also resembles Simpson in being a European rather than a British sports personality. (Given that he has an American sponsor and wins stages in US

events, his fanbase must actually extend far beyond
Europe.) He persistently comments on the fact that he is
better known in Belgium than in Britain, and has put down
roots in Tuscany. In the UK, his four stage wins in the 2008
Tour de France were overwhelmed in a few weeks by the
ecstasy that greeted the performance in Beijing of the Great
Britain track cycling team. Cav was allotted all of four
seconds at the BBC's Sports Personality of the Year round-
up while in 2009 he finished second in Sports Personality to
the ageing soccer player Ryan Giggs, whose achievements
were underwhelming in comparison to Cavendish's stellar
record. That, if anything, looked like more of a kick in the
teeth.

Most of all, however, Cavendish is reminiscent of
'Tommy' in his total certainty that he was born to be a
champion on two wheels. Simpson was never in any doubt
that that was his destination: Cavendish is the same. His
early encounters with his future mentor Rod Ellingworth at
the Great Britain academy in 2004 are now the stuff of
legend. Back then, Ellingworth recalls Cav as 'an eighty-
five-kilos lad' – he raced the 2009 Tour at sixty-seven kilos
– 'saying how quick he was, how he would never let me
down. You go "yeah, yeah, yeah" and accept it, pay a bit of
lip service. But looking back, he believed in himself and was
already a winner.' At his interview for the Great Britain
cycling academy, the eighteen-year-old Cavendish did not
mince his words about his goals: winning Tour de France
stages and an Olympic title. So convinced was Cavendish of
where he was heading that he spent his junior years working
in a bank to squirrel away money to pay for racing in
Belgium as a senior, when he planned to make his big push
for a pro contract. He knew that his junior results would
suffer, but believed they did not matter in the long term.
Such clear thinking and sense of direction is rare indeed,
reminiscent of Simpson and Robert Millar.

'He's got a boxer's attitude, massive self-belief,' said

Ellingworth. But Cavendish is also one in a long line of fine cyclists to emerge from the Isle of Man, going back to Peter Buckley, Commonwealth Games road-race winner in 1966. The 'pocket rocket', Steve Joughin, was another fine sprinter and there are more following Cavendish: Jonny Bellis, Peter Kennaugh and his brother Tim, and Mark Christian. They are all part of a cycling history on the island that goes back to the 1950s, when Fausto Coppi would visit to race on the TT circuit. Cavendish reckons the weather is partly responsible: if you want to train, you toughen up or you do something else. And like the foreign legion of the 1980s, the Manxmen don't have it easy, because to race at any level, they have to travel, as young Cavendish did once he had begun winning races and grown out of the ballroom dancing in which he was an intense competitor in his early teens.

Cavendish has more than fast legs and a mercurial temperament. He knows how to suffer for his sport. At the 2005 Tour of Britain, Herety – then the manager of the GB road team – pointed him out as a star of the future. Perhaps, but Cav was a doubtful starter on day one due to a stomach upset, he then struggled through the stage, and spent most of the ensuing night on the toilet. On day two, as the race travelled through the Lake District, any talk of the youngster centred on whether his antibiotics would arrive at the stage finish. In spite of all this, he took third on the stage behind Hammond. At the end of the week, the race finished on a circuit in Central London. Cav had targeted the stage, had told the world about it, then was roughed up by the opposition and fell off his bike (Herety's view was that he had yet to earn his place at the front, and was being made to earn it the hard way). He looked as heart-broken as if he had just lost a world title. Clearly, this dumpy youth had guts and passion that went beyond the norm.

Two stage finishes in the 2009 Tour de France explained why Cavendish is not a run-of-the mill sprinter. Stage 19 to

Aubenas crossed a second-category climb just before the descent to the finish. The climb was not particularly steep or narrow, but it was long and relentless enough to put any sprinter in peril. Not only did Cavendish cling on, but he produced an astonishing turn of speed in the final metres to the line, turning a lower gear than usual at a rate that was more reminiscent of a pure track sprinter than a Tour de France fastman in the final week. Stage win number five demonstrated his ability to suffer, and his pure speed. Two days later, the Tour having been decided on Mont Ventoux – with Cav's fellow Briton Bradley Wiggins having clinched fourth place overall – the Manxman was the favourite for the finish on the Champs-Elysées, where no Briton had won before. Again, the manner of the victory was extraordinary: taking the final corner out of the Place de la Concorde on to the Champs, Cavendish was dragged clear of the field by his lead-out man Mark Renshaw, and the pair crossed the line twenty metres clear, both of them with their arms in the air. As a display of team work, it was superlative.

A little more than two years earlier, however, Cavendish was not even considered a likely Tour starter when he began his first year as a professional at the T-Mobile team. He was told that he was overweight at the pre-season training camp, then trained and dieted too hard and made himself ill. At T-Mobile, the management were more keen to back another young sprinter, Andre Greipel, and Cavendish initially had to work for him. But he was fit enough by April 2007 to be given his chance in the oldest one-day Classic in Belgium, the Grote Scheldeprijs. He won, ahead of the Australian Robbie McEwen, a multiple stage winner in the Tour, by a margin so fine that the Australian initially thought he had crossed the line first.

By early June, Cavendish had moved forward again, winning stages in the Four Days of Dunkirk and the Tour of Catalonia. He had suffered grimly in the Pyrenees to finish the latter event, and that prompted him to write to his managers at the T-Mobile team, requesting politely that they consider him for inclusion in their Tour team. While this sounds like nothing out of the ordinary, cycling is not a sport where the athletes tend to put themselves forward in this way. In fact, for a new professional, it showed massive self-belief and desire. But as Ellingworth told me after T-Mobile confirmed he would be doing the Tour, there were other emotions in play. 'He's not going to the Tour thinking "Great I'm riding the Tour",' said Ellingworth. 'He's thinking he's absolutely cacking himself, he seriously-doesn't know what he's getting into, he doesn't take it lightly at all, and in the next breath he says he's fast enough to win a stage.'

Again, the wind of circumstance was with Cavendish, showing that you make your own luck. T-Mobile had new management in place, and the head of the team was anything but a closed-minded European team boss. The American Bob Stapleton is a self-made businessman who had been brought in to relaunch the squad after drug scandals involving their former leader Jan Ullrich. And in marketing terms, T-Mobile knew that with the Tour starting in London, a Briton wearing their pink jersey made every kind of sense, the more so if he had the legs to be talked up as a possible stage winner.

The Tour's second visit to Great Britain in fourteen years happened against the odds. Whereas in the early 1990s, in the build-up to *Le Tour en Angleterre*, Robert Millar and Sean Yates were still racing strongly, the early noughties had witnessed the implosion of David Millar's career, after a spate of other doping scandals in cycling. It took a brave and insouciant character to bring the race to the British capital with that background, and the Mayor of London, Ken Livingstone, was that man. 'Red Ken' simply brushed off any questions about the Tour's tarnished recent past, preferring to focus on its undoubted economic benefits for the capital, and the galvanising effect he hoped it would have on Transport for London's policy of getting commuters on bikes after the inception of congestion charging. Ironically, the Tour needed a *départ* with the prestige of London as much as the British capital needed the Tour. By the early noughties the race was jaded by several years of drug scandals and was running short on glamour, notwithstanding Lance Armstrong's showbiz connections. In 2004, when a delegation from London visited the downbeat, gloomy *Grand Départ* in the Belgian city of Liège to see what could be learned, they were rightly struck by the lack of razzamatazz.

London, on the other hand, was probably the finest start *La Grande Boucle* has ever enjoyed, outstripping the centenary Tour's opener of 2003 by a mile or two. In a summer when one deluge followed another, the sun, incredibly, shone on the British capital on that first weekend of July. The backdrop to the eight-kilometre prologue route was a tourist board's dream: Buckingham Palace, Big Ben, the Serpentine, Admiralty Arch, Whitehall. The crowds were astonishing, estimated at over a million, lining the roads four and five deep, and thronging to watch the big screens set up in the Royal parks along the course in an ambiance that was as much rock festival as bike race. The 11,000 bike parking spaces set up by Transport for London soon filled up. It was quite a place to make your Tour debut, as Cavendish reflected: 'You just couldn't slow down. You couldn't hear anything, not even the sound of your tyres. It was a wall of roaring voices.'

It was a far cry from the empty Plymouth bypass thirty-three years earlier, but so was the Dover–Brighton–Portsmouth two-day visit of 1994. In 2007, however, there was a vital difference. The success of the London start was founded on a huge, sustained increase in cycling's popularity across the board, across the country. There had been a massive switch to cycling to work within the capital after the terrorist bombings of 2005. The results of the Olympic track cycling team in Sydney and Athens, spearheaded by Bradley Wiggins, Jason Queally and Chris Hoy, had increased the profile of the sport. Lance Armstrong's repeated victories between 1999 and 2005, and the massive sales of his books, had taken the Tour beyond the realms of mere sport. The Tour of Britain had been relaunched successfully in 2004 and had visited central London three times. Cycle use in the whole country had boomed, up by 40 per cent among adults since 2001. By the time the Tour came, more people in Britain were cycling regularly than jogging, playing golf, or even football. There had been a colossal increase in cycling among the over-thirty-fives, reflecting a surge in national affluence during the Brown– –Blair boom. Cycling was a costly sport calling for expenditure of thousands of pounds on bike bling, and people were happy to splash out. Cycling was trendy, reflected in the high-end kit produced by clothing companies like Rapha and the involvement of designer Sir Paul Smith.

The script in this West End spectacular called for a victory for Bradley Wiggins, who had spent most of his childhood within a couple of miles of the course. The Swiss Fabian Cancellara dominated, however, as he was to dominate time trials at all distances in pro racing for the next few years. The following stage through Kent needed a reaction from the British and it was provided by David Millar, who recalled watching the Tour in Brighton as a teenager in 1994. He escaped soon after the start in Greenwich, rode through Kent in the escape of the day, and ended the stage on the podium wearing the polka-dot jersey of best climber. No Briton had worn the measled vest since David's illustrious namesake Robert twenty-one years earlier.

Millar said later that riding at the front of the race

through Kent gave him goosebumps, and driving ahead of Millar in the race convoy offered the same surreal juxtapositions as in 1994. British bobbies were holding up the traffic at roundabouts and monitoring junctions in completely traffic-free suburban streets between the *départ fictif* at Trafalgar Square and the *départ réel* in Greenwich. Morris dancers frolicked on village greens and elegant ladies in twinsets waved champagne glasses among oast houses and tile-hung cottages. It was standing room only in the main streets of villages such as Marden, Bethersden and Tenterden, which seemed to have competed to produce the best French signs they could. *'Bienvenue à Bethersden, bonne route, bonne courage, bonne chance'* was typical.

Cavendish had plenty of courage, but little luck. He was knocked off his bike by a spectator on one of the final hills before the stage finish in Canterbury. To add insult to injury his team manager was not permitted to pace him back to the bunch behind the team car, as is normally the case when a rider crashes or punctures. 'I was crying my eyes out for those last fifteen miles, I was in the cars crying as I rode when the commissaire refused to let the cars in,' he wrote in the *Guardian*. 'I was distraught because everything had been going so perfectly, and I was so motivated. This will probably be the only chance I ever get in my career to win a stage of the Tour de France on my home roads and it's gone.'

For Cavendish, crashes dominated that debut. In Canterbury the wounds were psychological rather than physical, but he had a second horrendous fall approaching the finish in Ghent less than twenty-four hours later. There were worries about his hip joint which took most of the impact, but he survived to begin his apprenticeship for real at the finishes in Compiègne and Joigny in the next two days, where he finished ninth and tenth. His verdict? 'Nothing special. The other sprinters would all say I was capable of winning a stage, and I'm not happy going home without one top-five finish.'

By the Alps, Cav was spent and a wound in his knee was infected. After the first Alpine stage, he told the *Guardian*, 'I've never, ever dug that deep in my life. My heart was beating, bump, bump, bump in the side of my head, and it was hurting, really hurting. I was kind of blacking out, it wasn't exactly going dark but it was like I was seeing everything through blurred vision, like looking through dirty glass.' His race ended the next day, but he had, he said, learned one key lesson about the Tour's bunch sprints: the speed in the finish straight might be the same as in other races, but the run-up was faster, longer, and more hectic. 'In other races you can sit back until the final metres, but at the Tour the sprint starts with a kilometre to go so you are at your limit for longer.' As he had said in his letter to the T-Mobile management, he would return knowing just what he needed to do to win a stage. Or four.

Alongside Cav at the London start were four other Britons, all of whom had had the support of the Olympic team structure in one way or another in furthering their careers. Millar was one, so was Wiggins, while Charly Wegelius had come through the under-23 set-up before turning professional in 2000. Wegelius is a reed-thin climber, the son of a Finnish showjumper, whose mentor in Manchester, Mike Taylor, had also been close to Paul Sherwen and David Millar. He had turned himself into one of the finest mountain-climbing *domestiques* in Italian cycling, and as a result the Giro had always been his priority. The Italian squad Liquigas finally gave Wegelius a chance to ride for himself in that Tour, but he bit the dust on the second Alpine stage to Tignes, crashing on a roundabout with an impact that he described as 'falling out of a plane'. Even so, he completed the race, and returned in 2009 and 2010, working for the Australian Cadel Evans at the Belgian team

Silence-Lotto. By the end of 2011, however, he had retired, to join Millar's Garmin team as a *directeur sportif*.

The fifth member of the British contingent was barely twenty-one, the 'baby' of that year's Tour. Geraint Thomas was commonly known as 'Gee' but nicknamed 'the Penguin' by the English press. It was David Millar who came up with the name because Thomas resembled the penguins in the cartoon classic *Madagascar*: cute and cuddly on the outside, but with a killer spirit inside. Thomas was the first Welshman to finish the Tour since Colin Lewis. He was a precocious talent who had won the junior Paris–Roubaix in 2004 and missed most of 2005 after an operation to remove his spleen. He had then become an integral part of the British 4000-metre team pursuit squad that took gold in the 2007 world championship and would go on to take the discipline to new levels of speed in 2008, together with Wiggins. Thomas showed his inner steel in that Tour, battling through to Paris in spite of one horrendous day in the south of France, losing his chubby infant's cheeks along the way. He returned to the Tour in 2010 and 2011, riding strongly for the newly formed Team Sky and wore the white jersey of best young rider in the 2010 race. 2012 was spent focussing on his ambitions in Olympic track cycling, but he could surprise many in the future when he is given the chance.

Cavendish and Thomas had much in common. They had raced the British youth circuit together since their early teens and had both come through the under-23 academy founded by former pro Rod Ellingworth with help from John Herety. In London, the pair had found themselves together again at the front when the first road-race stage halted briefly at Tower Bridge, a moment Thomas described as 'special, quite surreal'.

The objective was to produce a string of youngsters who could excel for the Olympic track team in the endurance disciplines: individual and team pursuit, points race, scratch, and the two-man Madison relay. As well as specific track skills, the best way to gain a foundation of fitness for these events was professional road racing, so the best riders from the academy, the 'graduates', would have to be placed with pro-road teams. Thomas, for example, was found a place at the South African Barloworld squad, and was riding the Tour to build an endurance base for the following year's Beijing Olympics.

Cavendish was among the first intake of six academicians in 2004; Thomas followed in 2005. The process was geared towards producing what ACBB had turned out by accident in the 1980s: young professional cyclists capable of looking after themselves. The youngsters were taught French, cooking (initially by Herety, a trained chef), hygiene and bike mechanics. In various ways, they were made to realise this was merely a stepping-stone in the path towards Olympic (and, in Cavendish's case, world) stardom. Firstly, there were their salaries, set at £2,500 a year, or £50 a week, because Ellingworth wanted to ensure his protégés stayed hungry. Like Robert Millar, Herety, Graham Jones and Sean Yates in Paris a quarter of a century before, if they won cash prizes at races, they could afford to splash out.

The academy intake were given bikes with componentry that was a grade lower than standard Olympic team issue: Shimano's Ultegra rather than Dura-Ace. Ellingworth drove the riders to races, but one was nominated as navigator and there was no mechanic or masseur. They had first-category rather than elite racing licences, a step lower than might have been expected. The ethos was 'boot camp' said Olympic Performance Director Dave Brailsford, with Ellingworth enforcing rigid discipline. If a rider turned up for training five minutes late, he did not start the session. After one race where, in Cavendish's words, 'they rode like wallys', Ellingworth made his protégés train hard in the rain for four and a half hours on a small circuit. Every now and then he would disappear, then pop up somewhere unexpected to make sure they weren't slacking.

The most celebrated escapade came when Cavendish drew a horse on the window of their terraced house. Every anatomical detail was correct, but the landlord was not amused. Nor were the members of the public walking past to the church opposite the house, and synagogue down the road. That episode earned the academicians three hours' riding flat out round the top of the Manchester vélodrome and a week washing the Olympic team cars every day.

Cavendish says that he would have made it as a professional had he not had his academy place, which is probably true given his personal drive, his speed and forward thinking, but he adds that the British cycling system helped him break through far faster than might otherwise have been the case. He was their first major success story when he won the world Madison championship in 2005, aged just nineteen, partnered by Rob Hayles. Ellingworth remains his coach and confidant and helped him to construct his Milan–San Remo triumph.

In 2008, Cavendish returned to the Tour, and while he was the same mix of confidence and raw emotion, much had changed. He was visibly thinner after finishing the first major Tour of his career, the Giro d'Italia. He had established himself as a stage winner in major Tours after taking two stages in the Giro, turning down a third when it was clear his lead-out man Andre Greipel could win it. His team was in its third different kit in twelve months. T-Mobile had pulled out the previous November after yet another doping scandal and had been replaced initially by the name High Road, the management company owned by Bob Stapleton, who was left holding the baby when the sponsor cut and run. At that Tour start in Brest, however, Stapleton announced a new lead sponsor: American clothing company Columbia.

In his second year in the hotseat, Stapleton had turned his team into a polyvalent squad dominated by thrusting youngsters, and critically including a core of highly competent lead-out men who could set up Cavendish for sprint finishes. Some, such as Greipel, his fellow German Gerald Ciolek, and the Austrian Bernhard Eisel were fine sprinters in their own right; others, such as Lance Armstrong's former right-hand-man George Hincapie were vastly experienced. After every win, Cavendish would hug them and thank them publicly. As he said, their sacrifice merely increased his motivation. 'When people push themselves that hard for you, you feel obliged to come away with the win.' In his autobiography, *Boy Racer*, which was dominated by his fortunes in the 2008 Tour, he began the book with a pen-portrait of each teammate. His heart was permanently on his sleeve, but as far as building team spirit went, it was in absolutely the right place. Ellingworth had noted the previous year that his protégé already had a team leader's ability 'to put an arm round someone, give them a bit of sympathy, get behind them, which is why he will be a success'.

Cavendish went through that Tour like an emotional whirlwind. 'I expect to do it,' he said, when asked beforehand if he thought he could win a stage. 'I'll be the best sprinter on the Tour.' He was grumpy with a television reporter who asked him what he had learned after a stage win eluded him early on (his answer, 'nothing' was worthy of Robert Millar) but was ecstatic in Châteauroux, Toulouse – a horror of a finish in the wet – Narbonne and Nîmes. The margins of victory were never narrow, hinting at the total dominance of 2009. Columbia's team work was exemplary, if not as seamless as it was to be the following year.

Those who believe sprinting is all glamour should hear Cav's account of a stage in the Pyrenees where he crashed when a football went into the bunch as they were lined out at 45kph. He 'did a table-top' through the air, and had to scrap all day merely to finish the stage. He was given a painkiller by the doctor, his stomach reacted badly, and he 'got through, just about'. Even then, his passion shone through: 'It's what makes cycling beautiful – the joy of winning, the pain of survival.' Not to mention the poetry of Mark Cavendish.

With four stage wins in his pocket, the rocket went home, to focus on the Olympic Games, without having been beaten in a flat stage finish. Even without the Manxman there were still one and a half British finishers in that Tour. Millar was one, having ridden strongly in the opening week, while the other was the half: the Kenyan Chris Froome, who was in the process of obtaining his British passport and didn't really have either nationality. Only twenty-three, Froome had the look of a man for the future, but in the long term it would not lie with his Barloworld team. The South African squad was one of four teams that had riders test positive, and the sponsor duly pulled out.

Cavendish had his frustrations too that summer. Pulling out of the Tour to focus on winning a gold in the Madison at the Olympic Games was the logical thing to do – he and Wiggins had dominated the field in the world champion-ship that March – but emotionally, if it didn't work, it was going to be a body blow. And so it panned out. In Beijing, Wiggins was on a rare bad day. He had been ill in the build-up to the Games and by the time the Madison came, he had probably pushed his body too far in winning gold medals in the team and individual pursuits. The pair were never in the running, and Cavendish was as livid as might be expected, yelling an expletive when he missed a change right in front of Tony Blair in the VIP box, then stalking out of the track centre with a face like thunder. Typically he had made no bones about the emotional terms on which he was racing, when he wrote in the *Guardian*: 'if we do not get a medal, we will have failed miserably.' Salt was rubbed in the wound when British Airways initially refused him a club-class ticket home, on the grounds that he had not won a medal. 'He was on his knees, absolutely devastated,' said Ellingworth. For the first time since his early teens, he did not want to ride his bike.

That autumn he announced he would never race the track again, but that spring he was back, at the world Madison championships alongside another Manx prodigy, Peter Kennaugh. By then he had re-established communication with Wiggins, although the pair had not spoken for two months after the Games. He remained bitter about quitting the Tour, 'the biggest regret of my career', he said in October 2008. 'I feel massively let down, I'm still bitter now. To leave the Tour de France to do that. I left the Tour de France when I was fighting for the green jersey and I could have potentially won on the Champs-Elysées.'

That particular gap was filled, emphatically, in July 2009, but astonishingly, given his dominance in every flat sprint finish, Cavendish did not bring home the green jersey. That award went to the hulking Norwegian Thor Hushovd – who won only one stage, at the top of a hill in Barcelona – and was effectively decided at the stage finish in Besançon, where Cavendish was relegated to last place for allegedly moving off his line to block the Norwegian in the build-up to the sprint. He was unhappy about it, words were exchanged in the media, and then Hushovd settled the issue by escaping during an Alpine stage to gather up points at intermediate sprints. The judges' verdict cost Cav thirteen points. His final deficit was ten.

Cavendish's achievements that July inevitably prompted one question: how does he do it? There were several answers, but the best place to start was in his mind. Whether you love him or find him irritating, Cavendish is a unique character, even among sprinters who are themselves a special breed of cyclist. Theirs is the only side of the sport in which contact is common, and that can include anything from an elbow in the ribs, to a full body lean, to a head-butt – all at over 40mph. 'Kill or be killed,' Cavendish says. Chris Boardman – who would have stayed a million miles from the stuff that goes on in the Tour finish straight – compared Tour sprinting to fighting, in which a person is driven by adrenalin. 'If you have the slightest doubt, you think "I'm going to lose", your body starts thinking of alternatives, how to get away, it shuts things down.'

Boardman felt that Cavendish's amazing strike record in the sprint could not be separated from the raw emotion he showed at other times. 'Mark simply believes he is going to win, so all the adrenalin and everything else he needs to put himself in a position to win happens.' As Boardman said '[after a race] he comes across as a right dick sometimes, but it's because you have caught someone in a totally emotional state. That's where he has to be to do the job.' As Cavendish says, 'There's that little thing in your head that says: "If this happens now, I'm fucked." Well, I don't have that.'

Cavendish's character helped him overcome something else, something more insidious. Through the 1990s and into the noughties, cycling had become dominated by figures: power-to-weight ratio, pulse rates, power outputs. That was the case in professional cycling, and it was also the culture in the British track cycling team. 'Hitting the numbers' was what counted. It went back to Chris Boardman and Peter Keen and was clearly the best way to achieve results in most track disciplines. In the timed events in particular, the equation was simple: if a cyclist could produce a certain power output for a given time – 'hit the numbers' in other words – he or she could be a contender.

Cavendish ran completely counter to all that. He was not a lab rat who could produce a result on a treadmill, then replicate it in competition. He was rubbish at testing, but supremely talented when he had his race head on. As a result, he had a rocky relationship with Simon Jones, the GB head coach of the time, and in a similar vein, the physiologist at T-Mobile initially believed Cavendish's 'numbers' meant he would not even be able to stay with the bunch. Not surprisingly, in view of his character, the more he was written off, the more he wanted to succeed. Like Lance Armstrong, he has a 'list' of people who have written him off. Like Armstrong, when he has a point to prove he is 'six times stronger'. Additionally, at critical moments he was fortunate to find people who believed in him: Ellingworth and another senior GB coach, Heiko Salzwedel; Stapleton and the managers at T-Mobile/High Road/Columbia.

There are also elements of Armstrong in Cavendish's obsessive nature, which means he can recall every move in a sprint finish. This is reminiscent of Hoban as well. It also means he is a quick learner, whether it be in pro racing, or at the academy. While Cav hasn't bought into the number culture, he is a firm believer in the Great Britain philosophy of 'marginal gains', such as looking after your own feeding in a race, fitting just the right wheels for the conditions. He doesn't 'do' psychology, but does visualisation in the sense that he thinks intensely about every race finish. As he said in one interview, 'When I wake up at night, I'm not thinking about a woman, but the next finish.'

He has other assets, too: the empathy with his teammates that Ellingworth noticed early on must have helped to mould Columbia into the seamless sprint train that guided Cavendish to the finish straight all through 2009. But it's not just about his teammates. Cavendish has the right people around him in other areas. Ellingworth is one of the canniest and most imaginative coaches in cycling. Stapleton was the right boss for him in the right place, another example of the way cycling has opened up in the last decade. Hiring the Tour's most consistent sprinter of recent years, Erik Zabel, to advise Cavendish, looks to have been an inspired move.

Physically, Cavendish is nothing special in the sense that he is not imposing in the way Mario Cipollini was, for example. On the other hand, his size is another plus-point. He is stocky rather than the usual long-legged cyclist, and sits much lower on the bike than most. In a finish sprint he projects himself right over the front wheel, somehow managing to keep control while pedalling out of the saddle at up to 200rpm. His aerodynamic advantage is hard to quantify, but at a speed of 45mph, being smaller and lower makes a huge difference. It also lowers his centre of gravity. He has another, unquantifiable quality. Somehow, in a bunch, he has the ability to ride while expending less energy than the others. Cav says it's partly pedalling ability, partly a knack for finding the right place to be, and the latter is an X-factor that has been identified in other greats, the best example being Stephen Roche, Tour winner for Ireland in 1987.

The sheer level of Cavendish's desire for victory is constantly on show, and it goes back to his formative years. It made him a fixture on the ferries between the Isle of Man and the mainland as a teenager, because every racing trip was a major logistical exercise in itself. How many teenagers are happy to get a midnight ferry, arrive somewhere at dawn, eat, wait for their race, then catch another ferry home again, time after time, because they are certain that they will eventually be the best in their chosen field? On at least one occasion, aged just fourteen, he went alone when his father couldn't take him. His mother Adele recalled that at school, when Cav was asked to choose GCSE subjects, a teacher asked him what he wanted to be when he left. 'When Mark said he wanted to be a pro cyclist, the teacher asked him what he wanted to do if he didn't achieve that. Mark just said, "I want to be a pro cyclist."'

*

Cavendish's future in the Tour is open to any kind of speculation: the history books are there for him to rewrite given a fair wind and good health. To paraphrase the French saying, the more he gets the hungrier he becomes, or as he says, he needs new targets, all the time. In the 2011 Tour, the green jersey was his stated objective and it duly came his way, and could well do more than once. The yellow jersey should also fall to him along the way, as it has to other greats of the finish straight such as Maertens, Cipollini, Sean Kelly and Erik Zabel, although the sprinters are put at a disadvantage by the Tour organisers' decision to do away with time bonuses for stage victories. By the end of the 2012 Tour, Cavendish had taken his tally of wins on the Champs Elysées to four in a row, another record.

He had also worn the rainbow stripes of world champion after taking the title with aplomb to complete one of the most cohesive performances ever in the race by any team. Great Britain were ably marshalled by Millar and Wiggins, the culmination of a two-year plan devised by Ellingworth and labelled 'project rainbow jersey'. His green jersey win – the first by a Briton – and world title earned Cavendish the coveted BBC Sports Personality of the Year award.

At the Tour, given his relative youth, the Manxman should be able to aim for the history books' rankings of career stage wins.

His total of twenty-three stages in five years makes even Eddy Merckx's all-time tally of thirty-five look vulnerable. With reference to 'Big Ted', one of the most experienced observers of the sport, the *L'Equipe* writer Philippe Brunel, felt that Cavendish's Milan–San Remo victory had resonances of Merckx's first win in *La Primavera* in 1966, at which point the Belgian was pigeonholed as a mere sprinter. Cav may not know it, but when he says he needs to win every time he sees a chequered flag, that is the 'Cannibal' spirit. Longer-term targets include the world road title in 2010 or

2011, and the London Olympic Games, where he will be a favourite for the road race and may ride the omnium, a multi-discipline track event where his sheer speed will come into play.

Perhaps without realising it, Cavendish has already been an inspirational force. He was certainly a role model for the thrusting youngsters flocking to race on Britain's velo-dromes and road-race circuits from 2008 onwards. More tangibly, Cavendish's 'winningness' early in 2007 confirmed to the Great Britain Performance Director Dave Brailsford that now was the time to push on with his goal of setting up a professional road team with the aim of putting a Briton on the top step of the Tour de France podium.

Cav's four stage wins in the 2008 Tour clearly played a role in inspiring Sky Television to back Brailsford's baby, as he provided undeniable, uplifting evidence of what British cyclists could achieve without taking drugs. If a loud-mouthed 'fat banker' – as Cav described his eighteen-year-old self – could come from nowhere to be the fastest man in the world within two years of starting the Tour, why should British cyclists not aim for the yellow jersey? The world championship win was followed by Cavendish joining Sky in a multi-million pound deal, but it wasn't that simple. The same year saw him eclipsed by the main beneficiary of Sky's entry to the pro ranks, a name that would have seemed completely unexpected back in 2008: Cav's Beijing Madison partner, Bradley Wiggins.

CHAPTER FOURTEEN

The Sky is the limit

It was a throwaway comment, but not one you would expect from a cyclist who had won an Olympic gold medal, a silver and two bronzes by the age of twenty-five. At a stage start late on in the 2007 Tour de France, Bradley Wiggins was mulling over his fourth place in the time trial at Albi – which could be considered a second place given that two of the riders who finished ahead of him subsequently tested positive. The placing had surprised the Londoner, who had gone into the race principally to win the prologue time trial and had not expected to be so fresh at the start of the final week. 'You know,' he mused, 'I really didn't realise I was that good.' It was my companion who pointed out: "Mate, you've got to remember you are an Olympic champion."'

At the time, Wiggins had no idea that two years later he would match Robert Millar's British best placing in the Tour by finishing fourth in the 2009 race, earning the respect of Lance Armstrong, the best Tour de France specialist cycling has seen. Nor would he have predicted that he would end up spearheading a British assault on the race by a British team. No one else saw it coming either. We only knew that Wiggins, the Olympic pursuit champion in 2004, had unfulfilled potential in road racing. We had seen glimpses of what could be, but it was an open question whether Wiggins would ever manage to exploit his potential to the full and if he did, what the outcome might be.

As far as I am concerned, the Wiggins Tour of 2009 began in a car park in Abergavenny. That was a mini-milestone: it was probably the last time he could appear at a bike race in

Britain without being mobbed by autograph hunters. Wiggins was pinning on his race numbers in the back of his 4x4 before starting the national road championship, when I asked him about the Tour. 'I'm going for the top twenty, top fifteen, maybe even the top ten, but you had better only write top twenty,' he said. He had a plan: place in the top three in the prologue time trial in Monaco, then bank on his Garmin team doing a strong ride in the team time trial a few days later to take the yellow jersey. After that, who knew what would happen?

Road racing not being an exact science, I kept an open mind. On various occasions in the past Wiggins had told me that he was going to have a serious go on the road and I had duly run the stories in the paper, but it had never quite worked out. However, there had been interesting hints of what his physical ability could offer, beginning in 2005, when he won a mountain stage in the Tour de l'Avenir. During the 2007 Tour, there had been that time trial placing at Albi, but equally significant was the stage in the Alps when the Tour crossed the Iseran, the highest pass regularly climbed by the race. I remembered Wiggins telling me afterwards, quite casually, that he had remained in the lead group to the top, with no difficulty, then slipped to the back later to save his strength. In 2007, when he had been forced to leave the race with four days remaining, he was still fresh physically. Clearly, he could handle the day-to-day workload on the Tour.

But what about the mental side? The modern Tour requires continual focus for every minute of the three-and-a-half weeks, on and off the bike. There was nothing in Wiggins's road racing career to suggest this could happen, and no precedent to imply that a rider with outstanding ability to prepare for four years for the Olympic games could transfer that talent to the Tour at the drop of a hat. But the point is that Wiggins is a big event specialist. 'He likes to do one thing well, and there is no one better than him at making it happen,' said his trainer Matt Parker. As Wiggins told me, having achieved his Olympic goals by 2008 when he won two further golds, he felt he had no option but to move on, rapidly. 'The reason why this is happening now is that it has to. I need to do it. When I won Olympic medals on the track I needed to win for my own self-esteem, my ego. The road has always been fun, a bonus, so I'd go through the 2007 Tour getting up there in the time trials, making a big break one day, just enjoying it. After Beijing there were no more excuses. I couldn't just go and waltz around the Tour because there was nothing to drop back to. The time came when I had to put some effort into it.'

Wiggins himself said of the key final week of the race, when one important day is immediately followed by another, and another, that it was similar to 'going for three Olympic golds in four or five days. Mentally it's tough, you have to back up a mountain stage with a time trial, you've been doing the same thing for three weeks, eating the same omelette and rice but it's nothing mind-numbing.' By 2009, he had ample experience of 'backing up' in three Olympic Games, beginning with Sydney, where he had ridden the team pursuit and Madison. In Athens, he had taken gold, silver and bronze in the pursuit, team pursuit and Madison. In Beijing, it had not quite worked out, but in the world track championship in Manchester, that spring, he had taken gold in all three events.

The Great Britain team psychiatrist Steve Peters had helped Wiggins to deal with the pressure of pursuiting, where a rider competes two or three times a day. He approached the Tour in the same way, again with support from Peters. 'In a race like the Tour, if you think three or four days ahead, you think it's an eternity and lose the plot. In a pursuit series I never think about the final, just about qualifying. Then you break it down, almost a hundred metres by a hundred metres. You don't think about the next stage until you've finished the one before.' Wiggins had taught himself to deal with a 4000m pursuit as two six-lap races of 1500m, with the final kilometre 'taking care of itself'. During the Tour, he noted that the press had become frustrated with his unwillingness to discuss the stages that lay ahead, but as he told me 'that's pointless. It's like climbing Kilimanjaro and thinking of the summit when you've barely begun. You don't do that. You set up base camp, then camp one, two and so on.'

The 2009 Tour was a classic example of events falling into place for a man in perfect shape to seize the opportunity. Although he had begun building to the race in December 2008, Wiggins said later that in January 2009 'I never expected to be in the top five at the Tour, no way, no way at all. I thought I'd do everything and see what happens, so I just ended up becoming a jack of all trades. [In January 2009] I didn't know if I was coming or going in the sport.' That lack of direction was reflected in the fact that he was riding for his third team in three years. He had quit Cofidis after the doping scandal to join Mark Cavendish at T-Mobile, then moved on at the end of 2008, because he saw the risk of being pigeonholed as a lead-out man for the Manxman.

So the start of 2009 was another new beginning, in the team that Jonathan Vaughters and David Millar had founded as Slipstream, which now had satnav company Garmin as its main sponsor. His first goal was the Paris–Nice prologue time trial, but defeat there rocked his confidence a little. 'I thought, "What am I going to do now?" so I went to the Classics, rode strongly there, thought, "Maybe I'll do Paris–Roubaix next year" because I finished twenty-third and hardly tried. Then I went to the Giro and was climbing well, and everyone was like "You're climbing well" and I was like "Well, but I'm not going to do anything am I?"'

In the Giro, eyebrows were raised when Wiggins out-climbed Armstrong on an early mountain-top finish, but his opportunity came after Christian Vande Velde crashed out, leaving the Londoner free to ride his own race. From his sofa, the American talked Wiggins through the race. 'He was watching the telly and kept texting me and ringing me up, he kind of coaxed me through the rest of it and gave me the confidence to hit the Tour and try to do something on general classification. So when I got to Monaco and stupidly said I thought I could get top twenty in the Tour and everyone burst out laughing, I was quite confident in myself because I'd seen the numbers and knew what I was at.'

Key among those numbers was his weight. When I saw him in that Abergavenny car park, he was emaciated even by professional cycling standards. The day before, he had had his final check-up with the Great Britain team dietician, Nigel Mitchell, who had told him he was at his target fat level, 4 per cent, and his target weight, seventy-one kilos, seven kilos lighter than when he had crossed the Iseran with the best in the race in 2007. It was not a healthy fat level, but as he told me, 'When I get home, [my wife] Cath is going to force feed me cake.' It had taken nine months to achieve that weight, but it was critical. He estimated that one kilo of body weight equated to a minute in time up a thirty-minute climb. 'That adds up to about ten minutes over a three-week race, and if you start to add up the fact that you are shifting less weight every time you go up any little rolling hills, every time you sprint out of a corner, it accumulates to a lot of time and energy.'

With the help of Nigel Mitchell and his trainer Matt Parker, the weight loss had been achieved gradually. Part of it was simply down to stopping track racing, which had resulted in a reduction in his upper body muscle (pursuits include standing starts, which call for strong shoulders and biceps). Relatively little of his power output had gone:

Parker estimated that at his Tour weight he could have done 4min 17sec for the 4000m pursuit, a couple of seconds slower than in Beijing. Just before the Tour, according to Vaughters, Wiggins had managed to hold 482 watts for twenty minutes in a time trial, figures comparable with those of a Tour winner such as Armstrong.

His third place in the opening time trial, to the London winner Fabian Cancellara, showed he was at the right level, as did Garmin's storming ride in the team time trial at Montpellier a few days later. With the time for the stage taken on the fifth rider, the American team took a huge gamble by racing the later part with the bare minimum: Wiggins, David Millar, Vande Velde, another American David Zabriskie, and the Canadian Ryder Hesjedal. The other four Garmin riders had been unable to hold the pace in the strong winds, on a difficult course of twisting lanes. But if one of the quintet had punctured or crashed, valuable time would have been lost. By the end of the team time trial, Wiggins was in sixth place overall. It was not quite as he had planned, but he could not have expected Cancellara's amazing form, nor that the Swiss's team, CSC, would put up a strong ride for second place in Montpellier.

So far, the script envisaged by Wiggins had been followed with one minor glitch. That came on the pancake-flat stage to La Grande Motte, when Cavendish and his teammates were joined in a late attack by Armstrong as the front of the race split in a strong crosswind. Armstrong was too seasoned a campaigner to ignore the opportunity to gain a little time and the 40 sec he gained on all the other overall favourites had ramifications later in the Tour for Wiggins.

For the Briton, however, the first step into the unknown came when the Tour entered the Pyrenees three days later, finishing up a long, steady climb to the Arcalis ski resort in Andorra. Since the days of Miguel Indurain the first summit finish in the Tour has tended to dictate the pattern for the rest of the race, and at Arcalis the eventual winner Alberto Contador sprang clear, while behind Wiggins rode strongly in an eleven-man group that included all the race favourites. That moved him up to fifth overall, and the question now was how far would he get before he cracked? Because surely he would crack at some point. Wouldn't he? But he rode strongly in the next day's stage over the Tourmalent, and come the Alps ten days later, there he was, showing no signs of pressure. His attitude to the race was summed up during a television interview when he was asked how he and his Garmin mates would deal with the day ahead. He responded with glorious British understatement. 'We'll eat our Weetabix and get on with it.' On the grimmest day between the Pyrenees and the Alps, a chilly, rain-soaked marathon through the Vosges, he showed no signs of stress.

This was a curiously constructed Tour, reflecting the desire of the new director Christian Prudhomme to shake up the race by breaking with the more predictable routes devised by his predecessor Jean-Marie Leblanc. In 2008 Prudhomme had temporarily dispensed with the prologue time trial; in 2009, he included only one full-length time trial stage, and that came between two days in the Alps and a final setpiece on the closing Saturday, up Mont Ventoux, no less. The Alpine stages opened with a summit finish at Verbier, and here something truly astonishing happened. Armstrong was dropped, and the man who upped the pace as the seven-times winner fell back was none other than Wiggins, who described watching himself dropping the great man at the finish as 'an out-of-body experience'.

According to Sean Yates, then a *directeur sportif* at Astana with Armstrong, the Texan and his team manager Johan Bruyneel were concerned about Wiggins in the final week of the Tour rather than more obvious candidates. 'They were most worried about him from Verbier, because he wasn't showing any cracks, he was following the pace. There was an element of uncertainty about him – he had come out of the woodwork to this point, how much more does he have?'

Wiggins was the focus of Armstrong's attention on the next day's stage to Le Grand Bornand, because he had climbed over the Texan in the standings, to third overall. That proved to be the toughest and most decisive day in the race, when Contador and the Luxembourgeois Schleck brothers, Frank and Andy, put the hammer down to clinch first place overall for the Spaniard and second for Andy. Armstrong, meanwhile, had to contend with Wiggins after they both fell off the pace on the Col de Romme, a short steep ascent off the Col de Colombière. That was closely followed by the Colombière itself, where Armstrong made a late attack to move into third overall, pushing Wiggins down to sixth.

The cards were shuffled a little again the next day, in the time trial stage around Aix-les-Bains. Here, Wiggins's third place to Contador and his old nemesis Fabian Cancellara meant he moved back up to fourth, setting the stage for the final showdown on the Ventoux. A searing pace was set through the vineyards to the foot of the climb, and, like Tom Simpson thirty-two years before him, Wiggins knew that his overall placing depended on the nine miles to the observatory. In a bizarre quirk of history, Wiggins was inspired by his ill-fated predecessor. He rode with a picture of the 'Major', and was duly inspired to hang on even though, for the first time in the race, he was struggling to hold the best in the field in the final couple of kilometres. 'It felt as if Tom was waiting for me,' he told *Guardian* writer Donald McRae. 'As I began the climb, it felt as if his spirit was riding with me. I imagined how Tom must have been feeling, riding towards his death, and the feeling grew as I climbed.'

Andy Schleck of Luxembourg, who was to finish second to Contador, attacked a dozen times in a vain attempt to break the Spaniard. That meant the rhythm was staccato rather than the sustained pace that would have suited Wiggins. 'It was horrible. I thought, "I can't go on, I can't do this any more . . ." But then I thought more vividly of Tom and how he must have felt that last day. It was like a reason not to give up. I felt I was doing it for his memory.' Wiggins was not the only one to pay tribute to 'Tommy' that day, although the Tour did not go to the trouble of laying an official wreath at his memorial (the organisers seem uneasy about recognising Simpson in any way, probably because of the drug connection, something which has offended the family). Mark Cavendish removed his crash helmet, while Charly Wegelius threw out a water bottle to be added to the tributes, and David Millar a cotton racing hat on which he had written 'Tommy Simpson RIP, David Millar'. Those tributes to the dead pioneer were followed by Cavendish's utter dominance the next day on the Champs-Elysées, marking an astonishing end to a Tour in which Wiggins and the Manxman had rewritten the history books and taken cycling in their country to a new level.

At the start of 2004, I began helping Wiggins produce a series of columns for the *Observer* that ran until 2009. To call it ghost-writing would be to do him a disservice: his ability to talk in depth about his sport meant that all I had to do was shuffle what he told me into what seemed like a sensible order. It was the job from heaven in some ways, because Wiggins is legendary for his encyclopaedic knowledge of cycling history. At times, he can seem almost trainspotterish. John Herety recalls that on early trips with Great Britain he would tell the older riders what kind of shoes they had been wearing ten years earlier when he was a kid with their poster on his wall. But his eye for detail meant he could explain to the readers in layman's terms what it was that made Lance Armstrong special, how a lead-out 'train' worked, or what it felt like to ride an Olympic pursuit.

Wiggins's fan-like knowledge is hardly surprising in one sense, given his background. His late father, the Australian pro Garry Wiggins, was one of the best riders in six-day track racing in the 1980s. Bradley was born in Ghent, erstwhile home of Tom Simpson and Barry Hoban. But after Garry walked out on his young family before Bradley's second birthday, his wife Linda might have been forgiven for keeping her son clear of her estranged husband's passion after she and Bradley returned to London. After all, the lad was keen on other sports, starting with the dog racing he watched with his grandfather, and, more seriously, football. Later, boxing would be another passion. But it was Linda who sat her son down to watch Chris Boardman win the pursuit gold medal in Barcelona, sparking the love of the Olympics that Wiggins still hopes will take him to five Games.

Young Wiggins began racing in club events on the unopened Hayes bypass in West London, where the facilities amounted to a table set up under an umbrella by the man who had run the Milk Race in the 1960s, Chas Messenger. He enjoyed a precocious rise. By 1997 he had won all there was to win in British junior racing – a year early. The junior pursuit world title followed in 1998, and that year, at eighteen, Wiggins was one of the England team who took silver in the Commonwealth Games in Kuala Lumpur. By happy coincidence, the start of his senior career coincided precisely with the formation of Peter Keen's Lottery-funded Great Britain team and he and the squad have grown hand in hand.

Like David Millar, like Cavendish, there is much more to Wiggins than just cycling: his young family, his vintage guitar collection – twelve or thirteen he estimated in 2009 plus the cheaper version that accompanies the team bus – his passion for the Jam, the Who and Oasis, his short-lived collection of Belgian beer. His guitar-playing has left him with a tight back and shoulder that have to be loosened up by a physio before a time trial. He is also modern cycling's most talented mimic. His Shane Sutton is a wonder, so too his Mark Cavendish, and he once completely spooked me by doing a perfect impersonation of David Millar down the phone from the Giro. Arguably his finest moment as a two-wheeled humourist was during the 2009 Tour when, after the French press alleged that Mark Cavendish was a 'racist' who did not like their country, he put the Garmin team bus's curtain over his head mimicking Ku-Klux-Klan headgear and baited the Manxman as he passed.

Wiggins is every bit as emotionally connected to his cycling as Cavendish, although he lacks the Manxman's willingness to put his emotions on public view. The Weetabix quote typifies the laid-back, stoic, very British persona he adopts in public. He can seem ice-cold, but can admit to being terrified before a time trial start or will rant for half an hour on the phone about something that has annoyed him. His 2008 autobiography, *In Pursuit of Glory*, went into detail about his ambivalent feelings about the death of his father, and explored the drink and depression that followed his 2004 Olympic gold medal in Athens. Back then, he came across as something of a dreamer. Over the years, however, the idealism has remained, but he has become more hard-headed about where his talent can take him.

There were times, many of them, when he would simply disappear and wouldn't answer his phone. I learned that there was no point calling him more than once. It was the Great Britain psychiatrist Steve Peters who pointed out that while many athletes can be said to resemble dogs, in that they are always around looking for attention, there are some who are like tigers. There are times when the latter retire to their lairs and then they come to you when they need you. He didn't mention Wiggins by name – or Robert

Millar for that matter – but the parallel was obvious. The only conclusion you can draw is that Wiggins is shutting out all distractions bar his family and getting on with his work.

If parallels are to be drawn, superficially Wiggins has a little in common with Chris Boardman. They share a background in track pursuiting, with gold medals at Olympic and world championship level. Both then used that talent to win time trials on the road. In the run-up to Wiggins's first Olympic title in the pursuit at Athens in 2004, Boardman played a valuable mentoring role for the younger man.

But the differences are as important as the similarities. Far more was expected of Boardman in the Tour de France. With hindsight, too much was expected of him given that his background was one where he rode time trials with occasional forays into road racing. Wiggins, on the other hand, was never seen as a contender for success in the Tour. It was never on his radar, in spite of the fact that as a youth he was a fearsome road racer who rode the 1998 world junior championships for Great Britain and by the end of 2000, aged all of twenty, he had a pro-road racing contract in his pocket with the ill-fated Linda McCartney team managed by Sean Yates. As an amateur, he won European stage races such as the Tour of Mallorca and the Flèche du Sud in Luxembourg. For ten years, however, the Olympics remained Wiggins's priority: road racing was what he did to get fit for the pursuit.

By 2006, when Wiggins made his Tour debut, he had been racing for European teams since 2002. He was the first and most high-profile example of the Great Britain team's philosophy that its track endurance riders would benefit from racing in Europe at the highest level. In essence, a Grand Tour was the best way to get the foundation for the intense work needed to win gold medals in the team and individual pursuits. He had got through the Giro d'Italia in

2003 – using it as preparation for the world pursuit championship – and had moved to Boardman's old team Crédit Agricole in 2004. He had not been happy at the French squad, and they had clearly not known how to deal with him.

When he made his Tour debut in 2006 for Cofidis, it was relatively uneventful. Wiggins was in awe of the great race. He told the *Observer* he was one of three *domestiques* in the team of nine and had spent the race fetching bottles for his team leaders, and towing his superiors back to the bunch after they punctured. He raced strongly in the time trial at Rennes in the first week but his task was solely to go hard in order to give the Cofidis team leader Sylvain Chavanel some times for reference. The only item he noted which had any significance with the benefit of hindsight was that he recovered well, 'waking before the alarm goes in the morning, falling asleep easily at night, and waking up really hungry'.

For Wiggins, that debut was ruined when the first man to Paris, Floyd Landis, tested positive for testosterone: he was even more devastated than when David Millar had been unmasked in 2004. Wiggins had suffered to finish the race, but Landis had ruined that achievement for him. He spoke briefly, in the heat of emotion, about quitting the sport, but the following year, he started as one of the favourites for the London time-trial prologue. He had reconnoitred the course at 3 a.m. one Sunday morning – the only time he could find when an absence of traffic meant he could go full pelt through the corners – and finished a worthy fourth.

His was a bizarre race that year. The high of London was followed by another fine moment, a 117-mile lone escape en route to Bourg-en-Bresse just before the race entered the Alps. It was the fortieth anniversary of Tom Simpson's death, but that was not in Wiggins's mind. Initially he hoped to take other riders with him, but once he embarked on his suicide mission, he knew how much television time he would earn, and this was his wife Cath's birthday: by being there in front of her on the box, they could share the day in a way.

By the Pyrenees, buoyed up by his fourth place in the Albi time trial, he was looking confidently at finishing in Paris and was expecting to push for the stage win in the final time trial at Angoulême. But as the tour descended once again into drug-related chaos, his race was cut short in the most bizarre way possible. With the man who had beaten him in Albi, Alexandr Vinokourov, out of the race after testing positive, and the race leader Mikael Rasmussen of Denmark under massive pressure after being misleading over his whereabouts for random testing, the atmosphere was frenzied when the announcement came that Wiggins's teammate Cristian Moreni had tested positive for testosterone.

No sooner had they finished the toughest mountain stage of the race, finishing on the Col d'Aubisque, than the entire Cofidis team were taken away for questioning by police, as was now customary. They then withdrew from the Tour, as was also now customary. It was utterly surreal to call Wiggins after that stage and hear him say: 'We are going somewhere with the police cars, no idea what is going to happen.' It was also profoundly disturbing on an emotional level. I liked the guy, and – unlike with David Millar – I had no doubts that he was clean: why the hell should he suffer and be besmirched because someone in his team was unable to race without doping? But any disillusionment in my mind was as nothing compared to how Wiggins obviously felt. His feelings were clearly summed up: before he boarded the aeroplane home the next day, he stuffed his Cofidis kit in an airport bin. To the best of my knowledge he was never seen wearing it again.

On 13 July 2007, as Wiggins was speeding on his lone break towards Bourg-en-Bresse, the Great Britain Performance

Director Dave Brailsford met the small British press contingent in a bar. There Brailsford told us of his plan to launch a British professional team to race the Tour, building on the structure that had helped form four of the five British starters in the race, and which had been behind the rehabilitation of the fifth, David Millar. The idea had first been mooted by Brailsford and his fellow manager at the Olympic team, Shane Sutton – he of the ANC squad back in 1987 – at the previous year's Commonwealth Games. Most dramatic of all was the goal Brailsford announced: to win the Tour de France within five years, with a British rider, and do it clean. 'We've had a feeling that the riders were coming through but having the feeling and having it confirmed are two different things. You see someone like Geraint [Thomas] charging down the prologue course and being best rider in his team at twenty-one and you realise it's on.'

On that day in Bourg-en-Bresse it was not obvious who that British rider might be. What was clear, however, was that, suddenly, British riders were moving through from track to road racing in ever-greater numbers. Wiggins, Cavendish, Thomas and Charly Wegelius were not the only products of the Great Britain set-up in the European professional ranks. Other track riders such as Paul Manning and Ed Clancy – future gold medallists in Beijing – and Steve Cummings were all racing respectably. The academy had another Manx star in the making in Jonny Bellis (whose career was ultimately to be stymied by an appalling moped crash), while the Yorkshireman Ben Swift was also forging ahead. Yet another Manxman, Peter Kennaugh, was waiting in the wings. All Brailsford was lacking was the sponsor, but the vast public support at the London start in 2007 had convinced him that big money backers would be interested. In the spring of 2008, with the world track cycling championships out of the way, and a massive haul of nine golds in the bag, he began to devote time to putting together a package for potential sponsors.

The obvious answer to the sponsorship question came in early June 2008. Just after Brailsford left a Sports Journalists' Association lunch in Fleet Street – where he had gone into further detail about the project – he was informed that British Sky Broadcasting had agreed to enter a major sponsorship deal with the Olympic team. Sky's backing for his professional team was not formalised until February 2009, but from late July 2008 it looked almost inevitable. Just before the British team left for Beijing, the satellite television company's deal with British Cycling was made public. Their 'multimillion pound' involvement ranged from backing the best track racers via the Sky+HD squad (confirmed after the Olympic Games) to running SkyRides, a series of mass participation events in major cities.

Putting the team together began, Brailsford said later, from the moment he got off the plane at Heathrow after directing the GB cycling team to eight gold medals in the Beijing Olympics. Most teams that compete in the UCI's ProTour have roots in some existing structure. They are developed from a lower-division team or are a breakaway from an existing squad. Brailsford was building from the ground up. By late September 2008 he had found the lead *directeur sportif* he thought he wanted: the Australian Scott Sunderland, a former teammate of Robert Millar at TVM and Chris Boardman at GAN. Sunderland had guided Carlos Sastre to victory in that year's Tour for the Danish team CSC, but by September 2009 the cracks were already showing and his time at Sky would be brief. CSC's logistics manager Carsten Jeppesen joined, so too their press officer Brian Nygaard and a handful of riders. Sean Yates, the legendary 'Tonk' himself, was a name that came up early on when possible *directeurs sportifs* were discussed: Yates was the only Briton to go on to a senior role with major European teams, having worked at CSC and with Lance

Armstrong at Astana and Discovery. His signing was announced at the end of 2009.

The way things were done at Sky mirrored the philosophy that had taken the British track cycling team to world domination: success is achieved by 'aggregation of marginal gains', by a multitude of tiny improvements that add up to a significant improvement. Looking for marginal gains means there are no givens. Tradition is thrown out of the window. Every detail had to be as perfectly performance oriented as could be, from the interior lighting of the team bus 'designed in conjunction with the team's psychiatrist' to the paint on the floor of the workshop (spotless white so that if any nuts or bolts were dropped they could be seen clearly and instantly picked up), and the selection of the team staff. The team's colours were based around a thin blue line (blue for Sky, natch), to represent 'the fine line between winning and losing'. The line went through everything to do with the team, down to the toothpaste and M&Ms in the riders' rooms at their first training camp. It extended to giving the riders 'ownership' over their racing and training schedules and consulting them over ground rules such as whether the team bus waited for late comers.

The difference between the British Olympic team approach and the traditional pro team had been summed up by David Millar in 2006. 'Instead of hiring big guns and expecting them to perform, British Cycling hire guys with expertise to get the best out of the riders. ProTour teams expect riders to get the best out of themselves but if Dave has an athlete in his charge, he sees it as his duty to get the best out of them.' Traditionally, *directeurs sportifs* had had a dual role: running the team on the road and giving training advice. Sky avoided any confusion by having *directeurs* to do the on-the-road stuff and a 'race trainer', the academy founder Rod Ellingworth. The fact that he was also still in touch with Mark Cavendish would prove to come in handy too.

Sky focused heavily on performance analysis – a vital element in the Beijing medal haul – with the team bus specially adapted to carry mainframe computers. Additionally, there was to be a 'battle bus' that would travel to the finish of a Tour stage, to feed television pictures on the run-in back to the riders' bus before the start so that the riders could be briefed by video rather than by looking at a plan in the race manual. As might be expected, Brailsford's team adopted the British Cycling philosophy on anti-doping. In June 2009, Brailsford underlined the basic rules: no riders or staff with previous doping convictions – in an ironic little twist, this disqualified David Millar – and no doctors who had any connection with cycling. Although he later softened the second rule when he controversially hired Dr Geert Leinders who had worked at Rabbank during the Michael Rasmussen days. The riders would be vetted before they were signed, and would be monitored in the same way as the Olympic squad, with their data examined by the then Olympic team doctor Roger Palfreeman.

At the world championships in Lugano in September 2009 a vast pile of rider contracts appeared on a table in the GB hotel for Brailsford to sign. The structure of the team was in place. A base was being planned in the Tuscan town of Quarrata, home to Max Sciandri, the GB academy, and academy alumni such as Swift, Cavendish, Thomas and Cummings. That included a performance laboratory on top of the usual elements such as workshops and stores. Most of the twenty-six riders had been named, with the biggest name among them the Norwegian Edvald Boasson Hagen, the hottest young property in the sport.

As far as the British contingent went, there were notable absentees, starting with Cavendish, who had made it clear he was happy at Columbia-HTC for the time being. Millar was out of the picture, so too Wegelius, who had been *persona non grata* with the Great Britain team management since the world championship in 2005 when he had worked for the

Italians while wearing a Great Britain jersey. Even so, the team included Thomas, Swift, Cummings and Kennaugh, another academy graduate in Ian Stannard, Chris Froome, who had taken British Nationality at the end of 2008. Most of the rest were Australians and Scandinavians, as English was the team's working language.

One thing was lacking: the Tour leader. The whole cycling world knew it had to be Wiggins, if the contractual wrinkles could be ironed out. Brailsford had told me the previous March he expected the pursuit champion to come on board, but that was before he became a hot property on the world stage. Shane Sutton had let it slip in June, then hastily retracted it. But from being another highly talented Briton with potential, Wiggins then suddenly became a contender for the podium in the Tour – and as Greg LeMond said, if you are going for the podium, you are going for the win. Not unreasonably, Garmin clung to the fact that their man had a second year to run on his contract, and a tug of love of football proportions was in the offing. It was new territory for British cycling, because the sport's transfer system is not straightforward, depending on a three-way agreement between the two teams involved and the ruling ProTour council.

After six months of speculation, Wiggins was finally presented to the press at a hastily convened briefing on 10 December 2009, just around the corner from the London hotel where he had worked as a carpenter in his amateur days. Asked what it had taken to make Garmin agree, Brailsford was tight-lipped: 'Common sense'. Plus, one suspected, a cheque. The deal had been on a knife-edge at times. Wiggins later revealed, 'It nearly didn't happen at one point; I didn't have a job for a week.' But whatever the ins and outs, the Sky chequebook was an enabling factor, not the main attraction. Wiggins felt he was returning to the people who had guided his career since he had turned to British cycling after the Linda McCartney team went bust in early 2001.

'Last year, the one thing I always came back to was the British team,' he said at the team launch. 'There was the British nutritionist, I had a trainer who was with British cycling – Matt Parker – I went on British Cycling training camps in January, paid for by British Cycling, all my nutritional products came from British Cycling, paid for by them. Between the Giro and Tour I stayed in Manchester and all the physiotherapy and stuff I had was from British Cycling. It almost feels like in 2010 I'm going to be working with exactly the same team behind me, apart from [not] riding with Garmin.'

By early 2010 the issue for Wiggins was the same one that had haunted Tom Simpson and Robert Millar before him. Finishing within reach of the podium in the Tour is all very well, but how do you repeat it or improve on it? Wiggins was adamant it could be done. 'Definitely, yeah,' he replied before the question 'Can you improve in 2010?' had ended. 'It's just knowing I can [do it] is the big thing. I know what weight I have to be for the Tour now, I know the process, how long that takes, the training I have to do, the bit more I have to do to improve in specialist areas. I hardly trained for it last year. Mostly we went training on the flat. I didn't really train in the mountains. I didn't look at any of the course. I didn't know the time-trial courses, I didn't know what mountains we were going up, just in terms of what gears you need for those things.' Hitherto, he pointed out, his priority had been to choose a low enough gear to keep him moving on the high passes, because in the back groups 'you were going so slow you didn't want to fall over.'

Yates felt the same. 'He will improve as a rider. There are a lot of variables that decide whether you are second, third or fourth, but I think he can do better. He knows he can do it and is confident and we know he can deal with the pressure. In theory that should push him up the podium, maybe not this year but next year or the year after. I can see a win in him.' As for Robert Millar, he may have been as surprised as anyone to see his record equalled, but he saw no reason why Wiggins should not better it.

Wiggins did eventually improve on it, but the process was a tortured one. 2010 turned into a vital year of learning for Team Sky and their new leader, but it was not billed as such. Expectations were very high, and Brailsford – surprisingly, given his attention to detail – was unable to manage them. The focus on Wiggins was intense, but the Sky leader did not rise to the task, by his own admission. The first hint that something might be awry came when journalists noted that he seemed off-colour when he and his 'bodyguard', the Canadian cyclist Michael Barry, reconnoitred vital Alpine stages. At the prologue he managed only a catastrophe: seventy-seventh place, after Sky had opted to start him early to avoid bad weather only for the rain to arrive ahead of forecast. He began struggling when the race entered the Alps at Morzine, cracking on the climb to the Avoriaz ski station, and after that proved unable to climb with the best.

There were tensions within the team as he struggled to come to terms with his lack of form, and at the finish in Paris he ended up in twenty-fourth place. For many riders that would have been respectable, but considering the hopes and hard cash that had been invested in him it was utterly disappointing. The irony was, said Wiggins's trainer Matt Parker, that he had not done much that was different from the previous year in terms of preparation. The difference, felt Parker, was that he had simply been busier throughout the year due to media and sponsor commitments stemming from his new found stature as a Tour contender, and the formation of Team Sky, and that had slightly reduced his training and recovery time. It boiled down to the law of marginal gains but applied in reverse.

Sky, meanwhile, were innovating furiously. My favourite 'marginal gain' was the rubber duck I saw placed jauntily in an ice-bath in the team doctor's room when I spent a couple of days with the team on the 2010 race. On a more serious note, Sky experimented with the baths to aid recovery, custom-made electrolyte replacement drinks, Normatec compression boots to aid circulation during recovery. Sky brought their own mattresses, duvets and pillows on the race. They were all hypoallergenic, so that the riders would not wake up with the sniffles hotel beds often produce. They were brand-new, so they contained less dust. And some of the pillows included built-in iPod speakers so that as the riders went to sleep, they could listen to what they wanted without disturbing their room-mate, who might well have been in a bed just inches away, dying for peace and quiet. It did not come easy: moving the panoply of bedding in and out of the hotel took a team helper an hour every morning and evening.

Under the influence of Formula One, the team bus was enhanced – most notably it included a 'bollocking room', as the meeting area became known. The briefings held on board were done using military terminology: wingman, assassin. But the question was: amidst all the planning and marginal gains, where were the results? At the Tour, when it really mattered, there was no stage win, and there was no rider high up the standings. It was partly that Wiggins wasn't firing, but also the contrast between the expectations raised around the team, and the reality that most of the management were still relatively new either to the Tour itself, or to the roles they were expected to play. Collectively, Brailsford described the whole four weeks as 'humbling', Wiggins's results as 'the first really big public failure of my career'.

The bigger, longer-term picture was hard for the media to keep an eye on within the Tour bubble, but Ellingworth and Brailsford were thinking of little else. 'If you look at the majority of us on the Tour, apart from the riders, we haven't done it before,' said Ellingworth when I visited Sky during the 2010 Tour. 'It is a big enough challenge for many teams, for us there's the moulding-together process, Sean [Yates] has never been a lead *directeur sportif* at the Tour and that needs developing, we are trying out different techniques, trying to find out what works best, whether it's equipment, bikes, clothing, trying to build a coaching model. In a business, the building period is 18 months from when you start, so that means two Tours. By the third, we should be bang on.' He could not have been more prescient.

CHAPTER FIFTEEN

Above Us Only Sky

Sleep does not come easy in the Hotel Parador, close to the summit of Mount Teide, the volcano in the middle of the island of Tenerife. When you wake in the middle of the night, the thin air at this high altitude, 2100m, causes you to gasp briefly for breath. There is a slight burning feeling in the lungs and throat as if breathing in acid, and a little more effort involved in going upstairs. There is one road past the Parador, and it goes from nowhere in particular to nowhere else. Outside, sudden winds whip up dust devils from the bare ground, which has never been cultivated and barely supports any vegetation. There should be tumbleweed. Clint Eastwood, Lee Van Cleef and Eli Wallach should be appearing from behind a lava flow accompanied by an Ennio Morricone score. This is spaghetti western country.

On a May weekend in 2012, instead of the Good, the Bad and the Ugly I had cyclists for company: Bradley Wiggins and the core of Team Sky's Tour de France squad. Kanstantsin Siutsou, Richie Porte, Mick Rogers, Christian Knees and Chris Froome were sharing a long training camp in Tenerife with Wiggins for the second time that year. They were sleeping high and riding low, using the variety of gradients that lead up to the Parador to work their muscles in a variety of ways.

I visited on a rest day, when time on the bike was limited to a thirty-minute spin to the nearest coffee bar while gossiping. The previous three days, however, had been six-hour stints, with some 4000m of vertical climbing per day. Wiggins was aiming for a total of 100,000m of climbing leading into the Tour. 'I said I wanted to train for the Tour without any compromise,' he told me. 'I'm getting to a point in my career where I want to look back with no regrets.' That meant beginning training earlier than usual in the previous winter, working at a higher intensity from the word go, and alternating long preparation camps at altitude with relatively few races, but which had to be tackled flat out, to win.

The training schedule devised by the physiologist Tim Kerrison and Wiggins's trainer Shane Sutton had begun on 1 November 2011. It used data garnered by Kerrison from the 2010 and 2011 Tours, which, he believed, illustrated the power outputs an athlete needed to produce at certain times in order to win the race. He showed me a graph – the same one which had been displayed to the Tour organisers ASO a week or two before – on which a red line tracked the power output levels against the time for which they need to be sustained. A second green line showed what Wiggins, or other Sky Tour riders, were able to achieve, putting those figures in relation to what they needed to do. That meant, said Kerrison, that he could tailor each rider's training programme to target specific areas of weakness. 'As a trainer, you try to make the curves meet, then you prioritise the areas you need.' There was specific Tour-related work: steep hill sessions that mimicked a mountain stage in the Tour, and structure that reflected the need to be consistent on a daily basis. One key factor, Kerrison felt, was training hard under fatigue, to replicate the kind of efforts a rider might be forced to produce during a third consecutive mountain stage in the Tour.

While during Wiggins' previous visit in April, the workloads had been 'mid-range', the intensity, pain and lactate in his legs had all been ramped up for this final camp before the Dauphin Libr stage race. 'Yesterday was twenty-five-minute efforts in thirty-five-degree heat, three of them,' he said. 'It's hard to tell a layman what it feels like: it's hard in a very sweet way, all mixed up with the endorphins.' The exertion was at the near maximal intensity he would adopt for a prologue time trial, followed at once by what equated to weight training on the bike. This was big gear efforts at low pedal revolutions, close to breaking point, all at an oxygen-deprived altitude between 1500m and 2200m above sea level. He would rest, then repeat what had come before. All this, Kerrison believed, would prepare Wiggins's legs for the steepest climbs on the 2012 Tour de France. 'When I came in, people believed Brad was only good up to about a seven per cent gradient; now he can cope with up to thirteen per cent.'

'Three of the lads were wasted by the end, but you realise that if you can do that effort now, it's the Tour winner,' said Wiggins. 'You can hardly breathe, but it's the kind of effort that wins the Tour.'

Working his body at this intensity, Wiggins emphasised, was only feasible after six months of continuous building to make sure that, when he finally put in those efforts, his body would be able to cope. He had also put time in in the gym, developing his upper body strength and his core fitness, all of which would help him to sustain this kind of toil. Wiggins and Kerrison believed his unexpected sprint stage win in the Tour of Romandie was a result of this intense training.

Asked to explain the improvement that took Wiggins to Britain's first victory in the Tour, Sutton, who had worked on and off with Wiggins since his arrival at British Cycling in 2003, had a simple answer: 'The key has been communication and compliance to work.' But another factor was the discovery of Kerrison, a sports scientist from Australia. He had trained Olympic swimmers and rowers, but knew nothing about cycling when he joined Sky in early 2010 and was given a simple brief: to look outside the traditional cycling box for ways of improving performance. He spent the 2010 race in Sky's camper, nicknamed 'Black Betty', travelling with Wiggins's trainer, Matt Parker. It took

Kerrison the best part of eighteen months to put his ideas together, helped by the data bank of Wiggins's power outputs for the 2010 Tour, and those of another Sky team member, the Colombian Rigoberto Urán.

2011 was largely experimental, but Kerrison uncovered one key thing: Wiggins responded well to hard training at altitude, which was put into his programme after the Australian realised it had not formed part of his preparation in the past and that he had tended to struggle when climbing over 2000m. The altitude training camps that year were a calculated gamble, but they worked: immediately after the first, in Mallorca, Wiggins rode to the biggest stage race win of his career, in the Dauphiné Libéré. That year's Tour was preceded by another session, at Sestriere in Italy.

Then Kerrison discovered Tenerife, already the venue of choice for Tour winners such as Lance Armstrong. Kerrison explained that Tenerife provided everything lacking for a Tour contender who lived in Lancashire: heat, high altitude and twenty-mile mountain climbs. There was also peace and quiet. The Internet in the hotel was intermittent, meaning the riders could do nothing after training other than eat, sleep, read and watch videos. The press were rarely invited. The benefit for athletes merely from being at altitude is that it enhances the body's ability to utilise oxygen, but there are other pluses at the Parador in the Teide massif. Unlike some high-altitude venues, the riders could go down to train at sea level, which is less damaging at high intensity and compared to Alpine locations the weather was relatively stable in April and May.

For at least half a century, the received wisdom in cycling had been that riders need to race for training. Kerrison and Sutton put their own twist on this, opting to put Wiggins in a small number of selected races in which he would ride flat out, no matter whether he was carrying fatigue from training. The idea was that he would become accustomed to competing while tired, precisely what is required in the Tour. As Wiggins explained later, what they had learned in 2011 was that racing could be counterproductive because the overload on the body was impossible to control: it was better to train harder than when racing, then use racing as further overload at selected moments. Racing flat out to win had another benefit: get a number of major wins under your belt and the pressure was off. The Tour, in essence, would become just another stage race, albeit bigger and far harder.

Conditioning for the Tour did not simply involve getting the body ready for its demands. Kerrison had the idea that wearing a race leader's jersey ought to become a matter of habit, so it helped that Wiggins and the core group of Tour riders won five stage races even before the main event. There was more: during 2011, when their leader won the Dauphiné, it had become clear that being a race leader entailed specific demands which had to be met. The idea behind having Wiggins win as many stage races as possible before the Tour was also that he and the team around him would develop ways of dealing with those demands. For example, it became routine for him to warm down on a home trainer before doing media work after the stages, while team personnel were delegated specifically to supply recovery drinks and rehydration while he spoke to the press, which could take up to an hour.

The contrast with our exchange in Pau in 2007 was stark. Back then, a couple of days before he was forced to leave the Tour, Wiggins had been blissfully unaware of what he might be capable of achieving. He was unable to see that his undoubtedly powerful engine and ability to focus unremittingly on a goal meant he fitted in the bigger picture of European professional cycling. That was hardly surprising in another sense: for years, the results in the Tour in particular had been distorted by doping. Any figures that were available had to be treated with a pinch of salt. Some were simply fantasy; others were physiologically unfeasible.

In Tenerife, Wiggins admitted that it had taken him several years to realise that his fourth place in 2009 might not have been a fluke. That was hardly surprising, given that he had spent his career working to evidence rather than blind faith, but no one, until Kerrison came along, could offer him a concrete, fact-based rationale to believe in. 'After 2009 I didn't really believe I could win the Tour. I thought, "That's for someone else, kids from Kilburn don't win the Tour." But I really believe I can win it now.'

The change in Wiggins had first become apparent when he met the press in Kew Gardens before the start of the 2011 Tour. He is not easy with media en masse at the best of times, but here he was a different man from the grouchy individual of 2010. He was open about the fact that at the end of the previous year he had received a 'severe bollocking' from Dave Brailsford and Sutton, who is celebrated for calling a spade a spade. He had, Wiggins admitted, not been behaving like a team leader should do, in spite of Sky's massive investment in him. 'I couldn't go on like that. It came down to the way I behaved after the Tour, the way I was racing, the role I was supposed to be fulfilling. I was so far away it was unbelievable. I decided I wasn't enjoying it. I had to make amends. It all started by accepting that I needed help.' Sutton was given an enhanced role – with an official title of head coach, his actual job at British Cycling since 2003 had been as 'troubleshooter', jetted in to turn around struggling elements within the set-up – and Kerrison was brought in to oversee the physiological side. 'I handed them my body, and said "train me, get this machine working".'

Critically, Wiggins travelled to the start of the 2011 Tour in the Vende with a game-changing stage race win under his belt. Part of the philosophy he had agreed with

Kerrison and Sutton was that there would be no targeting the Tour and the Tour alone in the way that had become conventional in cycling since Greg LeMond. The Tour would be the main goal, but he would race flat out to win in every event along the way. That translated to a third place in Paris–Nice – never his kind of race in the past – a stage win in the Bayern Rundfahrt, and, critically, victory in the Dauphiné Libéré, which put him on a level with Robert Millar and Brian Robinson.

While Wiggins turned up at the Tour start in a different frame of mind, Sky itself had been, inevitably, modified from its original prototype. The lead *directeur sportif*, Scott Sunderland, had not made it further than May 2010 after a clash of personalities and approach with Brailsford. A raft of the original riders were 'let go' when their two-year contracts ended at the end of 2011. More 'race coaches' were hired to work alongside Ellingworth as it became rapidly clear that he could not deal alone with the workload of coaching the whole team. The project to create a base for riders, staff and services in Tuscany had been quietly shelved. Ellingworth and Brailsford both maintained that the team was 'leaner and meaner' than in 2010, and had learned from that chastening experience. The core Tour team had been named early. There was less experimentation, more focus on racing for the sake of it rather than throwing everything forward to the Tour.

How Wiggins would have fared in the 2011 Tour remains a matter of speculation. The consensus was that he might have made the podium had he not broken a collarbone in a high-speed crash as the race headed for Châteauroux on 8 July, ironically enough on a stage that witnessed a British triumph as Cavendish surged to the inevitable bunch sprint win. Wiggins had ridden a faultless race for the first six stages and was lying sixth overall, just ten seconds behind the yellow jersey, Thor Hushovd, when his luck deserted him less than twenty-five miles from the end of a relatively innocuous flat stage. He was left lying in the road after a pile-up involving some thirty riders in the heart of the bunch on a straight section of road, just as the field was gathering speed for the day's intermediate sprint. Wiggins was the last of the victims to get off the deck, and when he did so he was clutching his left arm and shoulder, a classic sign that a rider has broken a collarbone or wrist. At first he appeared to be attempting to get back on his bike to finish the stage but then he climbed into the race ambulance, his Tour over.

Six weeks later, he was back in the saddle for the Tour of Spain, which finally provided him with the performance he had been looking for since his fourth place in the 2009 Tour: confirmation that that ride had not been a fluke. Recovery from the collarbone fracture had been more drawn-out than expected, meaning he could not race before the Vuelta, but even so he finished in third place overall, having led the race until the final week, and with Froome in a surprise second place after taking the final mountain-top finish. That was followed up with a silver medal in the world time trial championship to the German Tony Martin.

At the end of June 2012, Wiggins turned up at the start of the Tour de France in Liège as the overwhelming favourite. There was barely a dissenting voice: if he could keep in one piece, he was likely to deliver Britain its first Tour win. It was more than mere hype. As early as March, there had been a subtle difference in his racing style at Paris–Nice, where on day one he made it into the decisive move, and drove it on to the finish. He looked confident, aggressive, and he had the ability to seize the moment. Victory there had been followed by the overall at the Tour of Romandie, including something unprecedented: that sprint win from a large lead group. At the Dauphiné Libéré, Wiggins joined the select few who had won the French event twice, and did so with a dominant performance in the long time trial stage, where he came close to catching the 2011 Tour-de-France winner, Cadel Evans of Australia, who had started ahead of him. On the Col de Joux-Plane on the penultimate day, he and his Sky teammates Rogers, Porte and Froome dominated the lead group, with Rogers taking second overall and Froome fourth.

Perhaps surprisingly, Wiggins was unfazed by the label of favourite. As early as March, he had said of winning Paris–Nice, 'If I'm capable of winning it, I'm capable of winning the Tour de France.' There had been speculation that he had peaked too early, in spite of his continued assertions that each stage race was being ridden as part of his training plan. That meant he did not back off completely, and it also meant that he raced with what fitness he had at the time. At Romandie and Nice, it was sufficient to ensure narrow victories, but by the time the Dauphiné came round, it was clear he was well ahead of the opposition.

That competition, meanwhile, was thin on the ground. Alberto Contador was banned, following a positive test for Clenbuterol at the 2010 Tour. Andy Schleck had injured his pelvis in a crash at the Dauphiné. Evans looked a degree below his best after a lacklustre season. At Sky, meanwhile, insiders believed the team had moved up another level. 'The first year was average performance – not the best in the world but top five. People criticised ... but it wasn't that bad, the second year was better and this year the guys are riding bloody well,' summed up Michael Barry. 'The biggest change was the relationship between new people to the sport and people who'd been in it for a long time, acceptance of ideas by the old guard,' was the view of Rod Ellingworth.

The philosophy of naming the Tour team early had been refined: they were not merely selected at the start of the year, but five of the eight men who lined up with Wiggins had ridden most of his races with him and had shared his training camps in Tenerife and Majorca. Only Mark Cavendish, Bernhard Eisel and Edvald Boasson–Hagen had enjoyed different programmes. Indeed, if the Sky leader was the overwhelming favourite, the only questions on most lips concerned his teammates. It had been clear at the Vuelta the previous autumn that Froome had been climbing more strongly than Wiggins, and it was unclear how the partnership would pan out. And then there was Cavendish, who was starting the Tour with the goal of gaining fitness for the Olympic Games road race. He had only his close friend Bernhard Eisel for support and, as it was known that Sky would not be going all-out to ensure him stage wins or to win the green jersey – although that issue had been fudged all year, presumably to keep the sponsor happy – it was not obvious how his ambitions would mesh with those of his former Madison partner.

The Tour itself was to prove seamless, as Tour wins often do when a favourite applies himself to every detail on a route that plays to his strengths as the 2012 Tour did for Wiggins with its two long time trials. In the style of Miguel Indurain, he got through the race without losing time to any key rival in the mountains while gaining spadesful of seconds in the time trials. The process started in the Liège prologue with second place, after which he rode his luck through a first week where, as is always the case on the Tour, there were crashes galore.

Others were not so lucky. Froome lost over a minute on day one after a puncture as the race sped into Liège for the first road race stage finish; Wiggins, ironically, ploughed into the same pothole but his tyre stayed inflated. Sky were deprived of a key *domestique* when Kanstantsin Siutsou fell and broke his shin en route to Boulogne; in the same crash, Wiggins had to take to the verge, with his bike on his shoulder, to remain in the main group, where he was isolated towards the end of the race. A mechanical over the

Monts du Boulonnais would have wrecked his race. Critically, however, while Porte fell several times, Wiggins himself stayed upright, even avoiding the worst pile-up of the week, the '*massacre de Metz*', where the butchers' bill ran well into double figures.

The *maillot jaune* was his on the evening of 7 July, on the top of the steep climb to La Planche des Belles Filles, a ski station high in the Vosges. It was one of the steepest finishes the Tour had ever seen and it was dominated by Sky. Only Vincenzo Nibali, Evans and Froome survived the searing pace together with Wiggins, and it was Froome who won the stage. Those efforts in Tenerife had paid off. Evans, meanwhile, had shaped to make his move as the four leaders hit the steepest part of the final 'wall' but could not find the legs; Sky's head Dave Brailsford said later that he was almost certain from then on that Wiggins could win.

The following morning I met Kerrison outside Sky's hotel, a conveniently situated Novotel yards from the start in Belfort. I put it to him that few teams ever take the yellow jersey a week into the Tour and hold it to Paris; if Wiggins could manage this, he would be the first Tour winner to do so since Bernard Hinault in 1981. Kerrison's reply underlined how Sky's approach to the Tour had gained in sophistication: the core group of Tour riders, he felt, were actually more comfortable defending the yellow jersey, because having won five stage races that season – Porte had taken the Volta ao Algarve and Rogers the Bayern Rundfahrt – they had spent over seventy-five per cent of their season riding to protect a race leader.

The following afternoon, in Besançon, the yellow jersey reinforced his grip after the Tour's first long time trial. Over forty-five kilometres running northwards from the former royal salt production centre at Arc-et-Senans, Wiggins carved out a thirty-five-second gap on Froome, left his old nemeses Cancellara and Martin trailing, and most importantly extended his margin over Evans from

10sec to 1min 53sec. That left the Australian with a simple yet virtually impossible task. There was a longer time trial to come on the penultimate day between Bonneval and Chartres, in which Wiggins would open a gap that would be greater. With that in mind, Evans needed to gain well over five minutes on the Briton to have any margin for error. The rest of the field would need to do more.

Later in the week, after a rest day, the Alps beckoned. There, the challenges came: a neatly coordinated but ineffectual attack from the Italian Vincenzo Nibali, who went clear on the descent from the Col du Grand Colombier, then linked up with his teammate Peter Sagan of Slovakia; a pre-planned move on the Col du Croix de Fer by Evans and his teammate Tejay Van Garderen, which flopped when the Australian's legs gave out.

From then on, it seemed likely that barring those old saws, crashes or illness, the challenges to Wiggins would be internal. The Cavendish issue had been settled; the world champion was to be seen ferrying bottles at the back of the peloton. He did so with good grace, in the knowledge that Wiggins had made a massive effort to help him win the world title the previous September, and would repeat that in a couple of weeks when the Olympic road race came round. Indeed, his team leader would repay him before that, with two massive lead outs to enable his stage victories at Brive and on the Champs-Elysées.

The bigger question was whether Wiggins could withstand the psychological pressure that comes with leading the Tour. Life in yellow is demanding off the bike as well as on it. One of the great advantages of taking the *maillot jaune* relatively late in the race is that less time is spent dealing with the daily demands of the media. These cannot be underestimated: each day, the *maillot jaune* spends a good fifteen to twenty minutes wandering around the mixed zone, from one interview to the next, answering a series of questions which are usually the same. This is after live interviews – again at least five minutes – for French television, sometimes more. This is followed by a sit-down media conference – five to ten minutes – in the caravan for written press, transmitted to the press centre. This is all time when the race leader would, in an ideal world, be lying down in his team bus recovering from the day's effort and filling himself with recovery drinks. That's without beginning to ponder the mental demands of constant, daily questioning in a public forum. Since the great doping scandals of 1998 and 2006–8, drugs has been the prime topic, but as Chris Froome gained in strength, the question of what Wiggins thought his teammate was up to began to be thrown at the race leader as well.

Murmurings about Sky were inevitable, given cycling's recent history: with Lance Armstrong's all conquering US Postal Service team facing charges from the US Anti-Doping Agency, any team that performed strongly in the Tour could expect questioning. The first hint came after the stage finish at Porrentruy, when an Australian writer asked Wiggins how he felt about comparisons made between Sky and USPS on Twitter. He knew what he meant; Wiggins knew what he meant, and was angry. But by the middle of the second week, it was an issue he knew needed to be tackled head on, and he did so with a column in the *Guardian*. The most salient lines were these: 'nothing has changed [since the start of my career] in how I stand morally. Nothing has changed about the reasons why I would never dope . . . Doping would simply be not worth it . . . If I felt I had to take drugs, I would rather stop tomorrow, go and ride club ten-mile time trials, ride to the cafe on Sundays, and work in Tesco stacking shelves.' That only left mutterings here and there about Brailsford's decision to go back on his original team policy to avoid hiring doctors who had previously worked within cycling; the Sky head would, he said, re-examine his decision to hire, part-time, Geert Leinders, who had done a spell at the

Dutch team Rabobank. It was a live issue, if a minor one, but it would be dealt with after the Tour.

The Froome question was more intriguing because the Kenyan-born cyclist's obvious strength tapped into cycling history, instances when team leaders had had to contend with teammates who were their equal or, in some areas, stronger. The issue gained momentum as Froome made a brief attack on the climb to the ski station at La Toussuire in the Alps, before being reined in. That in turn prompted an exchange of views via Twitter between Wiggins's wife Cath and Froome's partner Michelle Cound, which, while brief, did hint at tensions behind the scenes. Wiggins himself appeared to have his doubts, although he did not let on in public.

If the affair never really moved beyond the realms of speculation, that was partly because Froome made an unlikely villain. A quietly spoken diplomat's son, he had come to cycling through mountain biking in Kenya, and had had to make his own way early on. Famously, at the world championship in 2006, he had been without support staff, and had had to attend the team managers' meeting himself, rather than have someone to do it for him. At Sky, he had been a mystery to the management, who could not figure out why immensely promising physiological tests did not translate into performances on the road. Eventually, he was diagnosed with the parasite bilharzia, which affects the immune system, and began treatment, after which his form had improved dramatically. He had signed a three-year deal with Sky after his fine run at the Vuelta in 2011, and although he had been adamant he would ride the 2012 Tour for Wiggins, in the future he was obviously a candidate for victory in a major Tour in his own right.

If the Froome question gained traction, that was inevitable: the 'official opposition' were not up to the task of taking on the Sky steamroller. Evans crumbled in the Pyrenees, where only Vincenzo Nibali was able to hold the pace with Wiggins and Froome; instead of attacks from their opponents, the centre of interest was Froome's apparent attempt to show his strength at the final summit finish, high above the Col de Peyresourde at the Peyragudes ski station. The Kenyan-born climber appeared to be ostentatiously waiting for his leader. He may have been – and Robert Millar was just one onlooker who found it all rather theatrical, if not downright disrespectful – but it was irrelevant to the outcome: Sky ended that stage with both their riders lying first and second overall. Wiggins had, he admitted, had tears in his eyes when he crested the Peyresourde to begin the last climb, with overall victory just three days away.

Those three days were all Sky, with Cavendish taking his brace of stages, thanks in part to massive lead-outs from the man in the yellow jersey, and Wiggins cementing his lead with his second time trial win between Bonneval and Chartres, the 53.5km stage which he had reconnoitred earlier in the year, and which had been in his mind ever since. Critically, he left Froome 1min 16sec behind, pushing his teammate to a deficit of 3min 21sec. In the last ten kilometres, he said, he had let his mind wander and recalled all that had led up to those final moments: 'My childhood, my father leaving us when I was a kid, my mum bringing me up in a flat, my grandfather, who was my role model and who died before the 2010 Tour, all the disappointments, crashing out of the Tour last year, watching Cadel Evans winning it and seeing how happy it made him, and wanting to feel like that – it's been a long journey.' The journey ended with him and Froome in first and second – the first time since 1984 that two riders from the same nation had occupied the top two spots overall in the Tour – and with no fewer than seven British stage wins from four of the five British starters.

*

Twenty-four hours later, Wiggins's final words from the 2012 Tour, as he bade farewell to the crowds from the podium on the Champs-Elysées, could never have fallen from the lips of Jacques Anquetil, Bernard Hinault, Alberto Contador or Lance Armstrong: 'Have a safe journey home, and don't get too drunk.' After a champagne reception at the Ritz (where the starving Sky riders eviscerated the finger buffet) he took a private jet home to his adopted Lancashire with Cath and his two children, Isabella and Ben, and was shocked to find a vast throng of press dogging his steps when he nipped out for a pint of milk or a gentle one-hour bike ride.

Given the reaction of the British media in the previous two weeks, that was hardly surprising. Wiggins's impending triumph had broken out into new territory: his progress in the Tour was a regular feature on BBC Radio 4's prime news programmes. On Monday 23 July, he deservedly made every front page: '£20m and a knighthood next for wonderful Wiggins' speculated one; 'Le Gentleman rides into Paris and history'; 'Magical History Tour'; 'King of France', 'Promenade des Anglais'. *The Times* went to town, devoting an entire wraparound souvenir spread to Wiggins. His triumph was truly timely, coming a few months after a disastrous rugby world cup for England, shortly after a shambolic showing from England's footballers in Euro 2012, and a couple of weeks after a brave near-miss by Andy Murray at Wimbledon. And it tapped perfectly into the nation's growing sense of anticipation before the London Olympic Games, something that was highlighted when he was asked to ring the bell at the start of the opening ceremony.

Once London 2012 got going, Wiggomania took hold. 1 August in Hampton Court took him to a new level of stardom. By day five of the Games, there had been no British gold medals, and a sense of slight panic was setting in. The *Guardian* devoted its centrefold to a Second World War-style poster stating 'Keep calm and carry on' with a footnote reminding readers 'we've still got Wiggo'. The first British gold came that morning in the rowing, but it was Wiggins's domination in the afternoon's time trial that caught the collective imagination; after winning the gold medal in the Olympic time trial to thunderous acclamation from a roadside crowd estimated at half a million, he made a point of doing a lap of honour through crowds who could not access the restricted start and finish area. The picture of him sitting on the gold throne set up for the winners doing a double 'victory' sign, became one of the iconic images of the Games.

By the end of the Games, the kid from Kilburn had become British sporting royalty. He had hobnobbed with his rock star idols at private parties thrown by the Stone Roses, visited a polo club owned by a former member of the Small Faces, and turned up at the velodrome (with Stella McCartney) to thunderous applause, while at the same time being rightly praised for having the common touch. He was, wrote the *Guardian*'s Zoe Williams, that rare thing: a sporting hero who one liked more on closer acquaintance. The mod 'airforce' roundel, which featured on his jersey and bike, began to appear on posters at races. His sideburns entered the national consciousness after the *Sun* and *Mirror* produced cut out and keep 'boards' for their readers. The Fred Perry top he wore to the velodrome prompted debate among fashion writers about whether the cardigan was 'back'. He was considered a shoo-in for BBC Sports Personality of the Year, although that changed a little after the spectacular achievements of Mo Farah and Jessica Ennis in the athletics stadium. There was a flip side: as a national celebrity, he could no longer move without a long lens capturing him for a tabloid newspaper; he was reduced to hiring a bodyguard, and at one point had to be smuggled out of his house in the boot of his car for an evening out. For a man who so valued his privacy and that of his family, it must have felt a high price to pay.

As for the man himself, he was not certain of his next move. At the Great Britain Olympic road race team's base in Surrey he told me he was uncertain as to whether he could summon the same massive level of motivation – and impose the same level of sacrifice on his family – that it had taken to win the Tour. This was a thought that his coach Shane Sutton had begun expressing out loud even before his protégé had won the Tour. So Wiggins speculated over other targets. His sense of cycling history and his desire to build the best all-round palmares in the sport prompted him to speculate about Paris–Roubaix and the Giro d'Italia. Six days later, he told the press in Hampton Court that nothing would ever top the Tour-Olympic double. But wherever he went, his place in British sporting history was assured.

The conclusion to the first edition of this book in 2005 was prescient in at least one sense. New pathways to the Tour were now available for Britons, I wrote, and that was to be proven correct, in spades. Cyclists as diverse as Charly Wegelius and Bradley Wiggins would indeed arrive at the race through their work with the British Olympic system founded by Peter Keen and perfected by Dave Brailsford. (It's also possible to speculate that without the support of that system during and after his ban, David Millar might have been lost to the sport after his arrest.) I noted that there were fears that the lure of Olympic medals might draw talented British cyclists away from the road, but pointed out that the opposite might happen: the Tour might become a career option that came after Olympic success (I've won the gold medal, now I need a new challenge). Again, the crystal ball was in order, as is shown by the stories of Bradley Wiggins and Geraint Thomas. On that note, watch out for Peter Kennaugh, gold medallist in London and tipped as a future Tour winner as far back as 2009.

Back then, however, there were merely hints of the talent that might be coming along behind Wegelius and Wiggins: Mark Cavendish's victory in the 2005 Madison world championship, Geraint Thomas's win in the junior version of Paris–Roubaix in 2004. The riders were coming through to British Cycling's academy but had yet to graduate. No one outside Kenya had heard of Chris Froome. There was no knowing where Mark Cavendish might end up, although Cavendish and Rod Ellingworth knew something special was brewing. Wiggins's mind was firmly set on becoming the first British cyclist to defend an Olympic title. There was not a hint of the British professional team project, not even a straw in the wind, although Brailsford's passion for pro cycling was obvious. Back in 2004 and 2005, with not a single Briton in the Tour, there was no sign that the talent would appear in sufficient numbers to field a competitive outfit.

The wheel has now turned full circle since the days of Brian Robinson, and even since the Foreign Legion era of the 1980s. Professional cycling worldwide is now talking about following the British model, rather than – to paraphrase the philosophy that guided Robinson and Robert Millar – the Brits having to 'go over there and live like the Europeans'. After the 2012 Tour, the issue for the traditional cycling world was no longer whether the British approach would work. The pressing question for the likes of Bjarne Riis, Alberto Contador, Cadel Evans et al was how to beat the Britons: how to match Mark Cavendish's imperious sprint speed and utter confidence, how to achieve the improvement that drove Wiggins to become the best in the Tour, not to mention how to look for the 'marginal gains' that drove Team Sky to dominate the 2012 race. That was not all. Given the massive public support for the London Olympics, not to mention the 'Wiggins factor', the Tour itself looked certain to return to Britain, with both

Yorkshire and Scotland pressing hard to host the *Grand Départ*, perhaps as early as 2014.

It was a footnote, but David Millar's stage win on 13 July 2012 probably marked the end of an era. It was, as the former Foreign Legionnaire Graham Jones sagely observed, probably the last stage win in the Tour by a British rider who had followed the route taken by the pioneers: going over to France and doing what the French did, getting a pro contract outside the British talent formation system. Future British Tourmen would be products of the British Cycling production line, living and racing in their home country, flying out to Europe without the need to go over the water and learn the hard way.

The timing with which two long-term trends have coincided could not be more perfect for the Britons. The sport seems to have finally turned the corner in its fight against the doping plague, thanks to two developments: a 'biological passport', which profiles significant changes to riders' physiological levels, which can indicate doping, and a ban on the use of needles. The long list of stars who have fallen to earth meant that by 2009 there was room aplenty at the top and the time was ripe for a complete culture change. The playing field had not merely levelled but had been left wide open. That happened precisely at the same moment when a new generation of Britons was emerging through a system in which needles had always been shunned. Listening to Cavendish, Wiggins and the likes of young Kennaugh express their distaste for drug-taking is heartening in what it says about the sport's future. Under the British system the doping issue had not been a matter of David Millar's 'why not dope?' but of Wiggins's 'why on earth would you want to?'

Back in 2005, it was clear that the Tour had become an integral part of the fabric of the British sporting summer as far as the fans and media were concerned. Lance Armstrong had played his part, so too outlets such as Radio Five Live, broadsheet newspapers such as the *Guardian* – the only one to employ a full-time cycling correspondent through the noughties – and television pioneers Channel 4 and Eurosport. The Wiggins Tour of 2012 gave massive impetus to a trend that had been gathering pace for the previous decade: cycling as part of the British sporting and cultural mainstream. The *Guardian* called for it to be declared the new national sport, while one member of the shadow cabinet stated the previously politically unmentionable: that cyclists should be given priority over motorists on the roads.

As Team Sky, Wiggins and Cavendish all went on to greater things there was a new risk, one that comes with celebrity and success. This was seen on day one of the London Olympics, when Cavendish was lambasted by the popular press for 'failing' to deliver a gold medal in the road race. The equation had been simplistically made by sports writers who knew little of the subtleties of cycling: if Wiggins had won the Tour, Cav would (not merely could) win at the Games. He didn't manage the gold, but that didn't mean he merited the derogatory headlines. That press reaction raised the prospect of the scenario I had predicted in the conclusion to the second edition of this book: that British achievement in the world's greatest bike race would suddenly be seen as a given, after almost sixty years in which it had been an exception.

Rafts of British stage wins from Cavendish, with Wiggins, Froome and – why not? – Peter Kennaugh or Geraint Thomas pushing for the overall title and the green jersey could well come to be expected as the standard July fare. There is nothing inherently wrong with that, as long as the background is never overlooked. The stories of Robinson, Barry Hoban, Tom Simpson, Robert Millar, Chris Boardman and David Millar and their companions over the last fifty years remain vitally important as British cycling progresses into the twenty-first century with Cavendish, Wiggins, Thomas, the sprinter Ben Swift and Kennaugh.

The efforts and sacrifices made by the pioneers should serve as a reminder that however straightforward it looks on television, success in cycling is a matter of degree. At the highest level it is always a question of slender margins: the judge's decision that may have lost Cav the 2009 green jersey, the temporary lack of concentration that cost Wiggins 40sec and perhaps third place that year, a pothole in which Chris Froome punctured and Wiggins didn't. The story of British cycling over nearly sixty years serves as a reminder that success is always dearly bought. For some the price is heartbreak and frustration, for others it 'merely' requires years of sacrifice for the champion and his family, with a certain amount of good fortune along the way.

In times of rapid change, history is easily overlooked, but it is then that it has its greatest significance. This book's original purpose was to serve as a record of the efforts made in the Tour by British cyclists for relatively small gains. Now, however, this book can celebrate twenty-first-century triumphs. If it can put them in context by ensuring that we do not overlook the blood, sweat and tears that went before, so much the better.

APPENDIX

British Tour de France cyclists

The following is a list of all the British cyclists who have competed in the Tour de France since its inception. Where appropriate, the winning time and the margin each rider finished behind the winner is also given.

1937 Bill Burl, Charles Holland (team: Empire Aces); both abandoned

1955 Dave Bedwell, Tony Hoar, Stan Jones, Fred Krebs, Bob Maitland, Ken Mitchell, Bernard Pusey, Brian Robinson, Ian Steel, Bev Wood (Great Britain)

1, Louison Bobet (France) 130hr 29min 26sec
29, Robinson at 1hr 57min 10sec
69, Hoar at 6hr 6min 1sec

1956 Brian Robinson (Luxembourg)

1, Roger Walkowiak (Nord-Est-Centre) 124hr 1min 16sec
14, Robinson at 33min 53sec

1957 Brian Robinson (Luxembourg-Mixed)

1, Jacques Anquetil (France) 135hr 44min 42sec

Robinson wins stage 7 from St-Brieuc to Brest

1958 Stan Brittain, Ron Coe, Brian Robinson (International)

1, Charly Gaul (Holland-Luxembourg) 116hr 59min 5sec
68, Brittain at 3hr 2min 32sec

1959 John Andrews, Tony Hewson, Brian Robinson, Victor Sutton (International)

1, Federico Bahamontes (Spain) 123hr 46min 45sec
19, Robinson at 1hr 12min 11sec
37, Sutton at 1hr 58min 34sec

Robinson wins stage 20 from Annecy to Chalon-sur-Saône

1960 John Andrews, Stan Brittain, John Kennedy, Harry Reynolds, Brian Robinson, Norman Sheil, Tom Simpson, Victor Sutton (Great Britain)

1, Gastone Nencini (Italy) 112hr 8min 42sec
26, Robinson at 59min 52sec
29, Simpson at 1hr 3min 43sec

1961 Stan Brittain, Ron Coe, Vin Denson, Seamus Elliott*, Albert Hitchen, Ken Laidlaw, Ian Moore, George O'Brien, Pete Ryall, Sean Ryan, Brian Robinson, Tom Simpson (Great Britain)

1, Jacques Anquetil (France) 122hr 1min 33sec
47, Elliott at 1hr 51min 5sec
53, Robinson at 2hr 4min 23sec
65, Laidlaw at 2hr 45min 47sec

1962 Alan Ramsbottom (US Dunkirk-Pelforth-Sauvage-Lejeune-Wolber), Tom Simpson (VCXIIème-Leroux-Gitane-Dunlop)

1, Jacques Anquetil (ACBB-St Raphaël-Helyett-Hutchinson) 114hr 31min 54sec
6, Simpson at 17min 8sec
45, Ramsbottom at 1hr 50min 19sec

Simpson wore yellow jersey during stage 13 from Luchon

---

* Elliott was actually Irish

to Superbagnères

1963 Alan Ramsbottom (Pelforth-Sauvage-Lejeune-Wolber)

1, Jacques Anquetil (St-Raphaël-Gitane-Dunlop)
   113hr 30min 5sec
16, Ramsbottom at 30min 36sec

1964 Vin Denson (Solo-Superia), Barry Hoban (Mercier-BP-Hutchinson), Tom Simpson (Peugeot-BP-Englebert), Michael Wright (Wiels-Groene-Leeuw)

1, Jacques Anquetil (St-Raphaël-Gitane-Dunlop)
   127hr 9min 44sec
14, Simpson at 41min 50sec
56, Wright at 2hr 19min 8sec
65, Hoban at 2hr 36min 43sec
72, Denson at 2hr 57min 23sec

1965 Vin Denson (Ford-France-Gitane-Dunlop), Tom Simpson (Peugeot-BP-Michelin), Michael Wright (Wiels-Groene-Leeuw)

1, Felice Gimondi (Salvarani) 116hr 42min 6sec
24, Wright at 40min 11sec
87, Denson at 1hr 46min 36sec

Wright won stage 20 from Lyon to Auxerre

1966 Vin Denson (Ford-France-Géminiani-Hutchinson), Tom Simpson (Peugeot-BP-Michelin); both DNF

1967 Peter Chisman, Vin Denson, Peter Hill, Albert Hitchen, Barry Hoban, Bill Lawrie*, Colin Lewis, Arthur Metcalfe, Tom Simpson, Michael Wright (Great Britain)

* Lawrie was Australian

1, Roger Pingeon (France) 136hr 53min 50sec
62, Hoban at 1hr 17min 29sec
69, Metcalfe at 1hr 22min 27sec
84, Lewis at 1hr 59min 50sec

Wright won stage 7 from Metz to Strasbourg; Hoban won stage 14 from Carpentras to Sète

Simpson died on stage 13 from Marseille to Carpentras

1968 Bob Addy, John Clarey, Vin Denson, Derek Green, Derek Harrison, Barry Hoban, Colin Lewis, Arthur Metcalfe, Hugh Porter, Michael Wright (Great Britain)

1, Jan Janssen (Holland) 133hr 49min 42sec
28, Wright at 38min 53sec
33, Hoban at 42min 28sec
62, Denson at 2hr 23min 29sec
63, Clarey at 2hr 43min 28sec

Hoban won stage 19 from Grenoble to Sallanches

1969 Derek Harrison (Frimatic-Viva-De Gribaldy-Hutchinson), Barry Hoban (Mercier-BP-Hutchinson), Michael Wright (Bic)

1, Eddy Merckx (Faema-Eddy Merckx-Clement) 116hr 16min 2sec
32, Harrison at 1hr 58min 24sec
67, Hoban at 2hr 53min 46sec
71, Wright at 2hr 56min 47sec

Hoban won stages 18 and 19 from Mourenx to Bordeaux, and Bordeaux to Brive

1970 Barry Hoban (Sonolor-Lejeune); DNF

1971 Barry Hoban (Sonolor-Lejeune)

1, Eddy Merckx (Molteni) 96hr 45min 14sec
40, Hoban at 1hr 34min 59sec

1972 Barry Hoban (GAN-Mercier-Hutchinson), Michael Wright (Gitane)

1, Eddy Merckx (Molteni) 108hr 17min 18sec
55, Wright at 2hr 8min 31sec
70, Hoban at 2hr 28min 20sec

1973 Barry Hoban (GAN-Mercier-Hutchinson), Michael Wright (Gitane-Frigecrème)

1, Luis Ocaña (Bic) 122hr 25min 34sec
43, Hoban at 2hr 3min
57, Wright at 2hr 23min 21sec

Wright won stage 10 from Nice to Aubagne; Hoban won stage 11 from Montpellier to Argelès-sur-Mer, and stage 19 from Bourges to Versailles

1974 Barry Hoban (GAN-Mercier-Hutchinson), Michael Wright (Sonolor-Gitane)

1, Eddy Merckx (Molteni) 116hr 16min 58sec
37, Hoban at 1hr 13min 11sec
57, Wright at 1hr 38min 11sec

Hoban won stage 13 from Avignon to Montpellier

1975 Barry Hoban (GAN-Mercier-Hutchinson)

1, Bernard Thévenet (Peugeot-BP-Michelin)
   114hr 35min 31sec
68, Hoban at 2hr 41min 17sec

Hoban won stage 8 from Angoulême to Bordeaux

1976 No British starters

1977 Barry Hoban (Miko-Mercier-Hutchinson), Bill Nickson (TI-Raleigh)

1, Bernard Thévenet (Peugeot-BP-Michelin)
   115hr 38min 30sec
41, Hoban at 1hr 39min 30sec

1978 Barry Hoban (Miko-Mercier-Hutchinson), Paul Sherwen (Fiat-La France)

1, Bernard Hinault (Renault-Gitane-Campagnolo)
   108hr 18min
65, Hoban at 2hr 6min 33sec
70, Sherwen at 2hr 18min 54sec

1979 Paul Sherwen (Fiat-France)

1, Bernard Hinault (Renault-Gitane-Campagnolo)
   103hr 6min 50sec
82, Sherwen at 3hr 3min 45sec

1980 Graham Jones (Peugeot-Esso-Michelin), Paul Sherwen (La Redoute-Motobecane)

1, Joop Zoetemelk (TI-Raleigh-Creda) 109hr 19min 14sec
49, Jones at 1hr 20min 33sec

1981 Graham Jones (Peugeot-Esso-Michelin), Paul Sherwen (La Redoute-Motobecane)

1, Bernard Hinault (Renault-Gitane-Campagnolo)
   96hr 19min 38sec
20, Jones at 41min 6sec
82, Sherwen at 3hr 3min 45sec

1982 Paul Sherwen (La Redoute-Motobecane)

1, Bernard Hinault (Renault-Gitane-Campagnolo)
   92hr 8min 46sec

111, Sherwen at 2hr 22min 54sec

1983 Graham Jones (Wolber), Robert Millar (Peugeot-Shell-Michelin)

1, Laurent Fignon (Renault-Elf-Gitane) 105hr 7min 52sec
14, Millar at 23min 29sec
69, Jones at 2hr 15min 3sec

Millar won stage 10 from Pau to Bagnères-de-Luchon

1984 Graham Jones (Système-U), Robert Millar, Sean Yates (both Peugeot-Shell-Michelin), Paul Sherwen (La Redoute)

1, Laurent Fignon (Renault-Elf-Gitane) 112hr 3min 40sec
4, Millar at 14min 42sec
91, Yates at 2hr 26min 41sec
116, Sherwen at 3hr 24min 48sec

Millar won stage 11 from Pau to Guzet-Neige and the King of the Mountains jersey

1985 Robert Millar, Sean Yates (both Peugeot-Shell-Michelin), Paul Sherwen (La Redoute)

1, Bernard Hinault (La Vie Claire-Wonder-Radar)
   113hr 24min 23sec
11, Millar at 15min 10sec
122, Yates at 2hr 37min 36sec
141, Sherwen at 3hr 28min 13sec

1986 Robert Millar (Panasonic), Sean Yates (Peugeot-Shell)

1, Greg LeMond (La Vie Claire-Wonder-Radar)
   110hr 35min 19sec
112, Yates at 2hr 15min 20sec

1987 Malcolm Elliott, Graham Jones, Adrian Timmis, Paul Watson (all ANC-Halfords), Robert Millar (Panasonic), Sean Yates (Fagor)

1, Stephen Roche (Carrera Jeans) 115hr 27min 42sec
19, Millar at 50min 47sec
70, Timmis at 2hr 19min 21sec
94, Elliott at 2hr 48min 39sec

1988 Malcolm Elliott, Robert Millar, Sean Yates (Fagor)

1, Pedro Delgado (Reynolds) 84hr 27min 53sec
59, Yates at 1hr 16min 6sec
90, Elliott at 1hr 44min 27sec

Yates won stage 6 from Liévin to Wasquehal

1989 Robert Millar (Z-Peugeot), Sean Yates (7-Eleven)

1, Greg LeMond (ADR-Agrigel-Bottecchia)
   87hr 38min 15sec
10, Millar at 18min 46sec
45, Yates at 1hr 27min 4sec

Millar won stage 10 from Cauterets to Luchon-Super-bagnères

1990 Robert Millar (Z), Sean Yates (7-Eleven)

1, Greg LeMond (Z) 90hr 43min 20sec
119, Yates at 2hr 5min 43sec

1991 Robert Millar (Z), Sean Yates (Motorola)

1, Miguel Indurain (Banesto) 101hr 1min 20sec
72, Millar at 1hr 36min 6sec

1992 Robert Millar (TVM), Sean Yates (Motorola)

1, Miguel Indurain (Banesto) 100hr 49min 30sec

18, Millar at 31min 19sec
83, Yates at 2hr 24min 44sec

1993 Robert Millar (TVM-Bison), Sean Yates (Motorola)

1, Miguel Indurain (Banesto) 95hr 57min 9sec
24, Millar at 44min 20sec
88, Yates at 2hr 16min 38sec

1994 Chris Boardman (GAN), Sean Yates (Motorola)

1, Miguel Indurain (Banesto) 103hr 38min 38sec
71, Yates at 2hr 4min 45sec

Boardman won the prologue time trial in Lille and wore the yellow jersey for three stages, finishing in Armentières, Boulogne and Eurotunnel; Yates wore the yellow jersey for one stage, Rennes–Futuroscope

1995 Chris Boardman (GAN), Max Sciandri (MG-Technogym)*, Sean Yates (Motorola)

1, Miguel Indurain (Banesto) 92hr 44min 59sec
47, Sciandri at 1hr 55min 10sec

Sciandri won stage 11 from Bourg-d'Oisans to St-Étienne

1996 Chris Boardman (GAN), Max Sciandri (Motorola)

1, Bjarne Riis (Deutsche Telekom) 95hr 57min 16sec
39, Boardman at 1 hr 27min 44sec

1997 Chris Boardman (GAN), Max Sciandri (La Française des Jeux)

1, Jan Ullrich (Telekom) 100hr 30min 35sec
67, Sciandri at 2hr 42min 24sec

* Sciandri also rode the 1990, 1992, and 1993 Tours under Italian nationality

Boardman won the prologue time trial in Rouen and wore the yellow jersey for one stage, finishing in Forges-les-Eaux

1998 Chris Boardman (GAN), Max Sciandri (La Française des Jeux); both DNF

Boardman won the prologue time trial in Dublin and wore the yellow jersey on the next two stages, the first of which finished in Dublin; he crashed on stage 2 to Cork and did not finish

1999 Chris Boardman (GAN)

1, Lance Armstrong (US Postal Service) 91hr 32min 16sec
119, Boardman at 2hr 47min 48sec

2000 David Millar (Cofidis)

1, Lance Armstrong (US Postal Service) 92hr 33min 8sec
62, Millar at 2hr 13min 3sec

Millar won the prologue time trial at Futoroscope, and wore the yellow jersey for three stages, finishing at Loudun, Nantes and St-Nazaire

2001 David Millar (Cofidis); DNF

2002 David Millar (Cofidis)

1, Lance Armstrong (US Postal Service) 82hr 5min 12sec
68, David Millar at 1hr 59min 51sec

Millar won stage 13 from Lavalanet to Béziers

2003 David Millar (Cofidis)

1, Lance Armstrong (US Postal Service) 83hr 41min 12sec
55, David Millar at 1hr 54min 38sec

Millar won stage 19 from Pornic to Nantes

2004 No British starters

2005 No British starters

2006 David Millar (Saunier Duval), Bradley Wiggins (Cofidis)

1, Oscar Pereiro (Caisse d'Epargne) 89hr 40min 27sec
59, Millar at 2hr 4min 10sec
124, Wiggins at 3hr 25min 32sec

2007 Mark Cavendish (T-Mobile), David Millar (Saunier Duval), Geraint Thomas (Barloworld), Charly Wegelius (Liquigas), Bradley Wiggins (Cofidis)

1, Alberto Contador (Discovery Channel) 91hr 00min 26sec
45, Wegelius at 1hr 46min 25sec
69, Millar at 2hr 32min 07sec
140, Thomas at 3hr 46min 51sec

2008 Mark Cavendish (Columbia Sportswear), Chris Froome (Barloworld), David Millar (Garmin-Chipotle)

1, Carlos Sastre (CSC) 87hr 52min 52sec
68, Millar at 1hr 59min 37sec
84, Froome at 2hr 22min 33sec

Cavendish won stage 5 from Cholet to Chateauroux, stage 8 from Figeac to Toulouse, stage 12 from Lavalanet to Narbonne, and stage 13 from Narbonne to Nimes, then withdrew

2009 Mark Cavendish (Columbia-HTC), David Millar (Garmin), Charly Wegelius (Silence-Lotto), Bradley Wiggins (Garmin)

1, Alberto Contador (Astana) 85hr 48min 35sec
4, Wiggins at 6min 01sec
59, Wegelius at 1hr 29min 37sec
85, Millar at 2hr 15min 04sec
131, Cavendish at 3hr 21min 54sec

Cavendish won stage 2 from Monaco to Brignolles, stage 3 from Marseilles to La Grande Motte, stage 10 from Limoges to Issoudun, stage 11 from Vatan to Saint Fargeau, stage 19 from Bourgoin-Jailleu to Aubenas, and stage 21 from Montereau-Fault-Yonne to Paris. He finished second to Thor Hushovd in the points jersey competition, 10 points behind

2010 Mark Cavendish (HTC-Columbia), Steve Cummings (Sky Procycling), Jeremy Hunt (Cervelo Test Team), Dan Lloyd (Cervelo Test Team), David Millar (Garmin-Transitions), Geraint Thomas (Sky Procycling), Bradley Wiggins (Sky Procycling)

1, Andy Schleck (Saxo Bank) 91hr 59min 27sec
24, Wiggins at 38min 45sec
67, Thomas at 1hr 59min 26sec
151, Cummings at 3hr 45min 08sec
154, Cavendish at 3hr 50min 44sec
158, Millar at 3hr 56min 07sec
163, Hunt at 4hr 1min 42sec
164, Lloyd at 4hr 2min 20sec

Cavendish won stage 5 from Épernay to Montargis, stage 6 from Montargis to Gueugnon, stage 11 from Sisteron to Bourgs-lès-Valence, stage 18 from Salies-de-Béarn to Bordeaux and stage 20 from Longjumeau to Paris. He finished second in the points jersey competition to Alessandro Petacchi, 11 points behind

2011 Mark Cavendish (HTC-Highroad), David Millar (Garmin-Cervelo), Ben Swift (Sky Procycling), Geraint Thomas (Sky Procycling), Bradley Wiggins (Sky Procycling)

1, Cadel Evans (BMC Racing) 86hr 12min
31, Thomas at 1hr 00min 48sec
76, David Millar at 2hr 14min 56 sec
130, Cavendish at 3hr 15min 39sec
137, Swift at 3hr 18min 7sec

Millar won stage 2 team time trial from Les Essarts to Les Essarts with Garmin-Cervelo. Cavendish won stage 5 from Carhaix to Cap Fréhel, stage 7 from Le Mans to Châteauroux, stage 11 from Blaye-les-Mines to Lavaur, stage 15 from Limoux to Montpellier, stage 21 from Créteil to Paris. He won the points jersey competition

2012 Mark Cavendish (Sky Procycling), Steve Cummings (BMC Racing), Chris Froome (Sky Procycling), David Millar (Garmin-Sharp), Bradley Wiggins (Sky Procycling)

1, Bradley Wiggins 87hr 34min 47sec
2, Chris Froome at 3min 21sec
95, Cummings at 2hr 47min 3sec
106, Millar at 2hr 55min 24sec
142, Cavendish at 3hr 28min 36sec

Wiggins won stage 9 from Arc-et-Senans to Besançon and stage 19 from Bonneval to Chartres. Cavendish won stage 2 from Vise to Tournais, stage 18 from Blagnac to Brive-la-Gaillarde and stage 20 from Rambouillet to Paris. Froome won stage 8 from Tomblaine to La Planche des Belles Filles. Millar won stage 12 from Saint-Jean-de-Maurienne to Annonay/Davézieux

Bibliography

Adrian Bell (ed.), *From the pen of J. B. Wadley*, Mousehold Press, 2002

Jean Bobet, *Demain on Roule*, La table Ronde, 2004

Pierre Chany, *La Fabuleuse Histoire du Tour de France*, La Martinière, 1997

Jeff Connor, *Wide-Eyed and Legless*, Simon & Schuster 1988

Pierre Daninos, *Les Carnets du Major Thompson*, Hachette, 1954

L'Equipe, *Tour de France, Cent Ans*, 2003

Rupert Guinness, *The Foreign Legion*, Springfield, 1992

Barry Hoban with John Wilcockson, *Watching the Wheels Go Round*, Stanley Paul, 1981

Rene Jacobs, *Vélo Gotha*, Presses de Belgique, 1984

Paul Kimmage, *Rough Ride*, Stanley Paul, 1990

Ron Kitching, *A Wheel in Two Worlds*, 1993

Robin Magowan, *Tour de France: The Historic 1978 Event*, Velopress, 1996

Chas Messenger, *Ride and Be Damned*, Pedal Publishing, 1998

Geoffrey Nicholson, *The Great Bike Race*, Hodder & Stoughton, 1977

Geoffrey Nicholson, *Le Tour*, Hodder & Stoughton, 1991

Chris Sidwells, *Mr Tom: The True Story of Tom Simpson*, Mousehold Press, 2000

J. B. Wadley, *My 19th Tour de France*, Wadley Publications, 1974

Jeremy Whittle, *Yellow Fever: The Dark Heart of the Tour de France*, Headline, 1999

Les Woodland (ed.), *The Yellow Jersey Companion to the Tour de France*, Yellow Jersey Press, 2003

INDEX

Index

Index